Torture

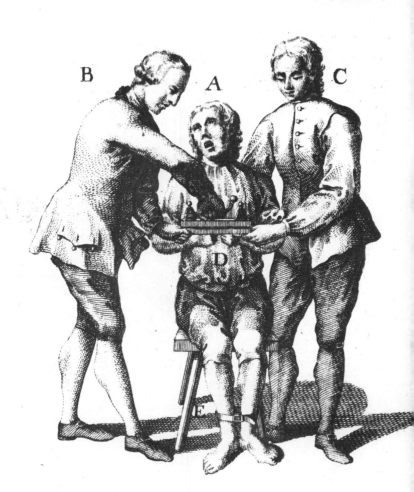

Torture and the Law of Proof

and the Law of Proof

John H. Langbein

Europe and England in the
Ancien Régime

The University of Chicago Press
Chicago and London

The University of Chicago Press, Chicago 60637
The University of Chicago Press, Ltd., London

©1976, 1977 by The University of Chicago
All rights reserved. Published 1977
Printed in the United States of
America
81 80 79 78 77   9 8 7 6 5 4 3 2 1

Library of Congress Cataloging in Publication Data

Langbein, John H
  Torture and the law of proof.
  Includes bibliographical references and index.
  1. Torture—Europe—History. 2. Torture—Great
Britain—History. 3. Evidence (Law)—Europe—History.
4. Evidence (Law)—Great Britain—History. I. Title.
Law⁻   345'.36'064   76-58314
ISBN 0-226-46806-2

John H. Langbein is Professor of Law at the University of Chicago Law School. He writes in the
fields of trust and estate law, modern comparative
law, and English and European legal history. His
book, *Prosecuting Crime in the Renaissance:
England, Germany, France* (1974), was awarded the
Yorke Prize by the law faculty of Cambridge University.

Contents

Contents

Preface

This book is principally concerned to state a thesis about a seemingly technical and forbidding corner of legal history, the European law of proof. But the particular subject, the law of torture, has a fascination for readers who do not ordinarily take an interest in legal history. Accordingly, I have tried to organize and write the book in a streamlined way, and to remove to the notes the discussion of matters that are likely to concern only professional legal historians.

Nevertheless, this *is* a book about the history of the law of proof. My purpose is to straighten out the garbled historical understanding of a juridical institution. I have been determined not to submerge the thesis of the book by allowing the inquiry to turn into other channels. I have left it for others to draw the implications for European political, administrative, and intellectual history.

A more serious limitation is that the book (which has been largely researched and written at the University of Chicago) is based preponderantly on printed sources—the statutes, legal treatises, and published records of the ancien régime, supplemented by secondary sources. I am confident that this range of sources is appropriate and sufficient to substantiate the thesis of the book, although I have no doubt that future work in the European archives can illuminate and refine some of the issues and the analysis. I hope that this book will stimulate such research on the part of those best situated to conduct it.

The history of torture in England is a less important subject, and one on which the conventional understanding has been broadly correct although wrong in many points of detail. Again, my perspective is strictly that of a student of the history of the law of proof. This is not the book for storytelling about the legendary martyrs and rackmasters; people like Saint Edmund Campion and Mr. Thomas Norton can be little more than names on a chart in these pages.

In assembling the data for Chapter 6 I have relied considerably upon the resourceful detective work of two research assistants, law students at the University of Chicago Law School, Kathleen Bratton '74 and Barbra Goering '77. I have benefited materially from suggestions on prepublication drafts by R. C. van Caenegem (Ghent); Helmut Coing (Frankfurt); Charles Donahue (Michigan); Charles Gray (Yale); Thomas Green (Michigan); Stanley Katz (Chicago); Mark Kishlansky (Chicago); Bernard Meltzer (Chicago); and Bernard Schnapper (Paris). I am indebted to many others for supplying references, information, and suggestions, and I have tried to the extent possible to acknowledge their assistance in the notes.

Dean Phil C. Neal and the University of Chicago Law School supported this study in many ways—encouraging the work, lightening my teaching responsibilities, and defraying research costs. The Alexander von Humboldt-Stiftung, the University of Chicago Center for Studies in Criminal Justice, and the Max Planck Institut für ausländisches und internationales Strafrecht made possible a short period of research on this book in Freiburg.

I wish also to express my thanks for suggestions from learned audiences to whom I have presented papers based upon this research: the Max Planck Institut für Europäische Rechtsgeschichte (Frankfurt, 1973), the American Society for Legal History (Washington, 1974), the Renaissance Society/Newberry Library (Chicago, 1975), and the Cambridge Legal History Conference (Cambridge, 1975).

Throughout the book I have followed the practice of modernizing and Americanizing the spelling of quoted matter from English and antiquarian sources. Abbreviated words have been written out. Punctuation, capitalization, and italicization are original. When translating foreign-language matter, I have not adhered to the most literal rendering when a more idiomatic expression seemed better.

1

Europe
Judicial Torture

1   Torture and the Law of Proof

From the late Middle Ages and throughout the ancien régime, torture was an incident of the legal systems of all the great states of continental Europe. Torture was part of the ordinary criminal procedure, regularly employed to investigate and prosecute routine crime before the ordinary courts. The system was one of *judicial torture*.

There was in fact a jurisprudence of torture, with its own rules, treatises, and learned doctors of law. This law of torture developed in northern Italy in the thirteenth century within the Roman-canon inquisitorial tradition, and it spread through Europe in the movement that is called the reception of Roman law. By the sixteenth century a substantially similar law of torture was in force from the Kingdom of Sicily north to Scandinavia, from Iberia across France and the German Empire to the Slavic East. Well into the eighteenth century the law of torture was still current everywhere, and it survived into the nineteenth century in some corners of central Europe.[1]

We shall have a good deal to say in this book about the history both of punishment and of torture, but the two must not be confounded. When we speak of "judicial torture," we are referring to the use of physical coercion by officers of the state in order to gather evidence for judicial proceedings. The law of torture regulated this form of judicial investigation. In matters of state, torture was also used to extract information in circumstances not directly related to judicial proceedings. Torture has to be kept separate[2] from the various painful modes of punishment used as sanctions against persons already convicted and condemned. No punishment, no matter how gruesome, should be called torture.[3]

It is universally acknowledged that judicial torture as it existed in the national legal systems of western Europe in early modern times was the creature of the so-called statutory system of proofs—the Roman-canon law of evidence. But historians have generally pointed

3

to factors other than the law of proof as having brought about the abolition of torture. They have especially emphasized the forceful writing of publicists like Beccaria and Voltaire and the political wisdom of Enlightenment rulers like Frederick the Great and the emperor Joseph II.

A principal thesis of this book is that the conventional account of the abolition of torture in the eighteenth century is wrong. In Chapter 3 it will be contended that the explanation for the disappearance of judicial torture is neither publicistic nor political, but juristic. In the two centuries preceding the abolition of torture, there occurred a revolution in the law of proof in Europe. The Roman-canon law remained formally in force, but with its power eroded away. The true explanation for the abolition of torture is that by the age of abolition torture was no longer needed. The system of proof which had required the use of torture was dead.

The Jurisprudence of Torture

The Roman-canon law of proof governed judicial procedure in cases of serious crime, cases where blood sanctions (death or severe physical maiming) could be imposed. In brief, there were three fundamental rules.

First, the court could convict and condemn an accused upon the testimony of two eyewitnesses to the gravamen of the crime.

Second, if there were not two eyewitnesses, the court could convict and condemn the accused only upon the basis of his own confession.

Third, circumstantial evidence, so-called *indicia,* was not an adequate basis for conviction and condemnation, no matter how compelling.[4] It does not matter, for example, that the suspect is seen running away from the murdered man's house and that the bloody dagger and the stolen loot are found in his possession. The court cannot convict him of the crime.

At least, the court cannot convict him without his confession, and that is where torture fitted into the system. In certain cases where there was neither the voluntary confession nor the testimony of the two eyewitnesses, the court could order that the suspect be examined about the crime under torture in order to secure his confession.

However, examination under torture was permitted only when

there was a so-called half proof against the suspect. That meant either (1) one eyewitness, or (2) circumstantial evidence of sufficient gravity, according to a fairly elaborate tariff of gravity worked out by the later jurists. So, in the example where the suspect is caught with the dagger and the loot, each of those indicia would be a quarter proof. Together they cumulate to a half proof, and he could therefore be dispatched to a session in the local torture chamber.

Now what was the logic of creating a system of safeguards, followed by a system of coercion to overcome the safeguards? Manifestly, under sufficient coercion nearly anyone can be made to confess to anything. To the extent that the explanation is to be found in logic, it is that the system did not allow indiscriminate coercion. The coercion was carefully limited by rule in two important respects.

First, there was the threshold requirement of half proof. It amounted to what Anglo-American lawyers would call a rule of probable cause. It was designed to assure that only those persons highly likely to be guilty would be examined under torture.

Second, the use of torture was surrounded by various rules designed to enhance the reliability of the confession. Torture was not supposed to be used to secure what Anglo-American lawyers call a guilty plea, that is, an abject confession of guilt. Rather, torture was supposed to be employed in such a way that the accused would also confess to details of the crime—information which, in the words of the German *Constitutio Criminalis Carolina* of 1532, "no innocent person can know."[5]

To this end the Carolina forbids so-called suggestive questioning, in which the examiner supplies the accused with the details he wishes to hear from him. Further, the Carolina directs that the information admitted under torture be investigated and verified to the extent feasible.[6] If the accused confesses to the slaying, he is supposed to be asked where he put the dagger. If he says he buried it under the old oak tree, the examining magistrate is supposed to send someone out to dig it up. (The rules regulating the use of judicial torture are set forth in greater detail in Note I at the end of this chapter.)

The Origins of Judicial Torture

This curious system of proof developed in the thirteenth century, although it has some roots in the twelfth century. The Roman-canon law of proof was the successor to the ordeals, the nonrational proofs of Germanic antiquity. When the Fourth Lateran Council of 1215 abolished the ordeals, it destroyed an entire system of proof.[7] The ordeals were means of provoking the judgment of God. God revealed the innocence of an accused whose hand withstood infection from the hot iron; God pronounced the guilt of one who floated when subjected to the water ordeal.

The abolition of this system meant not only a fundamental change in the rules of proof, but a profound change in thinking about the nature of government and law. The attempt to make God the fact finder for human disputes was being abandoned. Henceforth, humans were going to replace God in deciding guilt or innocence, humans called judges. It is almost impossible for us to imagine how difficult it must have been for the ordinary people of that age to accept that substitution. The question that springs to the lips is: "You who are merely another mortal like me, who are you to sit in judgment upon me?"

Over many later centuries Western political theory developed its answer to that question. "I, the judge, sit in judgment upon you because I have the power to do so. I derive my power from the state, which selects, employs, and controls me." And the state now claims to legitimate its power by purporting to derive it not from God but from the consent of the governed. In the thirteenth century, however, the modern theoretical solution lay very far in the future. The problem that confronted the legal systems of the church and of the secular governments (initially in the North Italian city-states) was to make this fundamental change acceptable in the tradition-conscious and religiously devout societies of that day. How could men be persuaded to accept the judgment of professional judges today, when only yesterday the decision was being remitted to God?

The system of statutory proofs was the answer. Its overwhelming emphasis is upon the elimination of judicial discretion, and that is why it forbids the judge the power to convict upon circumstantial evidence. Circumstantial evidence depends for its efficacy upon the subjective persuasion of the trier, the judge. He has to draw an inference of guilt from indirect evidence. By contrast, the system of statutory proofs insists upon objective criteria of proof.[8] The judge who administers it is an automaton. He condemns a criminal upon the testimony of two eyewitnesses, evidence which is in the famous phrase "as clear as the light of day." There should be no doubt about guilt in such a case. Likewise, when the accused himself admits his guilt, there ought to be no doubt. (Even under the former system of proof, confession constituted waiver. If the culprit admitted his guilt, the authorities were not going to waste their time and God's by asking for a confirmation under ordeal.)

The Roman-canon law of proof solved the problem of how to make the judgment of men palatable. That judgment was to rest on certainty. It was to rest upon standards of proof so high that no one would be concerned that God was no longer being asked to resolve the doubts. There could be no doubts.[9] The difficulty with this system is to our eyes quite obvious. The jurists who devised it had solved one problem by creating another. They had constructed a system of proof that could handle the easy cases but not the hard ones. Their system could deal with most cases of overt crime but seldom with cases of covert crime—cases where there were no eyewitnesses. If that sounds completely absurd, do bear in mind that even today many cases are easy—crimes committed in anger or in haste, and either witnessed or voluntarily confessed in remorse.

Nevertheless, the Roman-canon law of proof was unworkable standing alone. No society will long tolerate a legal system in which there is no prospect of convicting unrepentant persons who commit clandestine crimes. Something had to be done to extend the system to those cases. The two-eyewitness rule was hard to compromise or evade, but the confession rule invited "subterfuge."[10] To go from accepting a voluntary confession to coercing a confession from someone against whom there was already strong suspicion was a relatively small step, indeed, one which was probably taken almost from the inception of the system. There is considerable evidence of the use of torture in northern Italy already in the first half of the thirteenth century. Pope Innocent IV issued a decretal in 1252 confirming the use of torture in canon procedure, and in the works of Gandinus and other thirteenth-century writers the kernel of the subsequent law of torture was well developed.[11] Actually, judicial torture may not have seemed to contemporaries to be very far from the ordeals. Both were physically discomforting modes of procedure ordered by the court upon a preliminary showing of cogent incriminating evidence, usually circumstantial evidence. In this sense, the ordeals may have helped suggest and legitimate the system of judicial torture that displaced them.[12]

The law of torture found a place for circumstantial evidence in the law of proof, but a subsidiary place. Circumstantial evidence was not consulted directly on the ultimate question—guilt or innocence. It was technically relevant only to an issue of interlocutory procedure—whether or not to examine the accused under torture. Even there the *ius commune* attempted to limit judicial discretion by promulgating predetermined, supposedly objective standards for evaluating the indicia and assigning them numerical values (quarter proofs, half proofs, and the like).[13]

The practice of coercing evidence from suspects did not need to be invented by medieval lawyers. "Dreadful or not, compelling a person through violence to admit or disclose something against his will is a method of procedure so humanly obvious that it proves difficult to imagine an age in which it could not have been known."[14] The Digest preserved many references to the use of torture in imperial Roman law, a convenient peg on which the Glossators hanged the thirteenth-century practice.[15] Eberhard Schmidt has convincingly shown that torture was in use in medieval Germany in advance of the German reception of the Roman-canon law of proof.[16] The crux of the relationship between torture and the Roman-canon system of statutory proofs was this: there could be torture without the Roman-canon system,[17] but the reverse was not true. The two-eyewitness rule left the Roman-canon system dependent upon the use of torture.

The Classical Critique of Judicial Torture

What was wrong with the law of torture, after all? Superficially, it looks like a surprisingly good system, both efficient and just. The accused will not be tortured unless there is cogent incriminating evidence against him. When he is tortured, he will be asked for information, not just for a guilty plea, and the information he confesses will be examined and verified.

From a purely practical standpoint, laying aside moral objections to the use of coercion, there were a number of things[18] wrong with the system. Inquisitorial procedure had a prosecutorial bias that torture magnified. "Only a judge equipped with superhuman capabilities could keep himself in his decisional function free from the . . . influences of his own instigating and investigating activity."[19] Because torture tests an accused's capacity to endure pain, not his veracity, innocent persons might yield to "the pain and torment and confess things they never did."[20]

Further, the safeguards that were designed to prevent the condemnation of an innocent man on the basis of a false confession extracted from him were quite imperfect. If the judge did engage in suggestive questioning, even accidentally, that could seldom be detected or prevented. If the accused knew something about the crime, but was still innocent of it, what he did know might be enough to give his confession verisimilitude. For certain crimes, especially heresy and witchcraft, there was seldom any objective evidence that might be used to verify the confession, and condemnation was allowed on the basis of an unverified confession. In many jurisdictions the requirement of verification was not enforced, or was indifferently enforced.

These defects were well known. Today we associate their denunciation with Thomasius,[21] Beccaria,[22] and especially Voltaire.[23] But those writers were in fact latecomers to a tradition as ancient as the system itself. The warnings from imperial Roman law[24] were never forgotten. The jurists of the ius commune report failings.[25] The English jurist Fortescue, writing about 1470, recounts many of the dangers of the system.[26] The treatise writers who elaborate the law of torture in northern Europe in the sixteenth, seventeenth, and eighteenth centuries admit the dangers.[27] Long before Voltaire, French writers of the sixteenth and seventeenth centuries are pointing to cases in which an innocent person confesses and is executed, after which the real culprit is discovered.[28]

The law of torture survived into the eighteenth century, not because its defects had been concealed, but rather in spite of their having been long revealed. European criminal procedure had no alternative; the law of proof was absolutely dependent upon coerced confessions.

By contrast, the British Isles and some peripheral parts of the Continent remained free from judicial torture throughout the later Middle Ages,[29] because the jury system rather than the Roman-canon law of proof replaced the ordeals. And, to this day, an English jury can convict an accused criminal on mere circumstantial evidence. It can convict on less evidence than the Glossators and their successors stipulated as a bare prerequisite for further investigation under torture.[30]

Another point which emphasizes the connection between torture and the Roman-canon law of proof is that in Europe itself, torture was not allowed in cases of petty crime, *delicta levia*. The statutory proofs pertained only to cases of capital crime. Delicta levia were governed by what would today be called *freie Beweiswürdigung* or *l'intime conviction*, that is, the subjective persuasion of the judge. Because conviction on less than full proof (meaning in practice conviction on circumstantial evidence) was unobjectionable, judicial torture had no sphere.[31]

Abolition and the Fairy Tale

In the middle of the eighteenth century the leading states of Europe abolished judicial torture within the space of a generation. Prussia all but terminated judicial torture in 1740; it was used for the last time in 1752 and authoritatively abolished in 1754. In 1770 Saxony abolished torture; in 1776 Poland and Austria-Bohemia; in 1780 France; in 1786 Tuscany; in 1787 the Austrian Netherlands (hereafter called Belgium); in 1789 Sicily. By the next generation, abolition was complete throughout Europe.[32]

How did this abolition movement happen, how was it possible? In all the literature that discusses and celebrates the abolition of judicial torture, one meets the same account. We call it the fairy tale, and it goes like this: (1) The system of judicial torture persisted into the eighteenth century unabated. (2) There then arose a series of able publicists, most notably Beccaria and Voltaire, who revealed the incurable deficiencies of the jurisprudence of torture. (3) These writers shocked the conscience of Europe, and inspired the great monarchs of the Enlightenment to abolish torture. (4) Having abolished torture, the Europeans found themselves in a bit of a mess. There were lots of manifestly guilty criminals who could no longer be convicted, suspects whom it had previously been necessary to torture. (5) Various stopgap remedies were tried. Physical coercion is not the only form of coercion. Psychological duress could still be used (for example, isolating a suspect and talking him into a confession). The courts even went so far as to impose punishments for failure to cooperate with the investigating authorities, called variously in the German sources *Lügenstrafen, Ungehorsamstrafen, Verdachtsstrafen* (punishments for lying, for insubordination, for suspicion). (6) Ultimately, however, the Europeans realized that the Roman-canon law of proof without torture was unworkable, and it would be necessary to introduce a system of free judicial evaluation of the evidence. Therefore, the system of statutory proofs had to be abolished—in the various German states in the middle of the nineteenth century, in France somewhat earlier (during the 1790s).[33]

Now there are two major reasons why, without any further historical evidence, this conventional account of the abolition of torture should be doubted. First, it posits as the decisive causative element the moral outrage awakened by the likes of Beccaria and Voltaire. The difficulty with that is plain. The eighteenth-century writers were advancing arguments against torture that had been known for centuries. It seems unpersuasive to say that the abolitionist critique be-came decisive in the eighteenth century when it had been brushed aside in the seventeenth century and before, even allowing for the changed world view that we customarily call the Enlightenment. To say that abolition was an idea whose time had come is to beg the question, why had it come?

Second, the fairy tale would have it that the abolition of torture *preceded* the abolition of the Roman-canon system of proof, in some states by nearly a century. In view of the function of torture, this must appear highly unlikely. The Roman-canon system, we have seen, was simply unworkable without torture. How could the European states abolish torture and still continue to operate under the Roman-canon law of proof?

That is the mystery that has inspired the fairy tale. For if we look at the sources, this sequence of events seems to be confirmed: the eighteenth century abolished torture, the nineteenth century abolished the Roman-canon law of proof. Consequently, it has been assumed that the abolition of torture was not to be explained in terms of the law of proof, and the fairy tale took on its plausibility.

The thesis of this book is that the Roman-canon law of proof lost its force not in the nineteenth century but in the seventeenth. A new system of proof, which was in fact free judicial evaluation of the evidence although not described as such, was developed in the legal science and the legal practice of the sixteenth and seventeenth centuries, and confirmed in the legislation of the seventeenth and eighteenth centuries.

This new system of proof developed alongside the Roman-canon system. The Roman-canon law of proof survived in form, but in the seventeenth century it lost its monopoly. Thereafter the standards of the Roman-canon law continued to be complied with for easy cases, cases where there was a voluntary confession or where there were two eyewitnesses. But for cases where there was neither, the Roman-canon standards no longer had to be complied with. That is to say, in just those cases where it had previously been necessary to use torture, it now became possible to punish the accused without meeting the evidentiary standards that had led to torture.

What happened was no less than a revolution in the law of proof. Concealed under various misleading labels, a system of free judicial evaluation of the evidence achieved subsidiary validity. This development liberated the law of Europe from its dependence on torture. Torture could be abolished in the eighteenth century because the law of proof no longer required it.

In Chapter 3 we shall see how and why that revolution in the law of proof took place. Chapters 3 and 4 will also have something to say about why our legal historical literature has misunderstood what happened and allowed the fairy tale to stand for so long. First, however, it will be necessary to describe in Chapter 2 another change in the administration of criminal justice that occurred in the sixteenth and seventeenth centuries and that constituted the immediate context for the developments in the law of proof: the development of new modes of punishment as partial replacements for the blood sanctions that predominated in the later Middle Ages.

Note I
The Law of Torture

The law of torture as it had developed by the end of the Middle Ages in the treatises and practice books of the later jurists has been compendiously described in Piero Fiorelli's *La tortura giudiziaria nel diritto comune* (1953–54). The present account draws heavily on that work and on two primary sources influential in transmontane Europe throughout the ancien régime: (1) the *Constitutio Criminalis Carolina,* the criminal procedure ordinance promulgated for the German Empire in 1532, which was mostly a codification of the Roman-canon ius commune; and (2) the treatise by Joost Damhouder of Bruges, *Praxis Rerum Criminalium* (1554), which appeared in Latin, Dutch, French, and German editions that were republished for a century and a half for circulation among the European magistracy.[34]

Capital crime. The sources are unanimous in insisting that investigation under torture be restricted to cases of capital crime—crimes for which the guilty could be punished by death or maiming.[35] For cases of petty crime, delicta levia, "on which neither life nor limb depends,"[36] investigation under torture was forbidden.

The last resort. Torture was not to be used unless other means of gathering evidence were lacking. This rule was a natural corollary of the subsidiary role of the law of torture in the system of statutory proofs. If there were two eyewitnesses or voluntary confession, investigation under torture was unnecessary.[37]

Immune persons. The law exempted various classes of persons from liability to be investigated under torture. Some exemptions were based upon the accused's physical frailty. A woman was immune while pregnant; children below the age of twelve or fourteen were exempt; the aged infirm should not be tortured if it would risk death. Other exemptions were based upon status. Aristocrats, higher public officials, clergy, physicians, and doctors of law were immune in many places.[38] (The jurists' prudence in fashioning an exemption for themselves invites comparison with the modern rule of English law that barristers are not liable for their malpractice.)[39] The status-based exemptions were widely disfavored in the ancien régime. Neither in the German Carolina nor in French practice of the sixteenth and later centuries are they recognized.[40]

Never on Sunday. Examination under torture was not to take place on legal holidays—Sunday and the principal holy days.[41]

Corpus delicti. The jurists characteristically distinguished two phases to the investigation procedure: the *inquisitio generalis,* in which the judge determined whether a crime had been committed, and the *inquisitio specialis,* in which he inquired whether the evidence pointed to the guilt of a particular culprit. Torture was, of course, incident to the latter phase. Nevertheless, the conduct of the inquisitio generalis could have an important bearing on the resort to torture. If a prosecution terminated for want of what was called the *corpus delicti,* no further investigation (and hence no judicial torture) could ensue. The requirement that the judge first establish the fact of the commission of a crime was meant as a safeguard for the accused. Had it been rigorously enforced, the European witch craze could not have claimed its countless victims. Unfortunately, an exception developed that gutted the corpus delicti requirement for those "occult" crimes such as witchcraft and sorcery that were *facti transeuntis,* whose "traces vanished with the act." For these *crimina excepta* a lower standard of evidence was accepted to establish that the crime had occurred.[42]

Probable cause. The critical chapter of the law of torture was the set of rules designed to determine whether there was sufficient suspicion against the accused to warrant examining him under torture. This was the point at which items of circumstantial evidence, called indicia, were permitted to bear on guilt by becoming the basis for a decree authorizing examination under torture. The Roman-canon law of proof that required full proof for conviction required half proof for torture. The testimony of two eyewitnesses constituted full proof; half proof was the testimony of one such witness or, more often, circumstantial evidence of sufficient quality. The jurists conceded from the outset that they could not prescribe rules for the evaluation of circumstantial evidence sufficiently detailed to predispose every case, although they tried to frame a scheme of rules and illustrations to guide the judge as much as possible. We have elsewhere described this body of law as it was codified in the German Carolina.[43]

The judge. The system of judicial torture made it the responsibility of the investigating magistrate to order and to supervise the administration of torture. He was forbidden to delegate either function. He conducted the interrogation, usually in the presence of two or more observers who were municipal or other public officers. He was accompanied by a clerk who transcribed the proceedings in an authoritative dossier. In some places it was directed that a physician be present when severe modes of torture were employed.[44]

Modes of torture. The medieval jurists and the Renaissance codes disdained to regulate the actual application of torture. The sources tell us that there was considerable local variation in both the instruments of torture and the intensity of their use.[45] When one of the draftsmen of the French criminal procedure ordinance of 1670 suggested that the new code should unify the standards for the conduct of torture in the kingdom, a colleague replied "that it would be difficult to render torture uniform [and] that the description that it would be necessary to make would be indecent in an ordinance."[46]

The commonest torture devices—strappado, rack, thumbscrews, legscrews—worked upon the extremities of the body, either by distending or compressing them.[47] We may suppose that these modes of torture were preferred because they were somewhat less likely to maim or to kill than coercion directed to the trunk of the body, and because they could be quickly adjusted to take account of the victim's responses during the examination.

Threaten first. Consistent with the principle that torture could be used only in the last resort, the jurists felt that the threat of torture should precede its application.[48] The threat, or indeed the sight of the torture chamber, might induce the accused to confess without more.

Suggestive questioning. It has been emphasized in Chapter 1 that the reliability of confession extracted under torture depended considerably upon the prohibition of suggestive questioning. The examining magistrate was supposed to elicit evidence, not supply it.[49]

Verification. The requirement that the court verify the details of the tortured confession was not universal, it was hard to enforce, and actual corroboration was not required.[50] Further, when suggestive questioning occurred, verification only compounded the underlying deceit.

Repetition of torture. When the accused resisted confession, the judge was commonly permitted to order the repetition of torture at least once, often twice, sometimes much more.[51]

Voluntariness of the confession. A curious and revealing feature of the law of torture was the insistence on making the confession wrung by torture appear voluntary. No confession made under torture qualified as full proof under Roman-canon law. The confession is valid, says Damhouder, only if the accused "publicly repeats it [in the courtroom] free of all torture within twenty or twenty-four hours, or as others say, a day and a night after [the torture]."[52] This feeble safeguard, like the rule forbidding suggestive questioning, reminds us once again that the architects of the law of torture understood the potential unreliability of coerced confessions.

Often enough the accused who confessed under torture did recant when asked to confirm his confession.[53] But seldom to avail: the examination under torture could thereupon be repeated.[54] An accused who confessed under torture, recanted, and found himself tortured anew learned quickly enough that only a "voluntary confession" at the ratification hearing would save him from further agony in the torture chamber.

Resisting torture. The accused who withstood all examination under torture without confessing was said to have purged the indicia against him, and was entitled to be acquitted and released unless new incriminating evidence was discovered thereafter.[55] We shall see in Chapter 3 that the abrogation of this rule in the practice of the sixteenth and seventeenth centuries was an important part of the development that ultimately destroyed the law of torture.

Note II
Torturing the
Convicted

The system of judicial torture incident to the Roman-canon statutory proofs did not prevent, and indeed probably helped inspire, some other uses of torture. Coercing people to do as the authorities desire was such a simple and obvious practice that it was hard to confine to the jurists' design.

Roman-canon law authorized the use of torture when full proof was otherwise lacking, in order to obtain a confession that would constitute full proof. In various European states, however, torture was sometimes used against persons already convicted.

Torture préalable. The criminal who had been duly convicted and was awaiting execution of a capital sentence had forfeited his life. Since the criminal was the state's to execute, the state might put him to some better use first. (We shall see in Chapter 2 that the state came to treat some capital convicts as a resource, better exploited by being kept alive.) The doctrine developed, prominently in France, that the condemned criminal could be examined under torture about other crimes and criminals.[56] As codified in the ordinance of 1670, the practice was limited to discovering the criminal's accomplices.[57]

In the French sources ordinary judicial torture is known as *torture préparatoire*, as opposed to this torture of a convict, so-called *torture préalable*, literally "preliminary torture" in the sense of being preliminary to the execution of the capital sentence. The safeguards of the ordinary law of torture, such as the requirement of probable cause, did not exist. Torture préalable was regarded as much less objectionable than ordinary judicial torture. Even Voltaire defended it.[58] When Louis XVI abolished ordinary judicial torture in 1780, he excepted torture préalable until 1788.[59]

Requiring confession for condemnation. A less functional practice was the usage, widely reported for Belgium, that treated confession as a prerequisite for condemnation even when full witness proof had been obtained.[60] This practice contradicted the rule of the ius commune that torture was a last resort, to be used only when full proof was not to be had by other means.[61]

Several of the more common torture devices are reproduced on the following pages from engravings appended to the Austrian Empire's criminal procedure code of 1769, the *Constitutio Criminalis Theresiana,* discussed infra page 50. The illustrations, which depict modes of torture employed in Prague and Vienna, are how-to-do-it guides for local craftsmen and court officers in constructing and operating the devices.

The accompanying text describes the various features of the devices and the tasks of the operators.

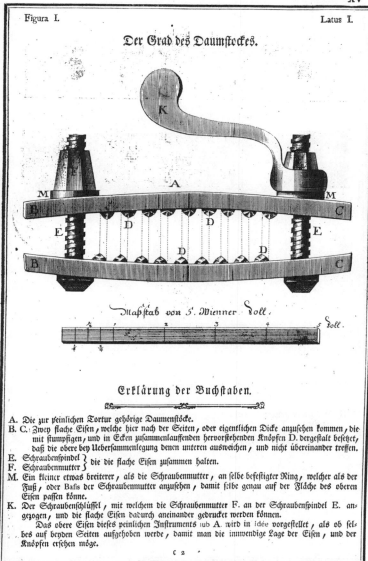

Figura I.   Latus I.

Der Grad des Daumstockes.

Erklärung der Buchstaben.

A. Die zur peinlichen Tortur gehörige Daumenstöcke.
B. C. Zwey flache Eisen, welche hier nach der Seiten, oder eigentlichen Dicke anzusehen kommen, die mit stumpfigen, und in Ecken zusammenlauffenden hervorstehenden Knöpfen D. dergestalt besetzet, daß die obere bey Uebersammenlegung denen unteren ausweichen, und nicht übereinander treffen.
E. Schraubenspindel } die die flache Eisen zusammen halten.
F. Schraubenmutter }
M. Ein kleiner etwas breiterer, als die Schraubenmutter, an selbe befestigter Ring, welcher als der Fuß, oder Basis der Schraubenmutter anzusehen, damit selbe genau auf der Fläche des oberen Eisen passen könne.
K. Der Schraubenschlüssel, mit welchem die Schraubenmutter F. an der Schraubenspindel E. angezogen, und die flache Eisen dadurch aneinander gedrucket werden können.
     Das obere Eisen dieses peinlichen Instruments sub A. wird in idée vorgestellet, als ob selbes auf beyden Seiten aufgehoben werde, damit man die innwendige Lage der Eisen, und der Knöpfen ersehen möge.

Thumbscrew: the suspect's thumbs are inserted in a vice and compressed between the metal-studded surfaces.

Vorſtellung auf was Weiſe, und auf welchem Platz des unteren flachen Eiſen die Daumen des Inquiſiten zu legen?

Das untere flache Eiſen.

Erklärung der Buchſtaben.

M. N. Das untere flache Eiſen von den Daumſtöcken, worauf der Ort angedeutet zu ſehen, wohin die Daumen Y. zu legen ſind.
R. Ende des erſten Glieds des Daumens.
Y. Die beyde Spitzen der Daumen.

The lower plate of the thumbscrew, with the two thumbs shown in place.

Vorſtellung der eigentlichen Anwendung des Daumſtockes, mit den hierzu nöthigen Perſonen.

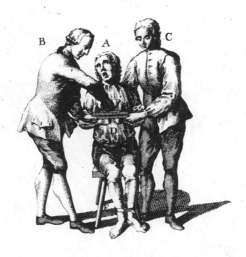

Erklärung der Buchſtaben.

A. Der Inquiſit, auf dem gleich hiernach des mehreren entworffenen Bankel, oder Schammel ſitzend.
B. Der Freymann, der mit der linken Hand den Daumſtock an einem Ende haltet, mit der anderen aber mit dem Schraubenſchlüſſel beyde flache Eiſen wechſelweiſe an den Schraubſpindeln immer mehr, und mehr zuſammen ſchraubet.
C. Der Freymannsknecht, welcher mit dem rechten Arm den Inquiſiten an den Schultern, und mit der linken Hand den Daumſtock bey dem anderen Ende haltet.
D. Des Inquiſitens Hände.
E. Ein Riem, womit dem Inquiſiten die Füſſe zuſammen geſchnallet ſind.

The thumbscrew shown being applied to the suspect, who is seated with his legs secured.

Figura IV.

Latus II.

Entwürff des obern Leibs des Inquisiten, wie selber nach vollzogener brennüng von vorne anzüsehen.

Entwürff dieses grads der peinliche Tortur neme: des Feuers.

Entwürff des nach der Seiten, und vollendeten Grad des Feüers anzüse; Senden Inquisitens.

Erklärung der Buchstaben.

A. Der Inquisite, wie selber von der Seiten in vollzogener Außdehnung bey diesem Grad des Feuers auf der Folter anzusehen kommet.
B. Der Scharfrichter, welcher also auf der Leiter stehet, daß selber des Inquisiten Fuße zwischen den seinigen habe, und mit dem rechten unten auf dem Sprossen aufstehet, mit dem linken Fuß aber auf die Sprossen kniet. In beyden Händen haltet er zwey angezündete Buschen Unschlittkerzen F. deren jeder aus 8. zusammen gebundenen Kerzen bestehet, und fahret mit selben dem Inquisiten auf die beyde Seitentheile der Brust, oder latera pectoria in der mitleren Gegend zwischen der Achsel, und der Weiche (oder Ilia) in die Rundung 3. bis 4mal beyderseits zugleich herum.
C. Die Achselhöhle, so von der ruckwärts gedrehten Schulterhöhe verdeckt.
D. Die Weichen, oder Ilia.
E. Die beyden Warzen, welche mit der Brennung verschonet werden müssen.
F. Die zwey angezündete, und etwas schief an den Leib des Inquisiten zuhaltende Buschen Unschlittkerzen, welche dergestalt angehalten werden müssen, damit die in den brennenden Buschen befindliche erste Kerzen mit ihrem Docht an den Leib des Inquisiten angehalten, von denen übrigen aber die Flammen auf die zubrennende Theile frey spielen können; diese Brennung, so auf beyden Seiten, gleichsam durch 3. runde Cirkeln L vorgestellet, wird während ausgesetzten Zeit der Peinigungssatz 10. bis 11mal widerholet.
G. Der mit Handhabel die Waisen fest haltende Knecht, damit sich selbe nicht umdrehe.
H. Der Inquisit, wie selber nach vollzogener Brennung seitwärts anzusehen ist.
K. Der von vorne anzusehende Inquisit nach vollzogener Brennung.
L. Die in allen 3. Vorstellungen A. K. und H. des Inquisten gebrennte Flecke, oder Cirkeln.
M. Der ruckwärts stehende Knecht, der in Erforderungsfall die Lichter abbutzet.

The rack: a flaming torch is being applied to the side of the suspect's chest while he is being racked.

Strappado: the suspect is hoisted by a pulley so that his weight is on his wrists. Weights are shown on the floor, ready to be attached to his feet to increase the strain.

Figura IV.   Maßstab von 6. Wienner Zoll.   Latus I.

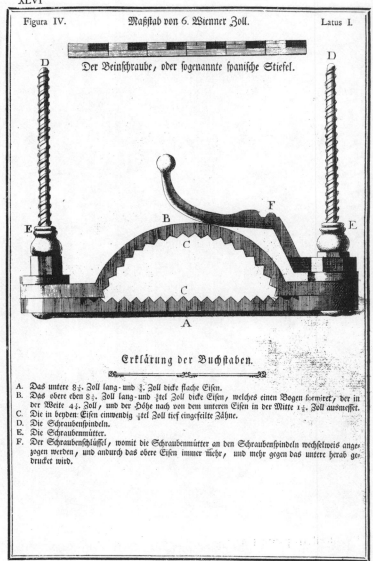

Der Beinschraube, oder sogenannte spanische Stiefel.

Erklärung der Buchstaben.

A. Das untere 8¼. Zoll lang - und ⅜. Zoll dicke flache Eisen.
B. Das obere eben 8¼. Zoll lang - und ⅜tel Zoll dicke Eisen, welches einen Bogen formiret, der in der Weite 4¼. Zoll, und der Höhe nach von dem unteren Eisen in der Mitte 1¼. Zoll ausmesset.
C. Die in beyden Eisen einwendig ⅛tel Zoll tief eingefeilte Zähne.
D. Die Schraubenspindeln.
E. Die Schraubenmütter.
F. Der Schraubenschlüssel, womit die Schraubenmütter an den Schraubenspindeln wechselweis angezogen werden, und andurch das obere Eisen immer mehr, und mehr gegen das untere herab gedrucket wird.

Legscrew: the suspect's leg is inserted in a metal vice whose inner surfaces are scored with sharp edges.

Figura IV.   Latus III.

Vorstellung der eigentlichen Anlegung des Beinschraubens, und der hierzu benöthigten Personen.

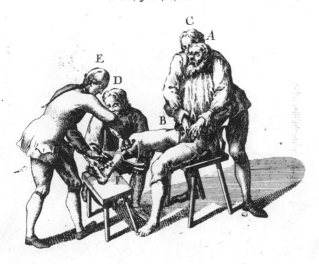

Erklärung der Buchstaben.

A. Der auf einem ordinari Lehnstuhl sitzende Inquisit.

B. Des Inquisitens auf einem etwas niedrigen Bankel, oder Schammel hindanngestreckter Fuß.

C. Ein Freymannsknecht, der Inquisiten von ruckwärts bey beyden Armen auf dem Stuhl niederhält.

D. Ein anderer Freymannsknecht, der mit der linken Hand Inquisitens Fuß auf dem Schammel nieder, und mit der anderen rechten jenseits des Freymanns den Beinschrauben hält.

E. Der Freymann, so mit der linken Hand den Beinschrauben haltet, und mit der Rechten mittelst des Schraubenschlüssels beyde Eisen wechselweis an den Schraubenspindeln immer mehr, und mehr zusammenziehet.

F. Der an den Fuß des Inquisiten dergestalten angelegte Beinschraube, daß das untere flache Eisen unten am Waden, und der Bogen von dem oberen Eisen über das Schinn- und Wadenbein zu liegen kommet.

Legscrew in operation.

Figura V.

Latus IV.

Entwurff der Anlegung der Schraubſtiefeln.

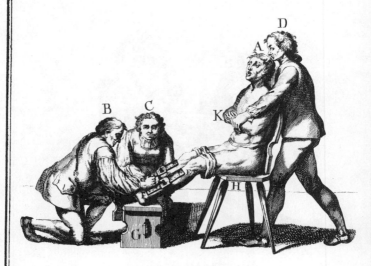

Erklärung der Buchſtaben.

A. Der auf einem Stuhl H. ſitzende Inquiſit.

B. Der Scharffrichter, welcher mit der linken Hand den Fuß des Inquiſiten haltet, mit der rechten aber den Schraubenſchlüſſel umdrehet, und dadurch die beyden Theile der Schraubſtiefeln aneinander ziehet.

C. Der neben der linken Seiten des Scharffrichters knicende, und dem Inquiſiten ſeinen rechten Fuß in der Lage haltende Knecht.

D. Der hinter dem Inquiſiten ſtehende Knecht, welcher demſelben die beyden Hände auf der Bruſt kreuzweis zuſammen haltet.

E. Der Ort, wo die Anlegung des oberen Eiſens, ſo einen ſtarken Mannszoll tief unter der Knieſcheiben geſchehen muß, weil anſonſten, ſofern das Eiſen an der Knieſcheiben zu liegen kommet, das Band der Knieſcheiben, oder Ligamentum patelæ gedrucket würde, wodurch die Articulation des Knies ſelbſten Gewalt leidete, folglich eine Extravaſation in der Höhle der Knie- Articulation entſtünde, wodurch eine Steiffigkeit, oder Anchyloſis erfolgete.

F. Der Ort oberhalb dem Knöchel, wo das End der Eiſen aufzuliegen kommet.

G. Eine halbe Ellen hohes Schämmerl, worauf die beyden Füſſe des Inquiſiten vorwärts gerad ausgeſtreckter mit den Ferſen aufzuliegen kommen.

H. Ein Lehnſtuhl, ſo eine Ellen hoch iſt.

K. Die beyden Hände des Inquiſiten, ſo von dem ruckwärts ſtehenden Knecht D. zuſammen gehalter werden.

A double legscrew of somewhat different construction being applied to the suspect.

2 The Transformation of Criminal Sanctions

The movement for the abolition of capital punishment is rightly associated with the writers of the Enlightenment, especially Beccaria, whose enormously influential tract appeared in 1764. Perhaps because the abolitionists drew so much attention to the gore of the capital sanctions of the eighteenth century, it has seldom been realized that capital punishment was already in a deep decline in the age of Beccaria and Voltaire. Writing to Voltaire in 1777, Frederick the Great boasted that in the whole Prussian realm executions had been occurring at the rate of only fourteen or fifteen per year.[1] When John Howard visited Bremen in 1778, he discovered that "[t]here has been no execution in this city for twenty-six years."[2] The abolition movement that we associate with Beccaria and Voltaire[3] was a second-stage affair. Indeed, it had to be. For abolition presupposes the existence of a workable alternative for the punishment of serious crime.

The Blood Sanctions

"The one punishment," said Maitland, "that can easily be inflicted by a state which has no apparatus of prisons and penitentiaries is death."[4] Another class of sanctions as easy to administer as death is physical mutilation of the culprit. These punishments, death and maiming, were the ordinary penalties for serious crime in the Western legal systems in the later Middle Ages.

At about the time that the medieval sanctions were entering their long decline, they were codified in the German Empire in the *Constitutio Criminalis Carolina* of 1532.[5] The statute provides a typical assortment of modes of capital punishment. An ordinary murderer or burglar merits hanging in chains or beheading with the sword. A woman who murders her infant is buried alive and impaled, a traitor is drawn and quartered. Other grave offenders may be burned to death, or drowned, or set out to die in agony upon the wheel with their limbs smashed. If the court thinks that the circumstances of the crime merit severer punishment, it may order that the criminal be dragged to the place of execution, and that his flesh be torn with red-hot tongs before he is killed. For less grave offenses the Carolina prescribes afflictive punishments—flogging, pillorying, cutting off the ears, chopping off the fingers, cutting out the tongue—usually accompanied by a sentence of banishment. The Carolina's catalog of sanctions for serious crime exemplifies not only German but general European practice of the age.[6]

The first comprehensive criminal code that completely abolished capital punishment was the *Leopoldina*[7] of 1786, promulgated by the future German (Austrian) Emperor Leopold II for the state of Tuscany, the region around Florence and Pisa which was then a Hapsburg duchy. In the Leopoldina a few of the punishments are familiar—flogging, pillorying, and banishment. But the Carolina's blood sanctions have disappeared. The principal sanction that has displaced capital punishment is imprisonment. (We shall be using the word "imprisonment" in the sense of the German *Freiheitsstrafe* to mean confinement anywhere, not just in prison, and to include both confinement simple and confinement subject to further conditions such as hard labor.) In the Leopoldina, confinement, sometimes at hard labor for terms up to life, has become the exclusive sanction for serious crime,[8] whereas two and a half centuries before, in the Carolina, death and maiming had been equally exclusive.

The substitution of various forms of imprisonment for the sanctions of the medieval law began in the sixteenth and seventeenth centuries both on the Continent and in England. By the middle of the eighteenth century, when the first demands for total abolition of capital punishment were made, the death penalty had everywhere ceased to be the exclusive punishment for serious crime. The abolition movement is much celebrated. In this chapter we shall be looking at the development that made it possible.

Medieval Imprisonment

Imprisonment had an important place in European criminal procedure in the Middle Ages, but not as a sanction. The rule of the ius commune, repeated incessantly by the jurists and codified in statutes like the Carolina, was that prisons were meant to detain and not to punish.[9] In cases of serious crime the only function that the jurists conceded to imprisonment was pretrial detention, keeping custody of the accused while the court decided whether to acquit him or to convict and punish him with a blood sanction. This "custodial"[10] or "preventive"[11] imprisonment is distinguished from the other common medieval usage that the jurists approved: "coercive" imprisonment designed to compel someone to take some other procedural step, characteristically the payment of a crown debt or a civil judgment debt.[12]

We are concerned with a third usage, so-called "penal" or "punitive" imprisonment,[13] confinement as a mode of punishment. Penal imprisonment first appeared in the Middle Ages in the legal system of the church. Ecclesiastical courts did not impose the blood sanctions, which in canon law were deemed inconsistent with the clerical station. Even when ecclesiastical proceedings led to a death sentence, as in the heresy inquisitions, the church courts "relaxed" the condemned heretic to the secular authorities for the imposition of capital punishment.[14] Incapable of employing the ordinary secular sanctions of the day, the church had a considerable incentive to develop an alternative. The church also had the elementary administrative capacity that imprisonment requires, to construct and maintain places of confinement and to care for those incarcerated.[15]

Penal imprisonment did enter the secular legal systems in the late Middle Ages, but not in place of the blood sanctions for serious crimes. Rather, penal imprisonment was imposed as a sanction for petty crime, often as a "surrogate penalty"[16] for a petty offender who was unable to pay a fine, sometimes as a "collateral penalty"[17] in addition to a fine. In Italy, France, Germany, and England the sources evidence growing use of short-term imprisonment as a sanction for economic and moral regulation from the fourteenth century onward.[18] When the Belgian jurist Damhouder summarized the practice of the mid-sixteenth century, it was still true that of the "several sorts of prisons," only those of the church were being used to punish serious crime. The secular prisons existed to guard serious offenders until their trials. Only for petty crime were the secular courts sentencing culprits to brief prison terms, occasionally on a diet of bread and water.[19]

The Galley Sentence

Over the course of the sixteenth and seventeenth centuries the foundations were laid at opposite ends of Europe for a new penal system for serious crime. The Mediterranean states introduced the galley sentence, and the countries of the North founded the workhouse. Both institutions arose to serve social purposes remote from the ordinary criminal law. Nevertheless, they converged under the ancien régime to form the prison system that displaced the blood sanctions from European law.

"The galley sentence arose not from the needs of criminal justice, rather its origin is most closely connected with the development of the medieval fleets of the naval powers of southern Europe."[20] Although sailing ships were coming into use by the end of the Middle Ages, galleys rowed by oarsmen continued to be important military vessels in the Mediterranean into the eighteenth century. Because galleys were highly maneuverable, they were more suitable for Mediterranean coastal waters than were the oceangoing ships of the Atlantic. Unlike wind powered craft, they could not be becalmed. Not until the eighteenth century did the superior size, speed, and firepower of the sailing ships fully overcome the military advantages of the galleys and render them obsolete.[21]

Galleys required several hundred oarsmen rowing in unison. The work was strenuous, dangerous, and severely disciplined.[22] Because volunteer oarsmen were seldom in sufficient supply, the fleets supplemented hirelings with galley slaves, usually Turks and North Africans either captured in war or bought for the purpose.[23] When these sources became inadequate to staff the growing fleets of the fifteenth and sixteenth centuries, the practice began in the West of forcing condemned criminals to serve as oarsmen.[24] Convicts whom the state had been eliminating through capital punishment were now regarded as a potential resource. From Spain,[25] Italy,[26] and France[27] the galley sentence spread to the North. It is reported in the Netherlands[28] in the 1520s, in Belgium[29] and Austria[30] in the 1550s.

Condemned criminals were at first obtained for the galleys by exercise of executive commutation power. In France, *lettres royales* commissioned "galley captains to procure oarsmen among the prisoners condemned to death or to another major bodily punishment."[31] In Belgium, then the Spanish Netherlands, Charles V and Philip II periodically authorized their governor in Brussels to commute capital punishment into sentences to the Spanish galleys.[32] The Austrian Hapsburgs were delegating their commutation power when they authorized local courts in their German, Austrian, and Bohemian lands to remit capital sentences into galley sentences for Philip's fleet.[33]

In France and the other states that made relatively sustained use of the galley sentence, the courts undertook to impose galley sentences directly.[34] However, the need for oarsmen fluctuated with the fortunes of the fleet. In France, for example, Henry III had to order the courts to cease sending men to the galleys in 1558, whereas in 1602 Henry IV was again demanding galley convicts.[35] In 1662 Colbert found it necessary to "reestablish" galley sentences for the wars of Louis XIV, imploring the courts to "convert the death penalty into that of the galleys...."[36] In Austria, which had no fleet of its own, the galley sentence was spasmodically employed for the benefit of allied fleets—in 1556, again in 1570, and variously in the seventeenth century.[37] After the Austrians acquired Naples in 1707, an imperial patent of 1716 instituted the export of convicts to the Neapolitan fleet.[38] By 1727 there was a surplus of Austrian convicts in Naples, and in 1728 the courts were ordered to cut back.[39] Courts in some regions of the Austrian Empire continued to sentence convicts to galley service in Venice until Maria Theresa forbade it in 1762.[40]

The motivation for the galley sentence was strictly exploitative. There was occasional lip service to reformative values, such as the Austrian King Ferdinand's pronouncement in a patent of 1556 that galley service would give the criminal an opportunity to atone for his misdeeds through hard labor.[41] Damhouder was more honest in calling the galleys worse than death,[42] and Ferdinand remarked in the Austrian patent of 1556 that since galley service was more feared than execution, changing capital sentences to galley sentences ought not to impair the deterrent force of the criminal law.[43] Ferdinand also ordered that convicts who were physically unfit for galley service should be executed as before.[44] Humanitarian considerations were equally distant in seventeenth-century France, where statute provided for one class of galley convicts to have their ears and noses cut off and to be branded with fleurs-de-lis on each cheek before being sent to the galleys for life.[45] We can imagine what conditions forced Louis XIV to issue a decree[46] in 1677 complaining that men sentenced to the galleys had been mutilating themselves in order to avoid galley service, and henceforth those who did it would be put to death.[47]

In periods when the need for oarsmen was intense, the authorities cast a very wide net for convicts. Men who merited the death sentence were sent to the galleys for life, lesser offenders were sent to the galleys for terms of years instead of being maimed or banished.[48] Vagabonds were conscripted.[49] On the other hand, the galley sentence did not wholly eliminate capital punishment, even when oarsmen were in great demand. The most heinous offenders continued to be subjected to capital punishment,[50] perhaps for deterrent purposes, perhaps for fear that they might escape from the galleys and return to their former ways.

The development of the galley sentence reflected not only the new needs of the Renaissance state but its new capacities as well. Convicts had to be selected, assembled, provisioned, chained, and marched to the ports.[51] The flow of convicts had to be adjusted to the fluctuating requirements of the fleets. The fleets had to be provisioned on a scale massive by comparison with former times.[52] The medieval state had been capable of nothing more than the blood sanctions. The galley sanction may not have been a humanitarian advance, but an administrative feat it surely was.

The galley fleets declined rapidly in the eighteenth century as refinements in sailing ships overcame the former advantages of the galleys. But although "galleys lost naval usefulness, their value as prisons remained."[53] In France, the galleys became "essentially prison hulks for the accommodation of convicts who slept aboard, and usually worked ashore by day."[54] When the supply of Austrian convicts began to exceed the demands of the Neapolitan fleet, the emperor ordered in 1728 that most convicts be diverted to work in the mines of Hungary or elsewhere.[55]

Throughout its history the galley system had many of the characteristics which would later be associated with the workhouse and the prison. The critical factor was the seasonal constraint upon the galleys' naval operations. In France, for example, "galleys normally went to sea only during the spring or summer of the year, for a campaign of two or three months at most; during the remainder of the year they were tied up in port (except for irregular forays near Marseilles to exercise or train their oarsmen), and the rowing force was employed ashore."[56] Bamford's recent book gives a fascinating account of the way galley service was extended into more general penal servitude. Although each galley convict received a daily ration of food, "the fare would not satisfy an able-bodied man," which "encouraged oarsmen to employ their extra time and energy earning money for supplementary food."[57] A remarkable variety of employment was found for the convicts. Some worked in "tiny shops . . . along the wharves adjacent to the galley anchorage; others labored daily . . . on the galley itself at some trade or handiwork. Some worked at widely scattered places around Marseilles. Others left the galley daily at dawn with [guards] accompanying them for regular or occasional work in the metropolis. Another group left the galleys to work in the naval arsenal itself."[58] In the eighteenth century as the galley fleet declined, the convicts were used largely on construction work in the port cities or in manufactures (bagnes) indistinguishable from the prison workhouses of the North.[59]

The Workhouse

In the second half of the sixteenth century the institution of the workhouse was developed. Like the galley sentence—"the great novelty"[60] in criminal sanctions of the first half of the sixteenth century—the workhouse also arose to serve social purposes somewhat removed from the ordinary criminal law. It was a response to "the problem of poverty and vagrancy [that] had reached an acuteness probably never before encountered."[61] Nevertheless, the workhouse like the galleys helped bring about a lasting alteration in the system of punishing serious crime. More than to any other source, the modern sanction of imprisonment for serious crime traces back to the workhouse for the poor.

The galley sentence was limited to the Mediterranean states and their allies; because the English navy did not have a galley fleet, the galley sentence could acquire no sphere in English criminal law.[62] Vagabondage, however, was a European-wide phenomenon, perhaps of particular intensity in England, and it was the English who devised the workhouse.

Throughout the sixteenth century "the position of the poorer classes"[63] was deteriorating and their numbers increasing. By the second half of the century, when Europe was "too densely populated for its resources and no longer riding a wave of economic growth, . . . the trend was toward the pauperization of considerable masses of people in desperate need of daily bread."[64] The causes were several. Because the European states had become "strong enough to preserve order and to control the power of the great lords,"[65] the feudal private armies were being disbanded as power "passed from the leaders of men to the holders of wealth."[66] Contemporaries all over Europe recorded that former retainers and sol-

diers were turning to begging and pillaging.[67] In the cities the growth
of manufacturing created a workforce more exposed to destitution
during declines of the business cycle.[68] In England the numbers of
this nascent urban proletariat may have been swelled by "agricul-
tural laborers and small yeomen"[69] displaced in the enclosure
movement. Simultaneously, the influx of bullion "from the New
World caused a general rise of prices. Food and clothing and rents
rose more quickly than wages, so that the poor could obtain fewer of
the necessities of life."[70] Finally, "[t]he agencies for giving aid to
the poor were themselves in a process of transformation."[71] The
dissolution of the English monasteries under Henry VIII was unique
in rapidity and extent, but elsewhere in Europe those "charitable
foundations, hospitals, and monasteries, which had reached their
greatest development during the preceding two or three centuries
under the aegis of the Church, were being dissolved or had deterio-
rated."[72] What poor relief there was seemed ill organized and
counterproductive—so "indiscriminate [that it] did nearly as much
to increase beggars as to relieve them."[73]

Although contemporaries applied the term "vagabond" to some
distinguishable types, there was a fairly consistent core notion. The
vagabond was poor, meaning not self-supporting; and he was usually
an outsider to the community that called him vagabond, a wanderer
from someplace else. Vagabondage tended to be an urban phenomenon. Throughout history surplus population has gravitated to the
cities in search of opportunity foreclosed on the land. The anonymity
of the cities also made it more difficult for the authorities to detect
and control vagabonds' movements. We think it no accident that the
workhouse movement originated in London, Norwich, Amsterdam,
Antwerp, Paris, and the cities of the German Hansa.[74]

Within the vagabond stream were several different elements.
"The first problem . . . is to know who the vagrant actually was, to
define his status. For vagrant and vagabond were emotive, elastic
terms."[75] There were the hopeless, those incapable of work by
reason of handicap. Second, there were those capable of work but
resisting—the "sturdy beggars" and "common soldiers" whose
presence was felt to be so disturbing. Third, some laborers temporar-
ily unemployed were reckoned among the vagabonds, people who
wandered occasionally because their permanent work was seasonal
or fluctuated with the business cycle.[76] Finally, contemporaries were
quick to lump with the vagabonds an element of professional petty

criminals—prostitutes, gamblers, petty thieves and the like.[77] There was a strong current of preventive criminal law in the regulation of vagabondage, a sense "that vagrants and bandits were brothers in hardship and might change places."[78]

The total social response to the problem of pauperism and vagabondage ranged far beyond the development of the workhouse. There were efforts to induce almsgiving and other charity, to generate tax revenue for poor relief, to restrict movement off the land, to control the price of food, and so forth.[79]

In England "the practice of London and certain other towns was in advance of the regulations of the statutes; the main feature of the period is the municipal organization of poor relief."[80] Bridewell, the former royal palace in London whose name became a generic term for later English houses of correction, appears to have been converted to the purpose by the 1550s.[81] The Bridewell in Norwich was operating in 1565.[82] Both cities instituted relatively benign schemes of public relief for the resident poor who could not work or who were in temporary distress;[83] both were alert to rid themselves of those recent immigrant poor whose place of settlement was identifiable.[84] To the Bridewells were sent the "sturdy beggars"[85] and "disordered" persons,[86] especially the young, and they were compelled to work for their sustenance. In Norwich the order of 1571 read: "The men to grind malt and other works, and the women to use their handedede [sic] and, except they work, not to eat."[87]

Unlike the galley sentence, the workhouse system was not wholly exploitative. There was present from the outset what we identify as the reformative policy of modern penology. The London order of 1579 prescribed: "Such youth, and other as are able to labor and may have work and shall be found idle shall have some manner of correction by the parents, or otherwise as shall be thought good in the parish. And if they will not amend, they shall be sent to Bridewell to be reasonably corrected there."[88] The workhouse would introduce the inmate to the regimen of honest labor, it would train him in a working skill, and it would reform his character through discipline and moral instruction. Thus equipped, he could be released, no longer a burden to his society. The workhouse would have reformed him.

The workhouse system that was instituted in Amsterdam in the 1590s is the subject of important studies by von Hippel[89] and Sellin,[90] work of a sort which has not been done on the English

Bridewells.[91] There were close trade connections between the Netherlands and England, especially Norwich and London.[92] It is widely supposed that the Amsterdam workhouses were set up in direct imitation of the English.[93] Another possibility is that the Bridewells served as the inspiration without being a detailed model: "once the idea of using labor and religious instruction as instruments of penal treatment arose, the translation of this idea into practice did not permit any great variety of means."[94]

From the outset the Amsterdam workhouse (*tuchthuis*) combined beggars and vagrants with petty criminals, a feature that was to become characteristic of English and German workhouses in the seventeenth century.

> Jan Van Hout, whose description of the [first Amsterdam] house [dating from 1597] is the earliest known, reported that among the inmates were vagrants without visible means of support, persons sentenced to terms of imprisonment by the magistrates; perpersons who had been publicly branded or whipped and then committed, and persons committed on petition by friends or relatives because of a dissolute or irregular life. The professional beggars furnished a sizable contingent. . . . The house was used also to punish runaway apprentices . . . . The aim was in many instances to provide an opportunity to learn a trade . . . . The terms of the sentences were from a few days to many years. While as the time went by ordinances were passed specifying the length of the imprisonment for certain offenses, most sentences could be imposed "at the discretion of the magistrates," permitting a certain amount of individualized punishment.[95]

Once the workhouse was devised for reforming the poor and the wayward, extending it to petty criminals was a small and almost obvious step. Imprisonment at forced labor commended itself as a via media between existing sanctions that were either too harsh for petty crime or else ineffectual. The blood sanctions seemed disproportionately severe, especially for youthful offenders.[96] On the other hand, banishment[97] and the lesser corporal punishments seemed inadequate. Banishment merely produced an "exchange" of such offenders "among the individual states . . . ."[98] Petty offenders could seldom afford money fines. For such reasons, we have already noted, the use of simple imprisonment had been growing in the later Middle Ages for some petty offenses.[99]

The workhouse offered two significant advantages over prior sanctions for petty crime. Because it was reformative, it meant to correct as well as to punish. The reformed man would emerge skilled for and reconciled to work. Second, because the workhouse was in fact a small manufactory, it might recover its costs from the labor of its inmates. This form of imprisonment would not burden the perpetually inadequate public revenues of the time. In Norwich the men were "to grind malt,"[100] in London some "twenty-five occupations were practised in Bridewell. Amongst these were such trades as the making of gloves, silk lace, pins, bays, felts and tennis balls . . . ."[101] The Amsterdam workhouses began with spinning and weaving. When the Dutch weaving industry declined, the women's house turned to the sewing of linen goods and the knitting of nets while the men's house was put to the rasping of imported dyewoods, that is, grinding logs into chips from which pigment could be extracted.[102] "The system of labor used would in modern terminology be called a contract system. The users of the rasped wood purchased it from the [workhouse] under contracts approved by the burgomasters."[103] It is a significant indication of the economic potential of the workhouse that inmates were paid in money for production above the minimum required of them in return for their daily keep. "This money constituted a small fund given to the prisoner on his discharge."[104]

The workhouse satisfied diverse concerns, humanitarian[105] and practical—for the relief of the poor, for preventive criminal justice, for reforming wayward youth—while happily paying for itself by extracting the labor of its inmates. It is easy to understand, therefore, why the workhouse system would be adopted widely in the age in which governments developed the administrative capacity to operate such an institution.

The Amsterdam workhouse system in fact exercised enormous influence in northern Europe. Within a few years it acquired such renown in the Netherlands "that near-by cities which had no similar facilities began to request permission to commit to it some of their offenders."[106] Numerous Dutch towns built their own workhouses early in the seventeenth century, and in the 1610s and 1620s the major Belgian cities (Antwerp, Brussels, Ghent) followed suit.[107] In France, workhouses were first organized in Paris in the 1610s, then in many other French cities later in the century.[108] The first German workhouse, in Bremen, was planned after consultation with the Amsterdam authorities and opened in 1613.[109] Thereafter Amsterdam and Bremen served as models for the German cities and states. Lübeck's workhouse was separate from an earlier shelter for the poor by 1613. Hamburg's workhouse was long in planning, and was in use by 1622 at the latest. Kassel's was built in 1617, Danzig's in 1629.[110] Later in the century after the Thirty Years War the foundations multiplied: Breslau and Vienna in 1670, Leipzig in 1671, Lüneburg in 1676, Brunswick in 1678, Frankfurt/Main in 1679, Munich in 1682, Spandau and Magdeburg in 1687, Königsberg in 1691.[111] The workhouse spread still more widely in the German states in the eighteenth century.[112]

Imprisonment

From the middle of the seventeenth century there is evidence that the workhouses for the poor were receiving some inmates who had been convicted of serious crime. By the end of the century specialized institutions were in operation in which serious offenders who would formerly have been subjected to the blood sanctions were confined for long terms at hard labor. The workhouse suggested the prison. This development recorded itself upon the German language. The Dutch *tuchthuis* became in German the *Zuchthaus*, a word which lost the meaning of "workhouse" for vagabonds and petty offenders and acquired the modern sense of "prison" or "penitentiary" for serious offenders.

In Bremen in 1648 a young man whose thieving merited death by hanging was, on account of his age and other mitigating factors, sentenced to perpetual imprisonment in irons, then put in the Bremen Zuchthaus to labor for his keep. He was released in 1652.[113] In Amsterdam one writer reported in 1663 that capital offenders were sometimes not executed, but sent to the tuchthuis for terms from two to twenty years. Another observer in 1696 reported "sentences of the same class of prisoners" from three years to life.[114] An ordinance of 1639 provided for ten- and fifteen-year terms in the Danzig Zuchthaus.[115] In the second half of the century Hamburg was replacing death sentences with long terms of confinement at hard labor.[116] The Prussian sentence to *Festungsarbeit*, forced labor on construction projects on the military fortresses and roads, was in use before 1685.[117] Sentences to forced labor on the highways were used in Nuremburg and Wurtemberg in the seventeenth century,[118] while at the same time Austria was employing convict labor in the mines and fortresses.[119]

When capital felons were rescued from death for a sentence of hard labor for life, the motive was strictly exploitative. Contemporaries understood that these schemes of lifetime confinement at hard labor were the German equivalents of the galley sentence.[120]

The rationale for the determinate sentences—that is, for terms less than life—was more complex. In Wurtemberg an executive rescript of 1627 instructed the courts to replace the blood sanctions with sentences to forced labor (except for criminals whose crime merited the most extreme death penalties), especially for skilled craftsmen for whose reform there was some hope.[121] The rescript was obeyed, and offenders who would previously have been banished or maimed or killed were instead put to terms of years or months at forced labor.[122] In Prussia, Frederick William I set up the prisons at Spandau and Magdeburg in order to develop a domestic woolen industry with convict labor.[123] We see, therefore, motives as diverse as for the workhouse: to reform offenders,[124] to save the lives of skilled workers who could contribute to the mercantilist state,[125] to render criminal sanctions more humane,[126] and to exploit forced labor.

By the middle of the eighteenth century, the combination of the galleys and the prisons had produced a drastic diminution in the use of blood sanctions. The maiming sanctions largely disappeared,[127] and the death penalty declined. Although careful statistical study is thus far lacking, we have enough snippets of evidence to see the pattern. For example, the Nuremberg executioner Franz Schmidt inflicted an average of more than eight capital sentences per year in that city alone from 1573 to 1617.[128] By contrast, in the 1770s executions averaged less than twelve per year for the whole of Prussia,[129] and just over thirty-one per year for Austria-Bohemia.[130]

Transportation

The workhouse system originated in England, but imprisonment at hard labor as a sanction for serious crime was not systematized there until the middle of the nineteenth century.[131] Nevertheless, the decline in capital punishment that we have observed on the Continent in the seventeenth and eighteenth centuries also occurred in England, although to a lesser extent.[132] As a base point, Stephen's suggestion[133] that executions were running at around 800 per year in England in Elizabeth's last years looks quite reasonable in the light of the evidence.[134] By contrast, in the year 1805 there were 68 executions,[135] hence a decline of better than 90 percent over the two centuries. Building on Jeaffreson's computations for the seventeenth century, Radzinowicz shows the following decline in executions for Middlesex and London: during the years 1607–1616, 140 executions per year; during the reign of Charles I, 90 per year; during the Commonwealth, 85 per year; during 1749–1758, 36.5 per year; during 1790–1799, 22 per year; and during 1800–1810, 12.3 per year.[136]

As on the Continent, the decline in England's "penal death rate"[137] came about because of the development of an alternative to the blood sanctions: transportation of convicts for terms of labor as indentured servants in the overseas colonies. Transportation of felons began as a trickle in the years 1615–1660, became substantial in the period 1660–1700, and expanded greatly after 1717.

English law was notorious for prescribing the death penalty for a vast range of offenses as slight as the theft of goods valued at twelve pence. Transportation was by no means the only mechanism for avoiding the imposition of the death penalty. Benefit of clergy permitted many first offenders to escape with their lives after being whipped and branded. Sympathetic juries might acquit the guilty or undervalue stolen goods in order to convict culprits of noncapital petty larceny. Royal pardons were surprisingly frequent.[138] However, it was transportation that gave England a via media between the blood sanctions and the petty sanctions, comparable to the French galley sentence or the Austrian and Prussian *Festungsstrafe*.

Curiously, transportation can be traced to a stillborn attempt to introduce the galley sentence in England. Near the end of the sixteenth century, plans seem to have been underway to create an English galley fleet. A statute of 1597 against vagabonds,[139] one of a group of statutes that formed "the great Elizabethan code"[140] of that year for dealing with the poor, authorizes the courts of quarter sessions either to banish certain incorrigible vagabonds or to send them to the galleys. This provision probably did not come into use, but there is evidence from Devonshire and elsewhere[141] that some convicted felons were reprieved for galley service, whatever that may have meant. Although England did not in fact construct a galley fleet, the prospect of doing so was imminent enough in 1602 to lead

Elizabeth to issue a commission to a group of privy councillors and
judges, authorizing them "to reprieve and stay from Execution
[felons] of strong and able Bodies to serve in Galleys...."[142] This
commission became the model for James' commission of 1615 to the
Privy Council that first authorized the transportation of felons "who
for strength of body or other abilities shall be thought fit to be
employed in foreign discoveries or other services beyond the
seas."[143]

Both commissions pertained to persons convicted of "robbery or
felony," but excluded the especially heinous offenses of "willful
murder, rape and burglary." (The 1615 commission also excluded
felons convicted of witchcraft.) Both authorized any six of the commissioners to act, and both had a quorum clause requiring that at least
two of those exercising the commission be drawn from a more select
group including the Lord Chancellor and the Lord Treasurer. Both
empowered the commissioners to reprieve felons for any mission and
for any length of service. Both provided for enrolling the orders of
the commissioners in the Crown Office of the King's Bench.

Most revealingly, the preamble of the 1615 commission declaring
its purposes follows the language of the 1602 commission, while
softening and amplifying it considerably. The "severity of our laws"
punishing felony with death make it "most requisite [that] some
other speedy remedy be added for ease unto our people." In order to
temper justice with mercy, the monarch orders that some of the
"lesser offenders adjudged by law to die" be punished instead in a
manner that will correct them "and yield a profitable service to the
Commonwealth in parts abroad...." We see the familiar congeries
of purposes that motivated the workhouse and the prison: to avoid the
severity of the blood sanctions, to correct the offender, to exploit his
labor.

The mechanics of sparing convicted felons for transportation went
through three phases. The first was the procedure of the 1615 commission, which depended on the initiative of the Privy Council to
institute reprieves and to arrange with contractors to export the felons
to the colonies. In his admirable study[144] of the seventeenth-century
transportation system, A. E. Smith discovered a number of relatively
minor revisions of this commission over succeeding decades.[145] He
computes that less than 200 convicts were transported in the forty
years to 1655.

In that year there first appeared the device of the conditional pardon. From 1661 to 1700 about 4,500 convicts were sent to the colonies in this way.[146] The form was a royal pardon, conditioned upon the convict being transported to the colonies for a fixed term, usually of seven years. This procedure eliminated the need to have the busy Privy Council propel the system. The initiative passed to the assize judges and the entrepreneurs:

> After a jail delivery or other major assize, the justices sent up to the secretary of state a pardon fully drafted for such of the convicts as they thought worthy of saving from the gallows. If sentence had already been passed on any of them execution was stayed. . . . This complete document was signed by the king and countersigned by the secretary of state. . . . The whole process became purely formal, and no case has been found where a pardon so recommended was refused, though the king frequently commanded that additional persons be included. The last step in the proceedings was for the prisoners to appear in open court and "plead their pardons," after which those who had been slated for transportation were available for shipment. . . .
> Actual shipment of the convicts was performed by merchants trading to the plantations, and it was enjoined in the pardon itself that they should give good security for the safe conveyance of their charges out of England. Arrangements with these merchants were entrusted to the sheriffs, or to the recorder of London, and the merchants made their profit by selling convicts as indentured servants in the colonies. It was thus essentially a private business, with which the colonial authorities had little or no concern.[147]

The transportation system seems to have declined at the end of the seventeenth century. In Maryland and Virginia, the two principal importers, the colonial legislatures passed hostile laws that "cramped the trade,"[148] while "the demand for white servants had lessened in the West Indies . . . ."[149] During the period 1704–1715 Smith found "negligible" evidence of transportation and some suggestion that men were instead being pardoned for service in the army.[150] (Marlborough's major campaigns in the War of the Spanish Succession ran from 1702 to 1709; the Treaty of Utrecht of 1713 ended the war.) Transportation revived somewhat thereafter; in 1715 and 1716 upwards of 100 convicts were pardoned for transportation.[151]

In 1717 the transportation system entered its third phase and acquired for the first time a statutory basis.[152] Trial courts themselves were empowered to sentence to transportation persons convicted of the property crimes which had theretofore been punishable by whipping and branding for first offenders on account of benefit of clergy.[153] (Benefit of clergy for such crimes had been extended to women in the seventeenth century and to illiterates in 1707.)[154] For nonclergyable offenses the former system of royal pardon on judicial recommendation continued. The 1717 statute empowered the court itself to "convey" the convicts to entrepreneurs "who shall contract" to transport them. The court was authorized to make these arrangements both for offenders whom it sentenced to transportation and for those guilty of nonclergyable offenses who pleaded conditional pardons.

The Act of 1717 was taken to overrule the Maryland and Virginia legislation preventing transportation.[155] Smith estimates that 30,000 felons were transported to the American colonies in the next sixty years, of whom more than 20,000 were sent to Maryland and Virginia, the rest mostly to the Carribbean.[156] As a result, one calculation for felony convicts in England in the later eighteenth century suggests that only 7.5 per cent were executed, and most of the remainder transported.[157]

The American Revolutionary War interrupted England's export of convicts in the 1770s. As a stopgap, which in fact lasted until the foundations of the modern prison system in the mid-nineteenth century, the government "decided to moor hulks on the Thames, put convicts in them and work them at hard labor."[158] When it became clear in the 1780s that the American colonies were lost for the purpose, the Australian penal colony at Botany Bay was established.[159]

Europe and England

The transportation system was England's analogue to the Continental galley and prison sanctions, and contemporaries knew it. For example, in a tract[160] written in 1725 Bernard Mandeville criticized various aspects of the transportation system. Convicts escaped before shipment, he complained, or returned to England prematurely. In the New World they were less an asset than a liability, corrupting the Negro slaves. By contrast, Mandeville pointed out, the French and Spanish "make use of Malefactors in their Galleys," and "the great Cities of [Holland] have all Work-houses for Criminals. At *Amsterdam* there is one, where Felons are kept constantly employed in rasping of *Brasil* wood."[161] Hence the author's modest proposal, to send English felons into galley service with the Moroccans in exchange for the captive British sailors now there.[162]

With Mandeville's suggestion we may contrast a message from the younger Colbert to a provincial judge issued in 1684, during Louis XIV's sustained effort to build up the French galley fleet: "The king has been informed that you have rendered several sentences to send to the American islands, as a manner of punishment, people who have fallen into disorder. And as this punishment has never been known in France, his majesty commands me to write you that he does not want you to order [it] any more."[163] Transportation could only have been instituted in France at the expense of the galleys.

The parallels between the European galley and prison schemes and the English transportation system are numerous and striking:

1. Both sanctions were introduced in the exercise of executive clemency for convicts who would otherwise have been subjected to the blood sanctions. In time, both were incorporated into the ordinary criminal process as sanctions imposed by the courts.

2. Both represent an administrative feat, in organizing and refining relatively complex schemes to extract convict labor.

3. Both were used as sanctions for serious crimes, but not the most serious. Transportation was overwhelmingly limited to property crimes,[164] and we have seen that the worst offenders continued to be executed on the Continent. Nevertheless, the new sanctions achieved a drastic diminution of capital punishment on both sides of the English Channel.[165]

4. Both served a similar congeries of purposes—to moderate the blood sanctions, to eliminate criminals from the society, to exploit convict labor, to reform offenders. Human life became more valuable in the mid-seventeenth century. The Europeans had suffered the catastrophic population losses of the Thirty Years War, and the English were trying to populate an empire while fending off the French.[166]

5. Both paved the way to the present systems of penal servitude. In the eighteenth century, French galley convicts and English transportees found themselves confined to hulks in domestic ports, from which they were led forth to daily labor on public works—like their counterparts in the fortresses, mines and prisons of Austria, Prussia, and the Netherlands.

3 The Revolution in the Law of Proof

In the doctrinal structure of Continental law the use of the various forms of imprisonment as punishments for serious crime fitted under the label of *poena extraordinaria*. In this chapter we shall see how the new criminal sanctions became the basis for developments in the law of proof that destroyed the Roman-canon system and made possible the abolition of judicial torture.

Poena extraordinaria

At an early stage in the elaboration of the ius commune the jurists were contending that all punishments are discretionary (*omnes poenas esse arbitrarias*).[1] The court should adjust the punishment to fit the circumstances of the crime. Even when statute or custom or the ius commune itself prescribed a particular penalty for a particular offense, the court should take into account mitigating or aggravating factors in order to ameliorate or intensify the punishment. A penalty imposed in the exercise of this discretion was known as a *poena extraordinaria* or *poena arbitraria,* an extraordinary or discretionary punishment. By the sixteenth century the principle of discretionary sentencing was well entrenched in the Continental legal systems.[2] Damhouder's practice manual from the middle of the century gives a succinct but typical account of the doctrine:

> The punishments are of two sorts, viz., ordinary and extraordinary. The ordinary are those that are set by law (*droict*), or that the Prince has ordained and decreed, or that custom and practice have introduced. The extraordinary are those that the Judge imposes at his discretion, because neither the Law (*Droit*), nor the Prince, nor Custom and practice have decreed them, or ordained anything. The judge in sentencing should always follow the ordinary punishments, and cannot increase, augment, diminish or change them without great and urgent cause and evident reason.[3]

The statutory penalty has presumptive force, but it yields to the need
to tailor the sanction to the crime.[4] In Jousse's formulation, "when
the circumstances [of the crime are not] those foreseen by the law
(*loi*) . . . the Judges may augment or diminish this penalty as justice
and equity require."[5] The judges' manuals of the seventeenth and
eighteenth centuries contain lengthy lists of aggravating and mitigating factors.[6]

The term poena extraordinaria was generalized to cover a variety
of situations in which the court exercised some discretion in sentencing. For example, statutes would occasionally characterize something as a criminal offense without fixing a particular penalty;[7] whatever sanction the court imposed was a poena extraordinaria. The
term was further used to describe the punishment imposed where the
governing statute expressly gave the court a choice. For example,
Article 131 of the Carolina stipulates that the mother who kills her
child should be punished either by drowning or by being buried alive
and impaled. Because the court had to choose between them, either
was reckoned a poena extraordinaria. Yet another usage was to describe any punishment imposed for what Anglo-American lawyers
call common law crimes, offenses not proscribed by statute but
punished by the courts anyhow.[8]

We have emphasized in Chapter 1 the preoccupation of the ius
commune with eliminating judicial discretion from the law of proof.
It is a striking contrast, therefore, to find an opposite rule (omnes
poenas esse arbitrarias) in the law of sanctions. There were some
limits to this discretion. The jurists mostly agreed that capital sanctions could not be imposed by the court when not foreseen by statute.[9] Further, the courts could not invent novel punishments—they
had to content themselves with choosing among the ghastly variety
that tradition bequeathed to them.[10] But these were slight constraints. The simple truth is that the contrast between fixity in the law
of proof and flexibility in the law of sanctions was not felt to be
disturbing.[11] In order to protect the innocent the procedure for guilt
determination required careful regulation, but the details of a convict's fate did not.[12]

So long as serious crime was punished exclusively with the blood
sanctions, the discretion to impose a poena extraordinaria was not
always of great moment. But the introduction of the various forms of
penal servitude into the catalog of recognized sanctions in the
sixteenth and seventeenth centuries gave the doctrine an enormous
practical significance. The choice of sanction for serious crime was

no longer between hanging in chains or beheading or whatever. A poena extraordinaria could now spare a convict from the blood sanctions.[13] Life or death lay regularly within judicial discretion.

Nevertheless, this was a discretion that left the Roman-canon law of proof undisturbed. These were cases of full proof. Conviction still required two eyewitnesses or confession; the law of proof was as dependent as before on investigation by torture. Only after guilt had been determined was the court exercising discretion to fit the punishment to the circumstances of the crime.

Punishment
without Full Proof

By the seventeenth century European courts had successfully implemented another usage of the term poena extraordinaria, the usage that subverted the Roman-canon law of proof.

In two types of cases the courts undertook to impose a poena extraordinaria *when full proof was lacking:* (1) the case in which sufficient circumstantial evidence to justify the use of torture was present, but the accused then withstood the torture without confessing; and (2) the case in which considerable and persuasive circumstantial evidence existed, but because it did not cumulate to half proof, it was insufficient to justify examination under torture. The power to impose a poena extraordinaria in these cases was subject to the important limitation that the punishment had to be less severe than that prescribed for full proof of the crime. Even for an offense that would normally be punishable by death, the death penalty could not be imposed as a poena extraordinaria when full proof was lacking.[14]

In these cases the accused was not technically said to be convicted. A true judgment of condemnation could only be passed on the basis of full proof. In order to achieve a verbal or formal harmony between the poena extraordinaria and the Roman-canon law of proof, it was said that the accused was being punished on account of the suspicion amassed against him, rather than condemned for the crime itself.[15] For that reason, the historical literature has been badly misled about the real nature of this version of poena extraordinaria. The practice acquired a pejorative label that has ever since operated to conceal its true significance. Writers called it the *Verdachtsstrafe,*[16] the punishment for suspicion.

The Verdachtsstrafe today is viewed in the literature[17] as yet

another barbarous practice of a cruel age: "Not only did those criminal courts use torture to make a man confess, but worse, they
punished him for being suspicious even if he was not guilty."

In truth, the Verdachtsstrafe was *not* a punishment for mere *Verdacht*, for being suspicious. It was a punishment imposed by the
court when the court was persuaded that the accused was guilty, but
when his guilt could not be established under the Roman-canon law
of proof. It was in fact free judicial evaluation of the evidence (*freie
Beweiswürdigung, l'intime conviction*). It was an alternative and
subsidiary system of proof, subsisting alongside the Roman-canon
law of proof. As a result, failure to meet the high standards of
Roman-canon full proof was no longer critical. The culprit could still
be punished if the court were persuaded of his guilt.

In this development were contained the seeds of the abolition of
torture. A new system of proof was appearing that did not require
confession in order to punish crime.

Like the Roman-canon system that it subverted, the new system
grew up in Italian practice. There are some earlier roots, but the
development came clear in Italy in the sixteenth century. Already in
the sixteenth century there are traces of it in French royal court
practice, and in seventeenth century Germany it is refined in the
scholarly and adjudicative work of Carpzov.[18]

We think that the most important factor in bringing about this new
system in the sixteenth and seventeenth centuries was the development of the new modes of punishment for serious crime—
imprisonment and the various forced labor schemes.[19] The Roman-
canon law of proof had formed at a time when all serious crime was
punished by death or maiming. The blood sanctions and the system
of statutory proofs had been defined in terms of each other.

When, however, the new punishments developed in the sixteenth
and seventeenth centuries, the courts were able to treat that relationship as a *restriction*. The *old* Roman-canon rules of proof pertained
only to the *old* blood sanctions. The courts deemed themselves able
to impose the new and less rigorous punishments according to a less
rigorous standard of proof—a standard of subjective persuasion
rather than objective certainty.

To understand this development, it is crucial to recall that the
courts did not have to invent the new lower standard of proof, they
had only to extend it. The lower standard—meaning free judicial
evaluation of the evidence—had existed throughout the Middle Ages

for cases of petty crime, *delicta levia*.[20] When the new modes of punishment appeared, there were already two distinct systems of proof in simultaneous operation. The one governed serious crime; it provided for blood sanctions, and hence it was encumbered with the Roman-canon rules of proof designed to assure certainty, complete with judicial torture. But the other system of proof was for petty crime, where only fines or minor corporal punishments were employed as sanctions. Here the standard of proof was not certainty, but rather the subjective persuasion of the trier. Not only was torture unnecessary, it was forbidden.

What happened in the sixteenth and seventeenth centuries was that the courts analogized the application of the new sanctions of imprisonment and forced labor, even in cases of serious crime, to the ancient procedure for petty crime, which *also* had employed noncapital sanctions. Where a noncapital punishment was being imposed, for whatever offense, the Roman-canon law of proof did not have to apply, because it never had applied.

Carolina to Theresiana

A convenient way to study the development is to contrast the beginning and the end. We take as our point of departure the two so-called codes of criminal procedure promulgated in the 1530s in the German Empire and in France. In both the *Constitutio Criminalis Carolina* (1532) and the *Ordinance of Villers-Cotterets* (1539), the Roman-canon law of proof is in exclusive force for serious crime.

The Carolina: Article 22[21] warns that no one is to be convicted on the basis of circumstantial evidence. Such evidence is relevant only to the question of whether there is sufficient suspicion to justify examination under torture. Articles 62 and 67[22] explain that where the accused will not confess, conviction requires at least two witnesses.

Villers-Cotterets: Article 164[23] says in effect that if the accused will not confess under torture, he must be released. (If the prosecution had been privately initiated, the released accused would then be allowed to sue his accuser.)

In these sources, therefore, we see the Roman-canon law of proof in its still-classical form: (1) punishment requires full proof, two eyewitnesses or confession; (2) circumstantial evidence bears only on whether or not to use torture; (3) if full proof cannot be obtained, the accused must be released.

If we now jump ahead more than two centuries to the *Constitutio Criminalis Theresiana* of 1769,[24] enacted in Austria a few years before the empress decreed the abolition of torture in 1776, we see a strikingly different picture. (The relevant passages are translated in the notes).[25] The Roman-canon law of proof is still in force, in the sense that a death sentence requires full proof through confession or competent witnesses; circumstantial evidence can justify examination under torture, but not capital conviction.[26]

However, when full proof cannot be obtained, the Theresiana leaves to the considered discretion of the judge the decision whether to release the man or to sentence him to an arbitrary punishment, that is, a poena arbitraria, a poena extraordinaria. The judge may do this either when the evidence is insufficient for torture,[27] or when torture is employed but the accused resists confession.[28] Further, it is a notable sign of the times that the statute prefaces these provisions with a recital that there has been "not insignificant doubt" about whether proof by circumstantial evidence might be as valid as proof by confession or by two witnesses.[29]

In the two centuries between the Carolina and the Theresiana a new system of proof achieved general, subsidiary validity. The Roman-canon system survived for the easy cases, but a court in the eighteenth century no longer faced the awful choice that the Roman-canon system imposed in the Middle Ages. The law used to be full proof or release, which is what forced the use of torture. Now, however, the choice was full proof *or poena extraordinaria* or release.

The former rules lost their monopoly. Even for cases of serious crime, the court could punish without complying with them, so long as the punishment was not death or maiming.

The New Law of Proof
in France

Everywhere one looks in the legal systems of the ancien régime, the pattern is similar. In Prussia[30] and elsewhere in the German states,[31] in Switzerland,[32] in Belgium,[33] the Netherlands,[34] and Italy,[35] poena extraordinaria has taken on the character of punishment short of death for evidence short of full proof.

The development of this system in France, under a distinctive nomenclature, is particularly instructive. Colbert's famous criminal procedure code of 1670 contains pieces of the new system, and numerous treatises written as commentaries on the ordinance describe something of the practice.[36] Again, we want to focus on two situations: (1) where there was evidence sufficient for torture, but the accused withstood the torture without confessing; and (2) where there was incriminating evidence, but not enough to constitute half-proof, hence not enough to justify examination under torture.

We have seen that Article 164 of the ordinance of Villers-Cotterets of 1539 provides that the accused who did not confess under torture was to be released. He was discharged for want of full proof. The ius commune said that he had purged himself of the suspicion.

To prevent the release of the accused in this situation, the French developed the practice that was codified in Title 19, Article 2 of the ordinance of 1670:

> The judges may also order that notwithstanding the order to Torture, the proofs shall subsist in their entirety, in order to be able to sentence the Accused to all types of monetary or corporal penalties; excepting, however, that of Death, to which the Accused who has undergone Torture without confessing cannot be condemned, unless new evidence appears after the Torture.[37]

When the court ordered examination under torture with the form of words *avec réserve des preuves en leur entier,* unsuccessful application of torture no longer purged the accused of the suspicion. The court could still order him put to any of the lesser sanctions short of death.

Of course, such an order did not comply with the Roman-canon law of proof in its classical sense. It was punishment based upon lesser proof, primarily circumstantial evidence, when the court was subjectively persuaded that the evidence established guilt. An eighteenth-century jurist records that judges "order it only when the evidence (*preuve*) approaches full and complete conviction, when they are intimately convinced that the accused is guilty...."[38] Jousse counsels that torture ought not to be ordered avec réserve unless the evidence (*indices*) against the accused was not only *considérables* (that is, sufficient for torture), but *très violents.*[39]

Because this practice makes Article 164 of the ordinance of 1539 more or less obsolete, we can infer that it became firmly established

in French law between then and 1670. The treatise writer Bornier
says that the practice originated in the usage (*style*) of the Parlement
of Paris.[40] Schnapper's study of the archives of the Parlement of
Bordeaux concludes that torture avec réserve appeared in that court's
practice between 1550 and 1565; his study of archive sources from
the Parlement of Paris dates its appearance there to before 1535.[41]

The treatises disclose that the usual punishment pronounced
against an accused who did not confess under torture was perpetual
galley service, or, in the case of a female, perpetual imprisonment at
hard labor.[42] Jousse reports a case that he had seen in Orléans in
1740 against a defendant "named Barberousse, accused of premedi-
tated murder, and against whom there was substantial evidence (*une
preuve considérable*), but not full proof. After he was put to the
torture avec réserve and confessed nothing, he was declared 'violently suspect' and sentenced to perpetual galley service."[43]

If the court could sentence an accused to such drastic punishment
after he failed to confess under torture, it could also sentence him
without bothering to use torture in the first place. Muyart de Vouglans writes that torture avec réserve "is ordered only when there is
evidence (*preuves*) so substantial (*considérables*) against the accused
that there lacks only the Confession in order to condemn him to
capital punishment, and that this evidence is, moreover, sufficient to
condemn him to any other punishment (*peine*). . . ."[44] Jousse explains that when full proof is lacking but the evidence is *considérable*,
the judge "may impose a punishment against this accused, but less
than that which he would impose upon him if there were a full proof
against him; this is then called punishing *pro modo probationum*."[45]

When we turn to the situation of incriminating evidence insufficient for torture, we find another variety of poena extraordinaria.
The court could impose a sentence called a *plus amplement informé*,
roughly translatable as an order "for further investigation" of the
accused. This practice seems to have originated as a genuinely provisional measure pending further investigation of a crime. But in the
sixteenth century it acquired the character of a punishment, usually
imprisonment.[46] Although the plus amplement informé had been
entrenched for more than a century, no mention of the practice is to
be found in the ordinance of 1670. Nevertheless, the draftsmen's
procès-verbal makes it clear that they knew how routine the plus
amplement informé had become,[47] and as Muyart de Vouglans
points out, the ordinance did not disapprove it.[48]

Jousse is explicit that the plus amplement informé "is imposed as a punishment (*peine*) rather than as a means of acquiring the evidence (*preuve*) necessary to the case."[49] Muyart de Vouglans, himself no enemy of judicial torture,[50] makes a revealing comment about the significance of the plus amplement informé. It "is a wise moderation [of the law of proof] which has been devised for the case where there is insufficient evidence (*preuves*) either to condemn or to acquit the Accused entirely; and primarily in order to spare him from investigation under torture."[51] Because a court could use the plus amplement informé to punish an accused whom it deemed guilty even when the evidence did not qualify for investigation under torture, the pressure to find or construe evidence sufficient for torture was relieved.

There were two distinct varieties of plus amplement informé— determinate and perpetual. The determinate version, called the plus amplement informé *à temps,* in which the accused was ordered imprisoned[52] for a fixed term, was the more common. It was imposed "only for major crimes, where capital punishment pertains, and when there is not sufficient evidence (*preuve*) to sentence the accused to investigation under torture."[53] The period of imprisonment was typically six months or a year.[54] When the plus amplement informé à temps "is imposed for a . . . substantial period, such as a year, and with the requirement of imprisonment, it is put among the infamous Punishments . . . ."[55]

The plus amplement informé à temps had another usage, which emphasizes its character as a penal sanction for evidence short of full proof. We have seen that when the evidence was sufficient for torture and highly persuasive of guilt, investigation under torture could take place avec réserve des preuves; if the accused did not confess, Title 19, Article 2 of the ordinance of 1670 authorized him to be sentenced "to all types of . . . penalties; excepting, however, that of Death . . . ." In such cases the penalty that the courts ordinarily imposed was the galley sentence, either perpetual or determinate, but they could instead impose a plus amplement informé à temps.[56] The plus amplement informé à temps had become merely a label for relatively short-term imprisonment imposed by the courts when the evidence was persuasive but short of full proof.

When the term of the plus amplement informé à temps had expired, the accused was normally released by a decree setting him *hors de cour,* literally, outside the court. This form of words carried with it the connotation that, although the crime had not been fully proved against the accused, neither had he been cleared of the incriminating evidence against him. It was a grudging acquittal, and in addition to its effect upon the man's reputation, it prevented him from suing his accusers for false imprisonment.[57]

The court could be harsher, depending upon the circumstances of the case. It could impose a second plus amplement informé à temps;[58] indeed, it could impose some other "serious punishment upon the expiration of the plus amplement informé, even when no further evidence (*preuves*) has arisen."[59] A final option open to the court at this stage was to sentence the same accused to the other variety of plus amplement informé, called *indéfini* or *usquequò*, meaning perpetual or indefinite.[60]

The plus amplement informé indéfini, says Jousse, "is a type of punishment (*peine*) whose effect is to leave the accused perpetually in the status of an accused, so that his fate remains uncertain on account of the evidence (*preuves*) that may arise against him. He is nevertheless released from prison during this time, [subject to rearrest if new evidence arises]."[61] Muyart de Vouglans explains that the plus amplement informé indéfini "is only pronounced in cases of very serious Crimes, which concern public order and of which the evidence (*Indices*) is substantial (*considérables*). . . . It can be said in effect that this is a punishment, not for the Crime, but for the violent presumptions and evidence which have not been purged, and which demand a *satisfaction particulière*."[62] The plus amplement informé indéfini imported infamy,[63] which meant more than disgrace in the community. The accused was rendered incapable of holding office or benefice, incapable of making a will or testifying as a witness in judicial proceedings.[64] In a case litigated in the Parlement of Paris in the 1740s, a woman against whom there was a plus amplement informé indéfini for suspicion of having poisoned a testator was denied her legacy under his will.[65]

In the archives of the Parlement of Bordeaux Schnapper has traced the plus amplement informé indéfini under a slightly different name well back toward the beginning of the sixteenth century. "[I]t was a condemnation by another name, with the result that between acquittal (*relaxe*) pure and simple and true condemnation there were inserted in the Parlement's hierarchy two types of decisions that allowed a doubt to hover over the honor of the accused: the setting hors de cour was nearly an acquittal, the plus amplement [informé indéfini], above all after torture, nearly a condemnation."[66]

Torture *avec réserve* and the *plus amplement informé* laid the basis for the abolition of judicial torture in France. They constituted the French *poena extraordinaria*, a subsidiary system of proof that permitted the courts to punish without full proof when there was persuasive circumstantial evidence. This alteration in the law of proof slowly made torture obsolete. Indeed, the draftsmen of the ordinance of 1670 already sensed the change. One of them, Pussort, is reported as reminding his colleagues that torture was *un usage ancien* of little utility in France.[67] Another, Lamoignan, First President of the Parlement of Paris, "saw great reasons for abolishing it, but that was only his personal opinion."[68] One hundred ten years later Louis XVI referred to Pussort's remark in the decree of 1780 that abolished torture. This decree is instructive in another respect: it propounds no alternative to torture, but it pointedly reminds the courts of their authority under Title 9, Article 2, of the Ordinance of 1670 to sentence an accused to punishments short of death even when he does not confess.[69]

Why Poena Extraordinaria?

We cannot say with precision why the revolution in the law of proof took place, for too much is yet unknown about how it took place. Legal historians have never digested the vast juristic literature on criminal procedure left from the Middle Ages and the Renaissance, and the court archives of the ancien régime remain all but wholly unresearched. Hence, much of the detail eludes us, although the outline seems tolerably clear.

The Roman-canon law of proof developed in the Middle Ages to serve the needs of the relatively weak governments then emerging.[70] We saw in Chapter 1 why the system of statutory proofs was, for all its rigidity, a great advance in its day. It laid to rest the barbarous ordeals of Germanic antiquity. It permitted the officialization and rationalization of criminal procedure.[71] In place of the ordeals that purported to invoke the judgment of God, the Roman-canon procedure legitimated fact-finding and adjudication by public officials, judges. The great and ultimately self-defeating safeguards of the Roman-canon law of proof were concessions made in order to implement this radical reorganization of criminal procedure. By forbidding judges to draw inferences of guilt from circumstantial evidence and by limiting the judges' power of condemnation to cases where there were two eyewitnesses or confession, the medieval law laid claim to certainty. Because the law of proof made judgment rest upon certainty, there would be less objection that mere mortals were displacing God from the judgment seat.

By the sixteenth and seventeenth centuries, when the revolution in the law of proof took place, the concerns that had produced the medieval emphasis on eliminating judicial discretion were long past. The ius commune had been entrenched for centuries, and rational adjudication was no longer a novelty that needed to be hobbled in order to find acceptance. Most importantly, in the age of the nation-state, judicial discretion could be tolerated because it could be controlled. The centralization and professionalization of the judiciary that occurred in the absolutist states of the sixteenth and seventeenth centuries was an essential prerequisite for a system of free judicial evaluation of the evidence. Such a system cannot be left in the hands of laymen.[72] Even the English did not do that: the professional judge in England exercised considerable control over the fact-finding of the jury through his power to control the framing of the indictment and to instruct the jurors; and he was exclusively responsible for sentencing.

In Europe the early modern absolutist states eliminated the remnants of private, feudal jurisdiction over serious crime; they rid the public courts of lay judges; and they subjected the professionalized public courts to central review.[73] The French ordinance of 1670 reflects in considerable detail the royal victory over the seignorial criminal courts and the growth of hierarchical control and review within the royal courts.[74] The more interesting development took place in the German states, where the problem was more severe. At the time of the Carolina, criminal jurisdiction was severely fragmented. Boehm computes that in Saxony alone there were in the early seventeenth century upwards of two thousand courts of first instance possessed of criminal jurisdiction.[75] Only a handful could ever expect to have a professional judge. The Carolina is overwhelmingly preoccupied with this problem. The preamble declares that the statute is being enacted in order to give guidance to the criminal courts, which are all too often staffed with incompetent laymen who hang the innocent and release the guilty.[76]

In the later sixteenth century and throughout the seventeenth century the German states worked to professionalize the criminal courts. Lay courts were suppressed outright, or they were required to associate a professional judge within them, or they were compelled to delegate serious cases to outside professionals. In Hesse, for example, as early as 1540 the regime was requiring the local courts to send up the file on every case of capital crime.[77] In Saxony by the time of Carpzov, the regime had imposed mandatory *Aktenversendung,*[78] and this, indeed, was part of the basis of Carpzov's influence. By about 1620, even the most powerful of the local criminal courts could impose only the most minor punishments. All serious cases had to be delegated to one of four superior courts staffed with professional judges, at Leipzig Carpzov himself.[79] This process of centralization and professionalization took place all over Germany, although not at the same speed or with the same thoroughness as in Saxony or Prussia.[80]

We must emphasize that the professionalized judiciary of the ancien régime had become long familiar with the use of circumstantial evidence, primarily for the delicta levia to which the requirement of Roman-canon full proof had not pertained. Even within the sphere of the Roman-canon law of proof, circumstantial evidence had a major although subsidiary role. The decision to investigate under torture turned primarily upon the cogency of circumstantial evidence, whose evaluation the jurists always conceded to involve considerable discretion.[81] Likewise, judicial discretion to adjust the punishment to fit the crime, the primary meaning of poena extraordinaria, characteristically required a review of circumstantial evidence.[82] This usage normalized the use of judicial discretion in the punishment of crime. At first that was a discretion which obeyed the Roman-canon law of proof and confined itself to sentencing rather than to determining guilt. But such lines blur when there is no compelling reason to maintain them. And there was in truth no longer any reason for the constraints of the medieval law. Judicial discretion was no longer a daring innovation, and the absolutist state could prevent it from being abused.

The professionalized judiciary wanted to escape the confines of the statutory proofs. The judges wanted the freedom to base judgments on compelling circumstantial evidence. They may also have been motivated by humanitarian grounds, for the new system of proof and punishment allowed them to decrease the use both of the blood punishments and of torture.[83] They had already used their discretion in sentencing after conviction, which was the main meaning of poena extraordinaria, to eliminate many of the most gruesome punishments.[84]

The limitations of the Roman-canon law of proof had outgrown their purpose. The weight of tradition kept them in force, but neither the political authorities nor the judiciary had any further interest in insisting upon the exclusivity of the medieval rules.[85] The situation invited doctrinal evasion, and the doctrine of poena extraordinaria had qualities that lent themselves to the extension from sentencing to guilt-determination.

As a practical matter, factors that bear on sentencing, such as the seriousness of the crime and the degree of the offender's culpability, are often relevant to guilt-determination. Hence, in a case of full proof, a poena extraordinaria imposed ostensibly as a sentencing decision (that is, reduced penalty for mitigating circumstances) might in fact reflect the judge's perception that the evidence, although persuasive of guilt, lacked the normal reliability of full proof.[86] This ambiguity in the doctrine of poena extraordinaria mirrored a similar ambiguity in the law of torture. Judicial torture was meant as a mode of investigation into potential guilt, and not as a sanction. Yet the simple truth was that torture hurt like hell, and everyone knew it. To be subjected to investigation under torture was to suffer a fate worse than most of the formal sanctions. That is why the ius commune insisted that torture could not be used to investigate petty crimes (delicta levia); otherwise the investigation would entail more suffering than the maximum permitted punishment.[87] The requirement of half proof for torture deepened the ambiguity. On the one hand, it merely set a precondition for interlocutory investigation. On the other hand, it authorized the infliction of physical pain when there was sufficient incriminating evidence against the accused. In this sense, judicial torture had always been a punishment imposed on account of the incriminating circumstantial evidence,[88] and we recall once again how candidly the juristic literature admits that judicial discretion is unavoidable in the evaluation of such evidence.

The doctrine of poena extraordinaria was manipulated in the seventeenth and eighteenth centuries to exploit this ambiguity in the law of torture. Although judicial torture continued to be viewed as a mode of investigation, hence of procedure, the practice and the legislation began to emphasize that torture was also a punishment, a poena, appropriate to a particular level of circumstantial evidence. Then, on account of the maxim omnes poenas esse arbitrarias, the courts could impose a poena extraordinaria, typically a form of imprisonment, where previously they used the poena of torture to coerce full proof.

This development stands out in the French ordinance of 1670.

Title 25, Article 13, provides a curious ranking of certain[89] of the criminal sanctions, which reads in its entirety:

> After the Death penalty, the most rigorous is that of torture *avec la réserve des preuves en leur entier,* perpetual galley service, perpetual banishment, torture without *réserve des preuves,* determinate galley service, flogging, *l'amende honorable,* and determinate banishment.[90]

The true function of this text is to confirm to the courts that they may impose sanctions less than death—typically galley service, the French variety of imprisonment at hard labor—on the same quantum of circumstantial evidence for which the medieval law permitted only investigation under torture to obtain full proof. Poullain du Parc, another of the French treatise writers, explains that since the statute defines torture avec réserve as "more rigorous than perpetual galley service, and since [torture avec réserve] can be imposed on the basis of substantial evidence (*preuves considérables*) which is nevertheless insufficient for a death sentence, it must necessarily follow that the judge can sentence to the galleys, even for an atrocious crime, on the basis of substantial evidence (*preuves considérables*), when there is not enough to impose the death penalty."[91] Punishment for serious crime no longer required full proof, hence in cases where the evidence was short of full proof it was no longer necessary to use torture to complete the proof.

The new law of proof enabled the judge to do what the ius commune supposedly forbade him to do: he could now sentence a culprit to punishment on the basis of circumstantial evidence. Circumstantial evidence is indirect evidence: it depends for its efficacy upon the subjective persuasion of the judge, who evaluates it and decides whether it raises a sufficient inference of guilt. Under the clumsy doctrine of poena extraordinaria for less-than-full proof, the subjective theory of proof found its way into European law. The objective theory of the ius commune lived on in form, but now fatally compromised by its antithesis. The seeds of the modern law of proof—freie Beweiswürdigung, l'intime conviction, the subjective persuasion of the trier—had been firmly planted for the nineteenth-century codes to harvest.

Of course, judicial torture continued to be permitted and employed in the ancien régime. But the revolution in the law of proof destroyed the raison d'être of the law of torture. When full proof was no longer

the exclusive prerequisite for punishment, the law of proof was liberated from its dependence on confession evidence. Judicial torture
was at last vulnerable to the ancient abolitionist critique.

4 The Abolition of Judicial Torture

The traditional account of the disappearance of judicial torture in the eighteenth century posits that a handful of publicists shocked the conscience of Europe with their critique of torture and inspired the lawgivers to eliminate torture from criminal procedure. We warned in Chapter 1 that this account would be shown to be untenable. In this Chapter we shall see how the revolution in the law of proof described in Chapter 3 led to the abolition of judicial torture. We shall also see why it has been mistaken to credit the abolitionist writers with the leading role.

The Abolition Legislation

When Frederick the Great acceded to the Prussian throne in 1740, judicial torture was still nominally in force, although since 1720 Frederick's father, Frederick William I, had required that all sentences to torture be submitted for royal approval before being carried out.[1] The codifying *Landrecht* of 1721[2] contained a classical scheme of regulation of judicial torture.[3] It carried forward the requirement of two eyewitnesses or confession for full proof.[4] Judicial torture was allowed in order to complete the proof when sufficient circumstantial evidence had established probable cause.[5] But the Landrecht also codified a system of poena extraordinaria so extensive that it rendered the requirement of full proof "almost illusory."[6] In cases of capital crime the statute authorized poena extraordinaria short of death both when the evidence would not permit torture,[7] and when torture was allowed but the accused successfully resisted confession.[8] Hence, by the time of Frederick the Great, the new law of proof had already displaced judicial torture from its former regularity in Prussia.

Within a month of his accession Frederick issued an order[9] abolishing torture except in cases of treason and "in those great murder cases where many people have been killed, or many culprits are implicated whose involvement has to be discovered."[10] We suspect that there may not have been much practical difference between Frederick William I permitting torture subject to royal review, and Frederick the Great abolishing it with exceptions that also continued to be subject to the requirement of royal review.[11] Torture may not have been used at all in the interval between 1740 and 1749, when Frederick wrote in a celebrated tract: "Eight years ago torture was abolished in Prussia, [where] it is certain that the innocent are not being confused with the guilty and justice is none the worse."[12]

In 1752 Frederick authorized the use of torture for the last time—in a case involving especially gruesome facts and cogent circumstantial evidence against the suspect.[13] But he took the occasion to express his hostility to torture and to delimit the alternative that he would formally propound two years later in his definitive abolition decrees. Confession should not be needed to convict, he said, when "the circumstances" (*Umstände*) are clear and fully proven against the culprit.[14]

Provoked by further requests for permission to put suspects to torture, Frederick ordered the complete cessation of judicial torture in decrees dated June and August 1754.[15] Frederick explained that he was abolishing torture because it was "gruesome" and "an uncertain means to discover the truth."[16] Henceforth,

> should the circumstances (*Umstände*) not quite wholly convict (*complicieren*) the accused, and yet the greatest suspicion (*Verdacht*) of his having actually commited the crime shall exist against the accused, and the circumstances raise such [suspicion] to the highest probability, then this accused must be sentenced to be chained in irons and imprisoned or put to fortress labor for life, even though he is unwilling to utter a confession.[17]

Of course, we see in Frederick's decrees the familiar device of poena extraordinaria, lesser penalty for cases short of full proof.[18] Now, however, the new law of proof was no longer a competitor alongside the law of torture; rather, it was displacing torture entirely.[19]

Elsewhere in Europe we see the same relationship. The abolition legislation substituted the new law of proof for the old law of torture. In Saxony, where poena extraordinaria had been employed in cases short of full proof since the time of Carpzov in the mid-seventeenth century,[20] the monarch abolished judicial torture in December 1770.[21] A set of instructions accompanying the abolition decree directed that in cases of half proof (where torture would formerly have been permissible) sentences to imprisonment at hard labor should henceforth be imposed—life imprisonment for the worst offenses, determinate terms for other serious crimes.[22]

In Austria the extensive system of poena extraordinaria in lieu of full proof contained in the *Constitutio Criminalis Theresiana* of 1769[23] paved the way for the abolition of judicial torture.[24] Maria Theresa's privy councillor Josef von Sonnenfels prepared a memorandum in the early 1770s for internal circulation within the Austrian regime, calling for the abolition of judicial torture; the document later became public and acquired a reputation as one of the leading abolitionist tracts.[25] Citing to the Theresiana's provisions for poena extraordinaria, Sonnenfels wrote that torture was now "superfluous for condemnation, because someone who is suspected can be punished without being brought to confession...."[26] Maria Theresa abolished torture in January 1776 at the behest of her son, Joseph II.[27] In 1788 Joseph recodified the system of poena extraordinaria:

> In addition to proof of a crime by means of confession or witnesses, a legal conviction can also be based upon the correlation of circumstances (*Umstände*) against the accused....
>
> If no proof of the crime can be established against the accused other than the correlation of circumstances against him, the punishment must always be reduced in length one degree below what the statute prescribes for the crime when it is proven by another means.[28]

Joseph II also issued the decree abolishing torture in Belgium (still the Austrian Netherlands) in 1787. As in Prussia, formal abolition was preceded by the imposition of executive review of sentences to torture. In 1784 Joseph ordered torture sentences submitted to his governing Council in Brussels, and the Council approved none thereafter.[29] The abolition decree of 1787[30] was resisted by the Belgian magistracy, in part because it was imbedded in a larger scheme of court reform that the Belgian judges opposed,[31] but also because it was viewed as Austrian meddling in local Belgian practice.[32] The decree of 1784 had been triggered by a case in which the Council had been moved to intervene to prevent a seignorial court from carrying out a proposed sentence to torture on a suspect accused of murder and church robbery. The Council reasoned that since the man was not "sufficiently convicted of the crime of which he is accused to impose a capital penalty, it is better to imprison him than to put him to the cruel test and uncertainty of torture." Accordingly, the governor general ordered him imprisoned in Ghent for a term of thirty years.[33] The abolition decree of 1787 led immediately to dispositions in the provisional code of criminal procedure of that year providing for poena extraordinaria in lieu of full proof.[34] (The abolition decree continued to be resisted by the magistracy and was set out of force not long thereafter. Torture was not eliminated from Belgian practice until the French conquest of 1794.)[35]

In France, conventional judicial torture (torture préparatoire) was abolished by decree of Louis XVI in 1780,[36] and we have said that the decree referred the courts to their authority under the Ordinance of 1670 to sentence an accused to punishments short of death even when he had not confessed.[37]

The Abolition Legend

These sources show unmistakably the causal relationship between the revolution in the law of proof and the abolition of judicial torture. Nevertheless, the historical literature contains hardly a mention of this remarkable development. The history books are busy telling a different tale, one that we have charitably called the fairy tale. They credit the abolition movement to the influence of Thomasius, Beccaria, Voltaire, and a few lesser writers, whose pens proved mightier than the rack. The publicists supposedly persuaded the monarchs of Europe of the wisdom and humanity of their cause, and they shaped liberal public opinion to pressure the rulers to act.

It would be possible to construct an historical explanation to reconcile somewhat the thesis that we have been demonstrating in this book with the traditional account that gives such primacy to the publicists. The abolition of judicial torture was both a juristic and a political event. While the jurists developed the new law of proof, it was the monarchs who rid the legal systems of torture. The new law of proof made the abolition of torture possible, but it did not compel abolition. Many an outmoded legal doctrine or institution lives on after a superior alternative should have displaced it. One thinkable historical scenario for the abolition of judicial torture in the eighteenth century is that the publicists demonstrated to the wielders of political power the ultimate implication of the new law of proof.

The trouble is that the event did not happen in this way. If it had, the historical literature could not have been so badly misled—it would not have overlooked so completely the revolution in the law of proof. There are in fact two reasons why the historians have not identified the revolution in the law of proof as the precipitating factor in the abolition of judicial torture. One we have previously mentioned: the new law of proof did not seem to conflict with the Roman-canon law of proof. The ancient requirement of full proof for poena ordinaria was left in force, and it was adhered to in the easy cases where there were two eyewitnesses or unrecanted confession. Because the requirement of full proof remained technically in effect until the nineteenth century in most Continental legal systems, the development and significance of the new system of proof tended to be obscured.

The more fundamental reason why historians have written hardly a word about the revolution in the law of proof is that they have followed the eighteenth-century abolitionist writers, who themselves said hardly anything about it. Most of them knew nothing at all about the change that had taken place, and the few who did had no conception of its significance. As a result of their ignorance of the law, the abolitionist writers impaired their own effectiveness. They made their job of persuasion immensely more difficult because they overlooked the most powerful argument that could have been made in behalf of their cause. They did not understand the place of torture in the traditional law of proof, and they did not understand that the new law of proof had liberated criminal procedure from its former dependence on confession evidence. No wonder, therefore, that when the nineteenth-century historians came to tell the story of the abolition movement, they had no inkling of the development that had really taken place. The paradox is that the abolitionist writers became all the more fabled in history as a result of being so much less effective than they could have been.

The eighteenth-century abolitionist literature is the product of its age in tone, but not in substance. The works of Thomasius, Beccaria, Voltaire, and the others do little more than restate the arguments that have been advanced against torture for centuries. Torture does not add to the certainty of judgments, they say, because it tests endurance rather than veracity. The stubborn will resist and the weak will confess. Further, the law of torture is unjust because it inflicts suffering, hence punishment, upon persons who have not been adjudicated guilty. These arguments are repeated incessantly, embellished and illustrated in countless ways.[38]

This classical critique of judicial torture had not succeeded in past centuries primarily because it did so little to demonstrate the workability of a criminal justice system shorn of the power to investigate under torture. In the eighteenth century, contemporaries were still deeply concerned that the social purposes of the criminal law might be unachievable without torture. The Belgian abolitionist writer de Fierlant, for example, as late as 1771 refers to the fear that without torture it would be difficult for the courts to convict hardened criminals such as killers, highway robbers, and arsonists. "This is the only difficulty [with abolition] that appears to me reasonable."[39] Sonnenfels, writing at about the same time, likewise wrestles with the objection that abolition would encourage potential criminals to hope for impunity, hence that criminality would increase. He replies with more cleverness than plausibility that such villains do not fear torture, rather they welcome it for the opportunity to resist confession and thereby to escape punishment.[40] (Sonnenfels' tract is virtually unique among the genre in perceiving that the new law of proof reduces the need for torture, but this argument is understated and was not absorbed by the other abolitionist writers.)[41]

In many of the Continental states, torture was abolished piecemeal, in order to give the regimes an opportunity to test the impact of abolition upon deterrence. We have seen that Frederick the Great excepted some major offenses from his decree of 1740, and he delayed fourteen years before abolishing torture definitively. Louis XVI suppressed only torture préparatoire in France in 1780. He abolished torture préalable in 1788; even that decree was made provisional, "reserving however regretfully [the option] of reestablishing torture préalable if, after some years of experience, we gather from the reports of our judges that it is an indispensable necessity."[42] The device of leaving the law of torture nominally in force, but subjecting torture sentences to executive review, reflects a similar caution about the consequences of abolition.[43]

Another indication of the concern that abolition might impair the deterrent efficacy of the criminal law was the practice of issuing abolition decrees to the courts in confidence. Frederick's initial order of 1740 was kept secret;[44] even the definitive abolition decree of

1754 was issued with a direction to the courts not to make it public.[45] When Maria Theresa forbade a particular variety of torture in Austria in 1773, her decree was communicated to the courts in confidence.[46] So too was the order of Joseph II in 1784 to the Belgian magistracy requiring executive approval for sentences to torture.[47]

The belief in the deterrent value of torture reflects again the curious double character of torture as both a means of investigation and a species of punishment. Although theory limited torture to a role in procedure alone, its quasi-sanctional character was always manifest. Both the fear of detection and the fear of suffering under torture might have deterrent force, and the eighteenth-century regimes were reluctant to dissipate it.

The abolitionist writers knew that they had to overcome this concern by demonstrating the workability of a torture-free criminal procedure. Had they understood the relationship of judicial torture to the law of proof, and had they appreciated the profound change that had overtaken the law of proof in the previous decades, the writers could have met the deterrence point squarely and defeated it. They could have replied that because criminals could now be punished on evidence short of full proof, confession was no longer essential. Thanks to the new law of proof the abolition of torture would not lead to automatic acquittals, but to condemnation and punishment based upon the circumstantial evidence that had previously been the basis for investigation under torture.

What is so remarkable about the abolitionist writers is that they overlook the revolution in the law of proof. They ignore the development that had liberated the legal systems from the former dependence on confession evidence and thereby made possible the abolition of judicial torture. Thomasius' *Dissertatio* of 1705, the first of the legendary abolitionist works, deals entirely with "the arguments of his predecessors, which like his own were directed in particular against the use of torture, but not against the then-current system of proof."[48] The romantic notion that Thomasius' little rehash of the traditional critique of judicial torture inspired Frederick the Great to issue his abolition decrees, though often repeated,[49] is improbable.

Beccaria also argues against judicial torture with no mention of its connection to the law of proof.[50] Beccaria is especially hostile to allowing "a magistrate to become arbitrary executor of the laws,"[51] which may have blinded him to an appreciation of the arbitraria of the judges. Without devising any consistent alternative, Beccaria was actually opposing the decisive element in the transformation of the law of proof that had made the abolition of judicial torture possible.[52]

Voltaire's critique of judicial torture is hopelessly confused. While repeating the traditional arguments about the unreliability of confessions extracted under torture,[53] he endorses the use of torture préalable in the case of the "assassination of Henry IV, friend of Europe and of the human race . . . . The interest of the world was to know the accomplices of [the assassin] Ravaillac."[54] Voltaire denounces the two-witness rule that lay at the heart of the problem of judicial torture—but on the ground that this standard was not strict enough! The two witnesses "may be villains"[55] testifying falsely. Consequently, Voltaire is driven to outbid the medieval jurists in his demand for certainty. "If against a hundred thousand probabilities that the accused is guilty there is a single one that he is innocent, that alone should suffice" for acquittal.[56] Such a position was hardly likely to reassure governments worried about impairing the deterrent efficacy of the criminal law.

Trapped by their ignorance of the law of proof, the abolitionist writers were able to formulate only one significant response to the contemporary concern about the workability of a torture-free criminal procedure. They pointed to the example of other states, initially England, later Sweden (where torture was largely abolished in 1734),[57] but most importantly Prussia. Prussia, the best-governed and most successful of Continental states, had proven that the ends of the criminal justice system were not dependent upon the continued use of judicial torture. This was the one genuinely novel theme in the eighteenth-century critique of torture. Thomasius and Montesquieu have only England to point to,[58] but by the middle of the century the impact of the abolition decrees of Frederick the Great was being felt everywhere. Thus Beccaria makes example of England, where achievements in literature and commerce "allow us no doubt of the excellence of her laws. Torture has been abolished in Sweden, abolished too by [Frederick the Great,] one of the wisest monarchs of Europe . . . ."[59] Voltaire points to the practice in England and elsewhere, and he emphasizes that torture "is abolished in all the states of the hero of the century, the King of Prussia . . . ."[60] Sonnenfels' work directed Maria Theresa's attention to Prussia's quarter-century of experience with abolition,[61] and in her abolition decree of 1776 she cites "the example that has already transpired in other states . . . ."[62] The Belgian de Fierlant and the Swiss writer Seigneux de Correvon advance the same argument.[63]

The abolitionist tracts give this central place to foreign, especially Prussian, example as a surrogate for reasoned analysis of the transformation of the law of proof. Foreign example demonstrated the workability of a torture-free criminal procedure. In a sense, therefore, the publicists made the abolition movement into one of the earliest exercises in comparative law. The lesson of one state's laws was held up for the instruction of the others. Nevertheless, we could hardly rate the abolition movement as an auspicious triumph for the methodology of comparative law, because the writers failed so completely to understand what they were describing. Their argument was conclusory: they knew that abolition worked in Prussia, but they had no idea why.

We do not doubt that the writers played some role in bringing about the abolition of judicial torture in the eighteenth century. Historians have rightly given weight to the publicists' campaign and to other factors outside the legal systems, for abolition was an event linked to many of the deepest themes of eighteenth-century political, administrative, and intellectual history. The historians' mistake, like that of the publicists, has been to ignore the enormous significance of developments within the European legal systems. We hope to have shown why the revolution in the law of proof must be the starting point for rewriting the history of the abolition of judicial torture.

2

England
The Century of Torture
1540-1640

5 The Torture-Free Law of Proof

By the thirteenth century, when the European law of torture took shape, the English common law had acquired most of the fundamental characteristics that would keep it distinct from the Continental ius commune.[1] Of the many differences that separated the two Western legal traditions, none is more striking than this: that the systematic use of torture to investigate crime never established itself in English criminal procedure.

Already in the fifteenth and sixteenth centuries, just as the Roman-canon law of torture was being extended to Germany,[2] the celebrated Renaissance "panegyrists"[3] of English law were noticing this contrast with the Continent and extolling the absence of torture in England. Sir John Fortescue, writing about 1470, points to the practice in France, where "criminals and suspected criminals are afflicted with so many kinds of tortures . . . that the pen scorns to put them into writing."[4] Sir Thomas Smith, writing from France in 1565, announces that: "Torment . . . which is used by the order of civil law and custom of other countries . . . is not used in England, it is taken for servile."[5] And Sir Edward Coke's *Third Institute,* written in the 1620s, cites Fortescue's remarks with approval and concludes that "there is no one opinion in our books, or judicial record . . . for the maintenance of tortures or torments . . . ."[6]

This self-congratulatory writing denying the role of torture in England is, however, quite false. The English did use torture. Indeed, both Sir Thomas Smith and Sir Edward Coke were themselves designated in commissions to examine particular suspects under torture.[7]

What the English did not do was to regularize the use of torture in their criminal procedure. Torture had a much shorter history and a much less central role in England, but it was employed. We have record of more than eighty cases from the century 1540–1640 in which the Privy Council or the monarch ordered torture (or the threat of torture) to be used against criminals or suspected criminals. The great majority of these cases involve crimes of state: sedition, treason, concerted activity against the established religion. Yet more than a quarter of the English torture warrants were issued in cases that we should call ordinary crime: murder, robbery, burglary, horse stealing.

The history of the use of torture in England has been carefully studied only once, in a remarkably sophisticated little monograph published in 1837 by the legal antiquary David Jardine.[8] He based his account firmly on original sources, the Privy Council registers and the State Papers Domestic, which were then unpublished and uncalendared. Working from the manuscripts and without indexes, Jardine identified about two–thirds of the eighty-one cases that we have been able to locate.[9] He established, therefore, the rough dimensions of the phenomenon; and many elements of his analysis, it will be seen, bear up in the light of the vastly greater modern understanding of Tudor-Stuart legal and constitutional history.

Jardine's achievement was to refute the lore from Sir Thomas Smith and such that torture was "not used in England." Understandably, therefore, Jardine emphasized how much torture there had been.[10] Yet his evidence also showed that while torture had been used enough in England to contradict the boasting about its absence, still it had been too rarely used to have been a systematic part of the criminal procedure. This paradox of steady yet infrequent use of torture Jardine left unremarked.

Later writers have exaggerated the extent and significance of torture in England.[11] The suspicion that torture was more used than recorded used (an issue we discuss in Chapter 6), has also helped writers avoid the question why torture, once in use in England, ran so confined a course.

Peine Forte et Dure

The tendency to overemphasize the amount of torture has been helped along by imprecision, some of it willful,[12] about what is really meant by the word "torture." Foremost among the practices of English law with which torture is sometimes confused is the *peine forte et dure*.

In our own day, when an accused felon is arraigned for trial, it is demanded of him that he "plead" to the crime or crimes charged in the indictment or information. He can waive adjudication by pleading guilty, which leaves only sentencing to the court. Otherwise, he will formally controvert the indictment by entering a plea of not guilty. The trier (prototypically the jury) then decides his guilt or innocence. Until the eighteenth century, however, the accused had a third option: he could refuse entirely to plead. In a modern English court, if a defendant attempts thus to "stand mute," the presiding judge will enter a plea of not guilty in his behalf, and the trial will go forward as though the defendant himself had voiced the plea. However, this solution was only devised by statutes of 1772 and 1827.[13] Before 1772 the defendant's refusal to plead prevented his trial.

The notion that jury trial was a consensual proceeding that the defendant had a right to decline was a remnant of the peculiar circumstances through which jury trial became the predominant determinative procedure in English law, the successor to the ordeals. When the Fourth Lateran Council of 1215 destroyed the ordeals, a different mode of proof had to be devised. Jury trial was already in use in English criminal procedure in some exceptional situations, as an option available to a defendant who wished to avoid the ordeals. The path of inclination for the English was thus to extend jury procedure to fill the enormous gap left by the abolition of the ordeals. But although trial by jury lost its exceptional character and became the regular mode of proof in cases of serious crime, it retained its consensual element. Because the criminal defendant had always had the right to choose jury trial, the right to refuse it was difficult to withdraw from him.

The government was for a time perplexed about what to do with defendants who refused to plead, hence who refused jury trial. Following some experimentation earlier in the thirteenth century,[14] legislation in 1275 directed that they be kept provisionally in *prison forte et dure*. Practice corrupted this phrase to *peine forte et dure:* the defendant who refused to plead to his indictment was subjected to physical coercion so terrible that it killed him if he did not relent and enter his plea.[15]

This barbarism would surely have disappeared within a few generations as the consensual origins of jury trial receded in popular recollection, had not another factor enhanced the value of the defendant's right to refuse jury trial. Conviction for felony entailed forfeiture of the felon's estate. A defendant who died under the peine forte et dure was not convict, and his estate descended to his heirs.[16] A propertied defendant had, therefore, an incentive to refuse jury trial. So long as he had not pleaded, the court could kill him, but it could not convict him.

Custom settled it that the defendant who was put to peine forte et dure was laid over with weights that would crush him to death unless he relented. The practice came to be called "pressing." In the seventeenth century the defendant could be pressed to death in a few minutes.[17] Pressing was not inevitably administered with such dispatch, however. If the crown had some interest in conducting a trial, it could protract the defendant's suffering in order to coerce a plea. When in 1615 Richard Weston, one of the Overbury murderers, initially refused at his trial to plead, Sir Edward Coke threatened him from the bench:

> For the first, he was . . . to be extended, and then to have weights laid upon him, no more than he was able to bear, which were by little and little to be increased.
> For the second, that he was to be exposed in an open place, near to the prison, in the open air, being naked.
> And lastly, that he was to be preserved with the coarsest bread that could be got, and water out of the next sink or puddle to the place of execution, and that day he had water he should have no bread, and that day he had bread he should have no water; and in this torment he was to linger as long as nature could linger out, so that oftentimes men lived in that extremity eight or nine days.[18]

Weston reconsidered and entered his plea.[19]

Even in exceptional cases like Weston's where the crown was genuinely concerned to coerce the defendant to stand trial before going to his death, we should not reckon peine forte et dure as torture. Despite fascinating parallels,[20] there remains the crucial distinction that in the peine forte et dure coercion was not being used to extract information, to gather evidence. The peine forte et dure is best regarded as a special kind of guilty plea. The defendant underwent a different mode of capital punishment in order to save his estate for his kin.[21]

We saw in Chapter 1 that on the Continent the Roman-canon law of proof with its dependence on torture was the successor to the ordeals. We should notice, therefore, that in some amateur English writing the ordeals themselves have been reckoned as torture, mostly on the expansive view that anything official and painful constitutes torture.[22] When someone was made to plunge his hand into boiling water or to grasp a hot iron, it may have hurt, but it was not torture. For all its evils, torture was employed in aid of a rational as opposed to a ritual mode of proof. The use of torture presupposed a legal system that wanted to base judgment on the truth and thought it feasible to get the truth in part by means of regulated coercion. Torture was an aid to fact-finding. The ordeals were administered by courts that did not engage in fact-finding. The ordeals were devices for obtaining the judgment of God. If the hand healed, God had adjudged the defendant innocent. The defendant was not being coerced to talk—indeed a misplaced "Ouch!" might violate the forms and cost him his suit.

Finally, torture has sometimes been confused with the afflictive sanctions. As late as the seventeenth century in England, traitors were still being castrated, disembowelled, and quartered, felons hanged, heretics burned at the stake;[23] lesser offenders were regularly whipped, their ears shorn, their noses slit. We repeat that no variety of punishment inflicted as a sanction following conviction, no matter how brutal, should be regarded as torture, because punishment is not directed to extracting evidence or information.

It should, however, be conceded that all of these practices—peine forte et dure, the ordeals, the afflictive sanctions—have this much connection to torture: they acclimated men to violence and suffering in criminal procedure. Torture by rack and manacles must have fitted more easily in a system that already knew the axe and the pillory.[24]

The Jury Standard of Proof

England was "not very far from torture in the days when the *peine forte et dure* was invented."[25] How then did medieval England escape the Roman-canon law of torture? Maitland's well known account has never been doubted. The English were not possessed of "any unusual degree of humanity or enlightenment."[26] Rather, they were the beneficiaries of legal institutions so crude that torture was unnecessary.

The Roman-canon law of evidence was devised on the Continent for a system of adjudication by professional judges. The English substitute for the judgment of God was the petty jury, an institution that retained something of the "inscrutability"[27] of the ordeals. The collective judgment of an ad hoc panel of the folk, uttered as the voice of the countryside, unanimously and without rationale, seemed less an innovation than the principled law of the medieval jurists. "Our criminal procedure ... had hardly any place for a law of evidence."[28] In lieu of the ordeals the common law accepted "the rough verdict of the countryside, without caring to investigate the logical processes, if logical they were, of which that verdict was the outcome."[29]

On the Continent, torture "came to the relief of a law of evidence which made conviction well-nigh impossible.... Luckily for England neither the stringent rules of legal proof nor the cruel and stupid subterfuge became endemic here."[30] The jury standard of proof gave England no cause to torture. When Sir Walter Raleigh, standing trial for treason in 1603, complained that there was but one witness against him, Justice Peter Warburton replied from the bench:

> I marvel, sir Walter, that you being of such experience and wit, should stand on this point; for so many horse-stealers may escape, if they may not be condemned without witnesses. If one should rush into the king's Privy-Chamber, whilst he is alone, and kill the king (which God forbid) and this man be met coming with his sword drawn all bloody; shall not he be condemned to death?[31]

To this day an English jury can convict a defendant on less evidence than was required as a mere precondition for interrogation under torture on the Continent.

The medieval English legal system not only presented no occasion to torture, it also developed no institutions to conduct torture. Torture is a mode of investigation conducted by public officers; "private torture" is simply trespass. Yet the Angevin system of self-informing juries required no outside officer to investigate crime and to inform the jurors of the evidence. Jurors "were men chosen as being likely to be already informed;"[32] the vicinage requirement, the rule that jurors be drawn from the neighborhood where the crime had been committed, was meant to produce jurors who might be witnesses as well as triers.[33] Denunciation (to the jury of accusation) and proof of guilt (to the jury of trial) operated informally, mostly out of court and in advance of the court's sitting. Medieval juries came to court more to speak than to listen. Apart from the State Trials, which were of no quantitative significance, there were no official evidence-gatherers. Thus, the institutions of the English criminal

process complemented the procedures: the English had no one to
operate the torture chamber that they did not need.

Public Prosecution
under the Tudors

When torture did appear in England in Tudor times, the procedures
and institutions had changed considerably. The juries had largely
ceased to be self-informing. The transformation of active medieval
juries into passive courtroom triers was probably completed in the
fifteenth century, certainly by the early sixteenth.[34] As the jurors
became bare lay judges, outside officers undertook to gather and
present evidence to them. Although there were earlier antecedents,
this prosecutorial function crystallized in the sixteenth century.[35]

The Privy Council itself took charge of investigating criminal
cases tinged with high politics, a category much expanded after the
English Reformation turned heresy into sedition. The Council sometimes undertook these criminal investigations as a body (''at the
Council Board''), but more typically it delegated them to ad hoc
commissions. The commissions commonly included the law officers
of the crown, the attorney general and the solicitor general, who took
increasing responsibility for courtroom prosecution when such investigations resulted in criminal trials.[36]

Of course, the vast bulk of ordinary felony continued to be local
business. The system remained rooted in private prosecution. Ag-
grieved citizens could inform the juries in court as in medieval times
they had informed them out of court. This scheme of citizen prosecution was, however, superintended by the local justices of the peace
(JPs), who were the real forerunners of the modern public pros-
ecutor. They bound over victims and other witnesses to testify, they
investigated in difficult cases, and where necessary they undertook
courtroom prosecution—that is, they led the evidence and argued it
to the jury. In an age when courtroom procedure was informal and
the rules of evidence still nonexistent, it mattered little that the prosecuting JP was usually a nonlawyer. Public prosecution by the JPs
was systematized by statute in 1555, although it had been developing
for over a century.[37]

It should be emphasized that even after the changes in the jury
system that led to the appearance of public prosecutorial institutions,
the jury standard of proof remained unaltered. The principal element

of the medieval system that had forestalled the use of torture in England in the thirteenth century continued into the sixteenth century and, indeed, into our own day. The trial jury required for condemnation not certainty, but only persuasion. Well into the eighteenth century there were no firm rules establishing minimum standards of evidence for conviction, and consequently no appellate review of verdicts for insufficiency of the evidence.

Nevertheless, while certainty is a much harder standard to satisfy than persuasion, persuasion is often difficult enough to achieve. Grand juries rejected bills of indictment and trial juries acquitted indicted persons in significant numbers.[38] English authorities in the sixteenth century must have been tempted to employ torture to uncover the elements of persuasion as their Continental brethren were using torture to establish certainty. For example,[39] in June 1570 the Privy Council intervened in the case of one Thomas Andrews, who was "vehemently suspected" of "a very heinous murder lately committed in Somersetshire, whereof the said Andrews . . . will confess nothing . . . ." The Council ordered Andrews brought to the Tower of London "to be set to the rack and offered the torture thereof . . . ." A Justice of Queen's Bench, John Southcote, was ordered to conduct the examination and was directed, "after he shall have taken his confession . . . to return him to [prison], to be further proceeded withall according to the order of the law." A later document records that Andrews confessed.

The jury standard of proof did leave room for the use of torture, yet instances of the use of torture like Andrews' case occurred rarely. Such cases occurred frequently enough to prove that there were no established procedural safeguards against the use of torture; but the cases are so infrequent that we can be quite certain that torture was not being routinized in English criminal procedure. Infinitely more cases of "vehement suspicion" were not investigated under torture, with the consequence that the evidence requisite for persuasion was not obtained and the suspect acquitted. With prosecutors now in the field and the use of torture underway, what stopped England's conversion to the law of torture? To deal with that question we need to examine what torture there was in England, and to inquire how it related to the criminal procedure of the time.

6 The Torture Warrants
1540-1640

In eighty-one cases over the years 1540–
1640 official warrants were issued authorizing the use of torture in
England. We know these cases primarily from the warrants or records of warrants in two surviving classes of public documents, the
registers of the Privy Council,[1] and the miscellany called the State
Papers Domestic.[2]

We shall never be able to say with precision in what number of
cases torture was used in England. The inference is inescapable that
some use of torture predates the surviving warrants. The Privy Council registers, our principal source, commence only in 1540.[3] In the
State Papers of Henry VIII there are a few earlier suggestions by and
to officials, including Thomas Cromwell, that torture be used in
various investigations.[4] There are hints that the rack may have been in
use in the Tower of London in the mid-fifteenth century.[5]

Not only does the use of torture appear to predate the authoritative
records, but the records are also incomplete for the century they
cover. In the State Papers Domestic we can find a Privy Council
warrant that is not recorded in the Privy Council register for the
time;[6] worse, there are a number of serious gaps in the registers,
periods as long as several years for which the registers are missing or
imperfect.[7]

Certain exclusions have also been made to reach our figure of
eighty-one cases. We have omitted six cases scattered over the years
1539–84 for which the evidence makes it seem probable that torture
was authorized but for which the warrants are not recorded.[8] Of
course, our total also excludes a number of less plausible but possible
cases.[9] Finally, art is occasionally required to decide what constitutes a case: in some instances we aggregate as a single case two or
more warrants directing the torture of the same suspect or related
suspects for the same matter,[10] whereas in two instances we treat as
separate cases a single warrant authorizing torture of two seemingly

unrelated suspects.[11] We have numbered the cases in sequence according to the dates of the warrants in the table at the end of this chapter.

Although the eighty-one cases constitute an incomplete data base, we think that they do not drastically understate the total. Torture in England remained a very exceptional practice of the highest central authorities. If there had been any massive use of torture before the records begin to evidence it in 1540, or after they cease to disclose it in 1640, or omitted from the records for the intervening century, literary and other sources would alert us. The issue, therefore, is whether the use of torture averaged about one case per year over the century as the surviving records suggest, or whether it occurred at some slightly higher rate—conceivably two or even three cases per year. The precise figure really does not much matter when contrasted with Stephen's computation that in late Elizabethan England about eight hundred felony convicts were executed each year.[12] Relative to the thousands of felony investigations each year, the number of torture cases was miniscule. Then why and under what circumstances was torture used at all?

The Gerard Warrant

The reign of Elizabeth was the age when torture was most used in England. Of the eighty-one cases, fifty-three are Elizabethan. To illustrate torture at work we shall take in detail a famous Elizabethan case, that of the Jesuit priest John Gerard (Case 69, 1597), and compare it with the data tabulated for all the cases. The Gerard case commends itself as our model in part because we also know it from a source beyond the warrant and the related State Papers: Gerard ultimately escaped from the Tower and wrote an autobiography recounting his victimization.[13] We shall be discussing the warrant in Gerard's case with a constant eye on the question how faithfully it typifies the other eighty. In this way we shall avoid rehearsing the factual detail of the whole string of cases. The Gerard warrant it will be convenient to reproduce in full:

> A letter to Sir Richard Barkley, Lieutenant of the Tower, Mr. Solicitor, Mr. Bacon and William Waad, esquire. You shall understand that one Gerratt [Gerard], a Jesuit, by her Majesty's commandment is of late committed to the Tower of London for that it hath been discovered to her Majesty [that] he very lately

did receive a packet of letters out of the Low Countries which
are supposed to come out of Spain, [he] being noted to be a great
intelligencer and to hold correspondence with Parsons the Jesuit
and other traitors beyond the seas. These shall be therefore to
require you to examine him strictly upon such interrogatories as
shall be fit to be [ad]ministered unto him and he ought to answer
to manifest the truth in that behalf and other things that may
concern her Majesty and the State, wherein if you shall find him
obstinate, undutiful, or unwilling to declare and reveal the truth
as he ought to do by his duty and allegiance, you shall by virtue
hereof cause him to be put to the manacles and such other torture
as is used in that place, that he may be forced to utter directly
and truly his uttermost knowledge in all these things that may
any way concern her Majesty and the State and are meet to be
known.[14]

Venue

The warrant to torture Gerard is typical in directing it to be done in
the Tower of London. In seventy-four of the eighty-one cases venue
was laid in London: the Tower in forty-eight cases, Bridewell in
twenty, and other or undisclosed London prisons in six. In one
early case there is no indication of venue (Case 3, 1543). In six
cases torture was authorized in the localities.[15]

Bridewell does not appear in the surviving torture warrants until
June 1589.[16] Thereafter for the rest of Elizabeth's reign, it was the
regular venue. The Tower, which had been the regular venue from
the beginning of the records, was used only twice more in the
reign.[17] With the accession of James, Bridewell disappears from the
torture warrants, the remainder all designating the Tower. No compelling explanation presents itself for the virtual disuse of the Tower
between 1589 and 1603.[18] In any event, sixty-eight of the eighty
cases with known venue designate these two London prisons, which
had specialized torture equipment.[19]

Only seven warrants permit local authorities to undertake torture
on their own—four of them early (Cases 4, 10, 19, 23), two barely
torture (Cases 37 and 41, which allowed youthful suspects to be
whipped to make them talk), and an anomalous case directing the
Lord Mayor of London to use torture on someone suspected of post-
ing placards to incite apprentices to disorder (Case 61). Even in cases
in which the Council authorized the use of torture to investigate local

felonies, it typically required that the suspects be sent up to London for examination under torture.

Modes of Torture

Regarding the varieties of torture instruments and the like, we incline to Pollock's view: "The details have no material bearing on the general history of the law, and may be left to students of semi-barbarous manners."[20] We pause over the subject for limited purposes.

The warrant to torture Gerard authorizes his examiners, "if you shall find him obstinate," to "cause him to be put to the manacles and such other torture as is used in [the Tower]." The warrants commonly contain some provision that torture be used only if necessary, in Gerard's case if he were "obstinate." This is an obvious limitation; it would have been pointless to rack a man who would talk without it. A number of the earlier warrants authorize only the threat, not the application of torture.[21] Hence in some of our eighty-one cases the screws were not actually turned. Nevertheless, we reckon these as cases of torture. Nothing significant to legal history depends on the distinction whether the wretch was actually racked or merely put in imminent fear of it.

More often than not the warrants prescribe a particular mode of torture, in Gerard's case the manacles, and typically either the rack or the manacles. Through 1588, when the Tower was the normal venue, the rack was—in the expression of one warrant—"the accustomed torture."[22] For the rest of the Elizabethan period, when torture was regularly conducted at Bridewell, "the torture of the House"[23] was the manacles. Apparently Bridewell was not equipped with a rack. The warrants under the Stuarts, which return venue to the Tower, mention both rack and manacles.

The manacles was the English term for the strappado—suspending the victim by his hands without foot support. Both the rack and the manacles involved distending the limbs, and it may have been that a warrant authorizing the manacles contemplated the rack as well. In William Monke's case (Case 80, 1626), for example, the warrant authorizes the examiners to use the manacles, whereas it was later reported that the victim was "tortured upon the rack and . . . thereby utterly disabled." In the case of Philip May (Case 75, 1603), the first warrant authorizes "the tortures of the rack." It was superseded a day later by a second warrant whose purpose was to make a change in the examining commission,[24] but which orders May put "to the manacles or such other torture as is used in the Tower." One is left with the impression that the Council did not much care about the choice of weapons. Often when a particular torture instrument was mentioned in the warrant, more general authority was also granted, in Gerard's case "the manacles and such other torture as is used in that place."[25]

The warrants do mention other tortures. Thomas Sherwood was ordered sent "to the dungeon amongst the rats," which seems not to have worked since the Council had to have him racked a couple of weeks later (Case 33, 1577). The priest George Beesley and his companion (Case 55, 1591) were ordered confined in the Tower to the "prison called Little Ease," a cell so cramped that the inhabitant could neither move nor stand in it.[26] A device called Skevington's Irons that survives in the museum of the Tower of London is not mentioned in the warrants, although other documents record that it was used in at least one of the warranted cases.[27] It operated by compressing rather than distending the body. Perhaps King James had it in mind when he instructed the examiners of Guy Fawkes: "The gentler tortures are to be first used unto him, *et sic per gradus ad ima tenditur* [and thus by degrees advancing to the worst], and so God speed your good work."[28]

Commissioners to Torture

The Council's warrant to torture Gerard issued to a commission of four: the Lieutenant of the Tower of London, Sir Richard Barkley; the Solicitor General, Sir Thomas Fleming; Francis Bacon (then still Mr. Bacon and without office); and Sir William Waad, clerk to the Privy Council. This group is in many respects typical.

In forty-four of the forty-eight cases where venue was laid in the Tower, the Lieutenant was named to the commission. In two early cases the Constable of the Tower, the Lieutenant's nominal superior, was named instead of the Lieutenant.[29] The Lieutenant was not likely to have been a clever interrogator; he appears as a sideline figure in Gerard's account of his examination. Some warrants make it clear that although the Lieutenant is associated, the other commissioners are to be the active examiners. Perhaps the Lieutenant was included mainly in order to absolve him from liability for allowing the active members of the commission to do their job on the Lieutenant's prisoner. Further, his were the jailors and the instruments of torture—somebody had to drive. On the other hand, the many warrants to torture at Bridewell never include the keeper of that prison.

The Solicitor General is designated in nineteen of the eighty-one cases, the Attorney General in fifteen (in 11 of which he overlapped the Solicitor). Common law judges are named in eight cases. The Recorder of London[30] is named in twelve warrants, various serjeants-at-law in nine, and common lawyers of lesser stature (such as Mr. Francis Bacon of 1597) in others. Civil lawyers are named, usually in company with common lawyers, in fourteen cases, mostly involving religious offenders.[31]

The inclusion of Waad, clerk to the Council, in the commission to torture Gerard was typical of the practice of those years. From 1581 onward in cases of state crime one of the clerks was often among the examiners. Such warrants frequently direct the commissioners to keep the Council informed of the investigation, and that must have been understood even when unmentioned. The clerk was a natural conduit between the Council and the commissioners.

In the warrants of the 1580s and 1590s three lesser Council servants appear recurrently: Thomas Norton, Richard Topcliffe, and Richard Young. The latter two were named so often that they may have been thought to be expert torturers.[32] For the rest, there was a miscellany of commissioners—a bishop, various diplomats and crown servants, some country justices, two mayors and an alderman. It is seldom clear why a particular person was named—why Bacon in Gerard's case, for example. Apart from the Lieutenant of the Tower, no officer is so consistently named in the commissions that his membership was really regular. The commissions number from one to eight members, but usually contain between two and four. Commissions of one or two men are common into the reign of Mary, much less frequent thereafter. As the commissions became larger a quorum clause was occasionally inserted, authorizing a number smaller than the whole group to conduct the examination.

The prominence of the law officers, judges, and other common lawyers in the commissions might suggest that they were being chosen in order to facilitate judicial torture. They best knew what went into an indictment and what proofs would sustain it at trial. On the other hand, we shall see that the English in fact made relatively little use of torture to gather evidence for judicial proceedings. We think it likely that the Council relied on the lawyers for lack of any better source of examiners. Lawyers are professionals at the business of fact-finding; and the prominent common lawyers were those whom the Council knew and trusted.

Gerard's autobiography and other records tell us that Attorney General Edward Coke took part in conducting Gerard's examination under torture,[33] although the warrant does not include him. We cannot say how common it was for persons not named in the warrant to join in the interrogation. The warrants themselves occasionally supplement the commissions in a different way, providing that the commissioners should base their examination upon interrogatories or articles to be devised by an outsider, for example, in the case of William Monke (Case 80, 1626), "upon such interrogatories as should be directed by the Lord Chief Justice of King's Bench."

Preconditions for Torture

The warrants from about the middle of Elizabeth's reign onward commonly contain some statement of the information against the suspect that led the Council to order torture, whereas the earlier warrants are often terser. Against Gerard "it hath been discovered to her Majesty [that] he very lately did receive a packet of letters out of the Low Countries which are supposed to come out of Spain, [he] being noted to be a great intelligencer and to hold correspondence with Parsons the Jesuit and other traitors beyond the seas." Sometimes, however, the warrant makes a point of not disclosing for the record the Council's suspicions. For example, Owen Edmondes (Case 59, 1592) "standeth at this present charged very deeply with matters concerning the State . . . and it seemeth there is good proof against him for the matters wherewith he is so charged." Recitals of this sort can be quite laconic. The accused robbers Mulcaster and Curate (Cases 12, 13, 1555) are, respectively, "vehemently suspect" and "vehemently suspected." Thomas Andrews (Case 26, 1570), accused of murder, "is vehemently suspected and will hitherto confess nothing." Against Richard Anger and another (Case 71, 1597) "there are great presumptions [that they] be the committers of [a] foul murder."

Jardine thought such expressions showed the "Roman origins"[34] of English torture practice. We shall dispute this view in Chapter 7, pointing out that the warrants make no effort to comply with the Roman-canon law of proof. But although the Council was not seeking to conform to any such external standard for the use of torture, it does seem to have found a rough standard of its own. The Council could impose torture without fear of formal legal or constitutional restraints, but it had practical incentives to use torture sparingly. The Council did not want to frighten or alienate any sector of the political community needlessly. Just as the Council so often instructed its commissioners not to apply the rack when the threat alone would suffice, it was unwilling to authorize any torture casually. The contrast with ordinary common law procedure must have appeared constantly to the members of the Council.[35] When, therefore, they took the exceptional step of ordering torture, it was natural for the register to reflect from time to time some element of self-justification. The standard for torture that can be inferred from the warrants is well removed from legal principle or doctrine. When the Council gives a rationale for a warrant, it seldom amounts to much more than an assertion that the Council took quite seriously both the offense and the circumstances inculpating the accused.

The Purposes
of Torture

Gerard's case was one of political or state crime. He was suspected of involvement in the running war of subversion that the English authorities were sure was being conducted by the Spanish and the Jesuits.

Political (including religious) offenders were the predominant subjects of English torture practice, although the undercurrent of torture in nonpolitical cases ran through the sixteenth century. In seven of our eighty-one cases the warrants and other sources disclose no information about the offenses involved.[36] Of the remaining seventy-four, however, twenty-two cases—more than a quarter—deal with ordinary felony, mostly murder and theft.[37] The other fifty-two cases concern state crime,[38] the doings of priests and plotters and the like.

In cases of ordinary crime the purpose of torture was primarily evidentiary. One Rice (Case 25, 1567), suspected of burglary, was ordered tortured "whereby he may be the better brought to confess the truth." Torture of a group of suspected murderers in 1579 (Case 36) was meant "to bring them to confess the fact, that thereupon (sufficient matter appearing) they may be further proceeded withall, according to the law." A boy, Humfrey (Case 37, 1580), thought to be in "privities" with the culprits who burglarized the house of Sir Drue Drury, was ordered whipped to "wring from him the knowledge of the persons and manner of the robbery, that thereupon order may be taken for their apprehension and punishment according to the laws."

The object of torture in the cases of state crime seems more diffuse. From Gerard there was sought "the truth" about his suspected conniving with other conspirators "and other things that may concern her Majesty and the state." Gerard had been held in jail for three years before he was put to torture,[39] during which time he could easily have been prosecuted to his death for violation of the statute forbidding priests to stay in England.[40] According to his autobiography, his examiners were primarily concerned to discover the whereabouts of Father Henry Garnet, the Jesuit superior in England.[41] In the case of Edmund Peacham (Case 77, 1615), the interrogatories have survived upon which the old clergyman was examined. Their main purpose is to discover accomplices and threatened sedition:

3. Whom have you made privy and acquainted with the said writings, or any part of them? and who hath been your helpers or confederates herein? . . .

9. What moved you to make doubt whether the people will rise against the king for taxes and oppressions? Do you know, or have you heard of any likelihood or purpose of any tumults or commotion?[42]

Peacham's supposedly treasonous writings had been discovered in his home in the course of a disciplinary proceeding against him in the court of High Commission. The writings alone were sufficient to condemn him for treason, it was held,[43] and he was convicted (he died of jail fever while awaiting execution). Again, torture was not really directed to gathering evidence for the trial.

For most of the earlier cases and some of the later ones the sources do not disclose enough of the detail that was known against political prisoners to permit us to say whether they could have been convicted without evidence secured through torture. Certainly many were doomed when they were apprehended, including such famous torture victims as John Hodgkins, the Marprelate printer (Case 52, 1589), and Guy Fawkes (Case 76, 1605). So was the pathetic prophet William Hacket (Case 56, 1591), who mounted a cart in Cheapside, the main thoroughfare of London, declared himself to be Jesus Christ, and denounced "the Lord Chancellor and the Bishop of Canterbury, whom [he] called traitors to God and the realm." The Elizabethan Council had no tolerance for such things. It ordered Hacket tortured "to utter and discover the bottom of his wicked and devilish purpose and the names of those that were authors, abettors or any wise privy to those his lewd intentions and doings . . . ." He was convicted and executed, but no further evidence was needed when torture was ordered. Torture was used not to procure courtroom evidence against the accused, but on the chance that accomplices and wider designs might be revealed. Likewise, the statute of 1584–85 that made it treason for Jesuits and other priests to remain in the realm made apprehension tantamount to conviction and eliminated the need to torture them for evidence.

The distinction between torturing for judicial evidence as opposed to other information was probably unimportant to the Council, although by the time of Peacham's case it had been casually formulated by Bacon (in a memorandum for King James): "In the highest cases of treasons, torture is used for discovery, and not for evidence."[44] The Council used torture to protect the state. Mostly that meant preventive torture to identify and forestall plots and plotters. Nothing kept the information thus extracted from being used at trial if it were needed, although there was a risk that an accused might persuade a jury that a statement made under torture was false.[45] Given the amount of torture that was authorized in these political cases, it is noteworthy that we know of so little evidentiary use. For that the explanation is doubtless still the ancient one that a jury could convict on scant evidence, and in treason cases the pressure to convict was intense.[46] Judicial torture was still unnecessary.

In the many cases of ordinary crime, however, torture for evidence-gathering seemingly had some utility. It remains to ask, therefore, in Chapter 7 how contemporaries justified the use of torture, and why under the supposedly absolutist early Stuarts torture in England came to an end.

The Table of
Warrants

Case number. The English torture warrants are listed below in the
table (pp. 94–123) in chronological sequence. We have numbered
each "case." Normally each warrant constitutes a separate case, but
in some instances where two or three warrants issued to investigate
the same offense (e.g., the Ridolfi Plot, Case 28) or offenders (e.g.,
Edmund Campion and companions, Case 42) we have treated multi-
ple warrants as a single case. In these instances we list the warrants
individually (e.g., 42A, 42B, 42C). The figures in parenthesis in the
"Case Number" column are the numbers assigned by Jardine to
those of the warrants that he knew and reprinted in the appendix to
his monograph. The notes to the table (infra pp. 192–205) contain an
entry for each of our numbered cases, citing at minimum the sources
of the warrants.

Suspects. The spelling of proper names has been modernized in relatively clear cases (e.g., Nichols for Nycholls, Heath for Hethe). We
have not eliminated the terminal *e* (e.g., Browne, Frenche) unless
the sources are inconsistent and use both forms (e.g., Bradshawe and
Bradshaw in Case 67), in which instances we use the shorter. A few
of these names (and some other data in the table) are derived not
from the warrants, but from related documents, cited in the notes to
the table. In cases involving several suspects we give the names in
the order in which they are set out in the warrants. Following the
table is an alphabetical listing of all named persons ordered tortured
(infra pp. 124–125), cross-referenced to the case numbers in the table.

Commissioners to torture. The information in this column in the
table has been supplemented considerably from sources beyond the
warrants. The warrants frequently designate some examiners by
office alone (e.g., the Lieutenant of the Tower, the Lord Chief Justice). We have generally been able to identify these officers. We
show the names in square brackets. Spelling has been conformed
where possible to the *Dictionary of National Biography*, Foss's *A
Biographical Dictionary of the Judges of England*, or Foss's *Tabulae
Curiales*; or to the variant preferred in the indexes to the published
Privy Council registers. Omitted Christian names have been supplied
in some cases, and these we do not show in brackets. We have

deleted titles of address (e.g., Sir, Dr., Mr.) and appositives of rank (e.g., esq., gent.,), but we have retained titles of nobility. We list the commissioners in the order in which they are designated in the warrants. An alphabetical compendium of all named examiners (infra pp. 125–127) is cross-referenced to the case numbers in the table.

Certain officers recur among the commissioners. We have established abbreviations for these titles of office, and we have interpolated them in the table in cases where the warrants give only the proper names. We also show which examiners were members of the civilians' inn, Doctors' Commons. The abbreviations:

AG	Attorney General
CPC	Clerk of the Privy Council
CT	Constable of the Tower of London
DC	Member of Doctors' Commons
JCP	Justice of Common Pleas
JQB	Justice of Queen's Bench
LCJ	Lord Chief Justice (of King's [Queen's] Bench)
LT	Lieutenant of the Tower of London
MR	Master of the Rolls
RL	Recorder of London
S	Serjeant at Law
SG	Solicitor General
SS	Secretary of State

We preserve without abbreviation other titles of office used in the warrants, save in a few cases where the officer also has one of the above abbreviated titles (e.g., Ralph Rokeby, identified as Master of St. Catherine's Hospital in the warrants, shown as member of Doctors' Commons, Cases 45, 52). We show only the more important title when the examiner held two or more, hence Attorney General or Recorder of London in preference to Serjeant.

In order not to clutter the table with information of relatively little bearing to this study, we have not supplied the titles of the many other dignitaries, crown servants, lawyers, and so forth when the warrants omit to mention them. By emphasizing officeholders we do not intend to slight the all-around Tudor statesmen (e.g., Thomas Bodley, Henry Killigrew, Richard Martin, Thomas Randolph, Ralph Sadler, Thomas Smith) and handymen (e.g., Thomas Norton,

Richard Topcliffe, Richard Young) who also figure prominently in the commissions. In contrast to the torture victims, very few of the examiners are unknown figures; the *DNB,* Foss, the Council registers, and the calendars to the public records identify most. We disclose in the notes to the cases when we have resorted to unconventional sources to identify the proper names or offices of commissioners. Members of Doctors' Commons have been identified through the kindness of G. D. Squibb, Q.C., who is presently preparing the Register of Doctors' Commons for publication. The manuscript is in Lambeth Palace Library.

Offense. We have not followed strictly the characterizations used in the warrants. When the facts indicate burglary although the warrant speaks of robbery, we use the former. There is no important line between the terms "sedition" and "treason," and not much of one between those two and the term "religious." The latter is somewhat more particular, so we use it when the sources permit. We use "treason" when the sources speak of it, and "sedition" as a catchall for crimes of state. In a few cases (e.g., Case 31) our characterization of the offense as sedition is an inference drawn more from the composition of the examining commission than the description of the suspect's conduct.

Mode of torture. Space does not permit us to disclose whether the warrant suggests, implies, or instructs that the torture be only threatened, or that it be threatened before being applied. We have said in Chapter 6 that nothing of legal historical significance turns on such distinctions.

Notes (infra pp. 192–205). In the notes to the table we have tried to summarize, or when convenient to quote from, the warrants regarding (1) the information that is recited to justify the use of torture, and (2) the particulars sought under torture. The warrants are in the main too imprecise about these matters to make it practical to devise a tabular presentation.

The Warrants

Case No.	Date of Warrant	Suspects
1	16 Nov. 1540	Thomas Thwaytes
2	15 Oct. 1541	unnamed thieves
3	14 Mar. 1543	unnamed
4	15 Aug. 1550	James (or John) Fowlkes
5	5 Mar. 1551	Reede
6 (1)	5 Nov. 1551	unnamed prisoners
7	16 Nov. 1552	Thomas Holland
8 (2)	7 Jan. 1553	Willson Warren
9	3 Jun. 1553	Robert Man James Gardener
10	27 Jan. 1555	an engraver and others unnamed

Venue	Commissioners to Torture	Offense	Mode of Torture
Tower	[Edward Walsingham], LT	sedition	the brake
Tower	Edward Seymour, Earl of Hertford William Paulet, Lord St. John	attempted robbery of Windsor Castle	torture
—	Charles, Duke of Suffolk The Council	sedition	tortures
Norwich?	John Robsarte William Fermour	concealment of plate, money and other treasure	torment
London?	Anthony Hungerforde	robbery	torment
Tower	Arthur Darcy, LT "certain commissioners"	—	tortures
Tower	[Edward Warner], LT	sedition	Little Ease
Tower	[Edward Warner], LT	murder	tortures
London	—	stealing hawks from the estate of Princess Mary	torture
Bristol	[John Smith], Mayor of Bristol	counterfeiting	rack

The Warrants (*continued*)

Case No.	Date of Warrant	Suspects
11 (3)	9 Jun. 1555	unnamed prisoners
12 (4)	4 Dec. 1555	Richard Mulcaster
13 (5)	11 Dec. 1555	Nicholas Curate
14 (5)	11 Dec. 1555	Hugh of Warwick
15 (6)	16 Feb. 1556	Barton Thomas Tailor
16 (7)	21 Jun. 1556	Richard Gill
17 (8)	29 Jul. 1556	Silvester Taverner

Venue	Commissioners to Torture	Offense	Mode of Torture
Tower	Edward, Lord North [Henry Bedingfield?], LT others	—	tortures
Tower	Henry Bedingfield, LT	robbery	rack
Tower	Henry Bedingfield, LT James Dyer, S [William Cordell], SG	robbery	rack
Tower	Henry Bedingfield, LT James Dyer, S [William Cordell], SG	horse stealing	rack
Tower	Henry Bedingfield, LT John Baker	—	torture
Tower	Robert Peckham [Henry Bedingfield], LT ''one of the Masters of the Requests''	murder	tortures
Westminster prison	Roger Cholmley, S Thomas Martin, DC	embezzling plate belonging to the Queen and others	tortures

The Warrants (*continued*)

Case No.	Date of Warrant	Suspects
18 (9)	19 Jul. 1557	"such as Sir Edward Warner shall inform them of"
19	24 Jul. 1557	unnamed prisoners
20A	18 Oct. 1557	Edward Newporte an unnamed servant to Newporte Cowley
20B	30 Oct. 1557	an unnamed servant to Newporte

Venue	Commissioners to Torture	Offense	Mode of Torture
Tower	[Robert Oxenbridge], CT	robbery	torture
	Thomas Pope		
	William Garreth		
	John Throckmorton		
	[Ralph Cholmeley], RL		
	John White, Sheriff of London		
Devon	Lord St. John, Lord Lieutenant of Devon	"riot and disorder ... upon the goods and corn of Jane Stourton"	torture
Newgate	[Edward Hastings], Master of the Horse	counterfeiting	torture
	[Edward Saunders], LCJ		
	Richard Southwell		
	John Nudegate		
Newgate	[Edward Hastings], Master of the Horse	counterfeiting	torture
	Richard Southwell		
	John Mason		
	Robert Peckham		
	John Nudegate		

The Warrants (*continued*)

Case No.	Date of Warrant	Suspects
21 (10)	13 May 1558	Richard Frenche
22 (11)	15 Mar. 1559	Pitt Nichols
23 (12)	22 Jun. 1565	Nicholas Heath
24	28 Dec. 1566	Clement Fisher
25	18 Jan. 1567	Rice
26	20 Jun. 1570	Thomas Andrews
27	25 Jun. 1570	John Felton

Venue	Commissioners to Torture	Offense	Mode of Torture
Tower	[Robert Oxenbridge], CT	—	torture
	Roger Cholmley, S		
	[Ralph Cholmeley], RL		
	Thomas Martin, DC		
	Mr. Vaughan		
Tower	[Richard Blount], LT	robbery	rack
	[Ralph Hopton], Knight Marshall		
provincial	Henry, Lord Scrope	vagabondage? sedition?	torture
Tower	John Walsh, JQB	—	rack
	[Gilbert Gerrard], AG		
	others		
Tower	[Francis Jobson], LT	burglary	torture
	others		
Tower	John Southcote, JQB	murder	rack
	[Francis Jobson], LT		
	others "as shall be appointed thereunto by Justice [Richard] Weston," JCP		
Tower	Thomas Wroth	sedition	rack
	[Francis Jobson], LT		
	others		

The Warrants (*continued*)

Case No.	Date of Warrant	Suspects
28A	26 Apr. 1571	Charles Bailly
28B (15)	15 Sept. 1571	William Barker Laurence Bannister
29	1 Apr. 1573	George Browne
30	29 Nov. 1574	Humfrey Nedeham
31	6 Feb. 1575	Cicking
32	25 Oct. 1576	Thomas Wells

Venue	Commissioners to Torture	Offense	Mode of Torture
Tower	[Owen Hopton], LT Edmund Tremayne	treason: the Ridolfi Plot	torture
Tower	Ralph Sadler Thomas Smith Thomas Wilson, DC [Owen Hopton], LT	treason: the Ridolfi Plot	rack
Tower	[Owen Hopton], LT [William Cordell], MR John Southcote, JQB Roger Manwood, JCP	murder	tortures
Tower	[Owen Hopton], LT [Thomas Bromley], SG Thomas Randolph Henry Knolles Thomas Norton	religious	rack
Tower	Francis Walsingham, SS [Thomas Bromley], SG Thomas Randolph, Master of the Posts [Owen Hopton], LT	sedition	rack
Tower	[Owen Hopton], LT [William Fletewoode], RL	robbery	—

The Warrants (*continued*)

Case No.	Date of Warrant	Suspects
33A (16)	17 Nov. 1577	Thomas Sherwood
33B (17)	4 Dec. 1577	Thomas Sherwood
34 (18)	4 Nov. 1578	Harding
35 (18)	4 Nov. 1578	John Sanforde
36	11 Jun. 1579	Robert Winter-shall Harvy Mellershe others
37 (19)	9 Dec. 1580	Humfrey, a boy
38 (20)	24 Dec. 1580	John Hart James Bosgrave Pascall

Venue	Commissioners to Torture	Offense	Mode of Torture
Tower	[Owen Hopton], LT [Gilbert Gerrard], AG	treason	dungeon amongst the rats
Tower	[Owen Hopton], LT [Gilbert Gerrard], AG [Thomas Bromley], SG [William Flete-woode], RL	treason	rack
Tower	[Owen Hopton], LT [William Flete-woode], RL	—	rack
Tower	[Owen Hopton], LT [William Flete-woode], RL	—	rack
Tower	John Southcote, JQB Owen Hopton, LT Thomas Browne Robert Levesey	murder	rack
Norfolk	Thomas Townsend Henry Doyley William Blennerhas-set	burglary	whipping
Tower	[Owen Hopton], LT George Cary [Gilbert Gerrard], AG [John Popham], SG	religious	tortures

The Warrants (*continued*)

Case No.	Date of Warrant	Suspects
39 (24)	3 May 1581	Alexander Briant
40 (25)	2 Jun. 1581	"a young maiden"
41 (21–23)	30 Jul. 1581	Thomas Myagh
42A (26)	30 Jul. 1581	Edmund Campion
42B (27)	14 Aug. 1581	Edmund Campion John Colleton, *alias* Peters Thomas Forde Paine
42C (28)	29 Oct. 1581	Edmund Campion Thomas Forde others

Venue	Commissioners to Torture	Offense	Mode of Torture
Tower	[Owen Hopton], LT John Hammond, DC Thomas Norton	religious	torture
Chester	[William Chaderton], Bishop of Chester	religious	whipping
Tower	[Owen Hopton], LT Thomas Norton Geoffrey Fenton, Secretary of the Council of Ireland	sedition	rack
Tower	[Owen Hopton], LT John Hammond, DC Robert Beale, CPC Thomas Norton	religious	rack
Tower	[Owen Hopton], LT John Hammond, DC Robert Beale, CPC	religious	torture
Tower	[John Popham], AG [Thomas Egerton], SG [Owen Hopton], LT John Hammond, DC Thomas Wilkes, CPC Thomas Norton	religious	rack

The Warrants (*continued*)

Case No.	Date of Warrant	Suspects
43 (29)	29 Apr. 1582	Thomas Alfield
44A (30)	10 Apr. 1586	Matthew Beaumond
44B	17 Apr. 1586	William Wakeman, *alias* Davies
44C	13 May 1586	William Wakeman, *alias* Davies Matthew Beaumond, *alias* Browne Pynder, *alias* Pudsey
45 (31)	23 Dec. 1586	Edward Wyndsor Edward Bently Ralph Ithell Thomas Tipping Anthony Tuchenor Thomas Habington Jerome Payne Sampsone Loane Hanry Foxwell Thomas Heath

Venue	Commissioners to Torture	Offense	Mode of Torture
Tower	[Owen Hopton], LT Thomas Randolph John Hammond, DC Thomas Owen	religious	rack
Tower	Owen Hopton, LT MacWilliams Richard Young	robbery	rack
Tower	Owen Hopton, LT MacWilliams Richard Young	robbery	rack
Tower	—	certain felonies	torture
Tower	Owen Hopton, LT Ralph Rokeby, DC John Popham, AG Thomas Egerton, SG Sandes, Clerk of the Crown Thomas Owen	treason	rack

The Warrants (*continued*)

Case No.	Date of Warrant	Suspects
46 (32)	24 Apr. 1587	Andreas van Metter
47 (33)	7 Jan. 1588	John Staughton Humfrey Fullwood others
48	14 Jan. 1588	Roger Asheton
49	16 Feb. 1588	George Stoker
50	8 Sept. 1588	Trystram Winslade
51	24 Jun. 1589	an unnamed goldsmith

Venue	Commissioners to Torture	Offense	Mode of Torture
Tower	Owen Hopton, LT Thomas Randolph Henry Killigrew Richard Young	sedition	rack
Tower	Owen Hopton, LT William Daniel Richard Young	sedition	rack and torture
Tower	Owen Hopton, LT Edward Waterhouse William Waad, CPC Richard Young	sedition	rack and torture
Tower	Owen Hopton, LT William Waad, CPC Thomas Bodley Thomas Owen Richard Young	sedition	rack
Tower	Owen Hopton, LT Richard Young James Dalton Richard Topcliffe	sedition	rack
Bridewell	Richard Young	burglary	"the torture of the House"

The Warrants (*continued*)

Case No.	Date of Warrant	Suspects
52	24 Aug. 1589	John Hodgkins Valentine Syms Arthur Thomlyn
53	1 Feb. 1590	Christopher Bayles, *alias* Evers John Bayles Henry Goorney Anthony Kaye John Coxed
54	18 Apr. 1590	William Browne three others
55	10 Jan. 1591	George Beesley, *alias* Passelaw Robert Humberson
56	20 Jul. 1591	William Hacket
57 (34)	25 Oct. 1591	Eustace White Brian Lassey

Venue	Commissioners to Torture	Offense	Mode of Torture
Bridewell	John Fortescue, Master of the Wardrobe Ralph Rokeby, DC [William Fletewoode], RL Richard Young, the Customer	religious: the Marprelate printers	torture
Bridewell	Richard Topcliffe Richard Young	religious	such torture as is usual
Bridewell	Richard Young other Middlesex JPs	robbery	rack and manacles
Tower	[Michael Blount], LT Henry Killigrew Robert Beale, CPC Giles Fletcher Richard Topcliffe	religious	Little Ease
Bridewell	Thomas Owen, S Richard Young others	sedition	manacles and other torture
Bridewell	Giles Fletcher Richard Topcliffe Richard Brauthwaut Richard Young	religious	manacles and other tortures

The Warrants (*continued*)

Case No.	Date of Warrant	Suspects
58 (35)	27 Oct. 1591	Thomas Clinton
59 (36)	4 Jun. 1592	Owen Edmonds
60 (37)	8 Feb. 1593	William Urmeston Edward Bagshaw Henry Aysh
61 (38)	16 Apr. 1593	unnamed suspect
62 (39)	11 May 1593	unnamed suspects
63 (40)	12 Nov. 1595	Gabriel Colford Thomas Foulkes
64 (41)	25 Jan. 1596	John Hardie
65 (42)	28 Feb. 1596	Humphrey Hodges

Venue	Commissioners to Torture	Offense	Mode of Torture
Bridewell	[John Popham], AG [Thomas Egerton], SG Richard Topcliffe Richard Young	sedition	manacles and other tortures
Bridewell	George Cary Richard Young	sedition	the torture accustomed
Bridewell	Richard Young Ellis [Thomas Egerton], AG [Edward Coke], SG	religious	torture
London	[John Spencer], Lord Mayor of London	sedition	torture
Bridewell	Richard Martin Anthony Ashley, CPC Cuthbert Buckle, Alderman of London others	sedition	torture
Bridewell	[Thomas Fleming], SG William Waad, CPC	sedition	manacles
Bridewell	Thomas Wilkes, CPC William Waad, CPC	sedition	ordinary torture
Bridewell	Richard Martin	burglary	manacles

The Warrants (*continued*)

Case No.	Date of Warrant	Suspects
66 (43)	21 Nov. 1596	some Gypsy ring-leaders
67 (44)	19 Dec. 1596	Bartholomew Steere James Bradshaw Robert Bradshaw Robert Ibell Robert Burton
68 (45)	2 Feb. 1597	William Thomson
69	13 Apr. 1597	John Gerard
70 (46)	1 Dec. 1597	Thomas Travers

Venue	Commissioners to Torture	Offense	Mode of Torture
Bridewell	[John Crooke], RL Richard Topcliffe Richard Skevington	their practices	manacles
Bridewell	[Edward Coke], AG [Thomas Fleming], SG Francis Bacon [John Crooke], RL	sedition	manacles and torture
London	[Edward Coke], AG [Thomas Fleming], SG Francis Bacon William Waad, CPC	sedition	manacles or the rack
Tower	Richard Barkley, LT [Thomas Fleming], SG Francis Bacon William Waad, CPC	religious	manacles and other torture
Bridewell	Richard Martin [John Crooke], RL Richard Topcliffe Thomas Fowler [Edward Coke], AG Vaughn Richard Skevington	"stealing a standish of her majesty"	manacles

The Warrants (*continued*)

Case No.	Date of Warrant	Suspects
71 (47)	17 Dec. 1597	Richard Anger, Jr. Edward Ingram
72	17 Apr. 1598	Valentine Thomas
73 (48)	4 Jan. 1599	Richard Denton Peter Cooper
74	14 Apr. 1601	Thomas Howson
75A (49)	19 Apr. 1603	Philip May
75B (50)	20 Apr. 1603	Philip May

Venue	Commissioners to Torture	Offense	Mode of Torture
Bridewell	[John Crooke], RL Richard Topcliffe Nicholas Fuller William Gerrard Altham	murder	manacles
Bridewell	Thomas Fleming, SG William Waad, CPC Francis Bacon	sedition	manacles
Bridewell	John Peyton, LT Richard Topcliffe	sedition	manacles
Bridewell	William Waad, CPC Thomas Fowler	sedition	manacles
Tower	John Popham, LCJ John Peyton, LT Edward Coke, AG Thomas Fleming, SG	sedition	rack
Tower	John Peyton, LT Edward Coke, AG Thomas Fleming, SG William Waad, CPC	sedition	manacles or other torture

The Warrants (*continued*)

Case No.	Date of Warrant	Suspects
76	6 Nov. 1605	Guy Fawkes, *alias* John Johnson
77 (51)	18 Jan. 1615	Edmund Peacham
78 (52)	19 Feb. 1620	Samuel Peacock
79 (53)	9 Jan. 1622	James Crasfield

Venue	Commissioners to Torture	Offense	Mode of Torture
Tower	Charles Howard, Earl of Nottingham Thomas Howard, Earl of Suffolk Charles Blount, Earl of Devonshire Edward Somerset, Earl of Worcester Henry Howard, Earl of Northampton Robert Cecil, Earl of Salisbury John Erskine, Earl of Mar John Popham LCJ	treason: the Gunpowder Plot	the gentler tortures first, and then by degrees
Tower	Ralph Winwood, SS Julius Caesar, MR Gervaise Helwys, LT Francis Bacon, AG Henry Montagu, RL Henry Yelverton, SG Randall Crewe, S Francis Cottington, CPC	treason	manacles
Tower	[Allen Apsley], LT Henry Montagu, LCJ Thomas Coventry, SG	treason	manacles or rack
Tower	Randall Crewe, S Thomas Coventry, AG	sedition	manacles and rack

The Warrants (*continued*)

Case No.	Date of Warrant	Suspects
80 (54)	30 Apr. 1626	William Monke
81 (55)	21 May 1640	John Archer

Venue	Commissioners to Torture	Offense	Mode of Torture
Tower	[Allen Apsley], LT	treason	manacles
	Francis Ashley, S		
	William Trumbull, CPC		
	Thomas Meautys, CPC		
Tower	[William Balfour], LT	sedition	rack
	Ralph Whitfield, S		
	Robert Heath, S		

Index (by Case Number) of Named Suspects Authorized to be Tortured

Index (by Case Number) of Named Commissioners to Torture

**Torture Warrants by
Year with Decade
Subtotals**

1540	1		1582	1
1541	1		1586	2
1543	1		1587	1
		3	1588	4
			1589	2
1550	1			16
1551	2			
1552	1		1590	2
1553	2		1591	4
1555	5		1592	1
1556	3		1593	3
1557	3		1595	1
1558	1		1596	4
1559	1		1597	4
		19	1598	1
			1599	1
1565	1			21
1566	1			
1567	1		1601	1
		3	1603	1
			1605	1
1570	2			3
1571	1			
1573	1		1615	1
1574	1			1
1575	1			
1576	1		1620	1
1577	1		1622	1
1578	2		1626	1
1579	1			3
		11	1640	1
				1
1580	2			
1581	4		Total	81

7 The Theory of Torture

By what right did the Privy Council (or occasionally[1] the monarch himself) order Englishmen put to torture? In the *Third Institute* Coke writes that "there is no law to warrant tortures in this land, nor can they be justified by any prescription, being so lately brought in."[2] Looking back at the practice of torture in Elizabethan times, Blackstone begged the question by labeling the rack "an engine of state, not of law . . . ."[3]

The Prerogative?

Because the torture warrants had been issued by the Council or the monarch, and because no law enforcement officer or court ever claimed the authority to use torture without such a warrant,[4] Jardine inferred that the power to torture was regarded as part of the royal prerogative. "This power of inflicting torture at pleasure at the mere instance of the Crown, has always appeared to me to be a very remarkable instance of the opposition of prerogative to law—of the existence in former times of a power above the law, controlling and subverting the law, and thus rendering its practical application altogether inconsistent with its theoretical excellence."[5]

One sign that Jardine's view is improbable is that the contemporary literature does not support it. The specialized treatises on the prerogative such as William Staunford's[6] do not reckon torture among the prerogative powers, although its use was notorious.[7] There is no mention of the power to torture in the little treatise[8] on the prerogative attributed to Francis Bacon, who elsewhere styled himself "a perfect and peremptory royalist"[9] and who was named as a commissioner to examine under torture in five cases.[10] The famous contemporary accounts by Sir Thomas Smith and Sir Edward Coke, we have seen, deny the existence or the legality of torture.

We suggest that the power to torture did inhere in the prerogative, not affirmatively but defensively. It derived from the doctrine of sovereign immunity.[11] The sovereign was immune from suit in his own courts. Not only were King and Council immune, they could immunize their agents. King and Council did not have to turn the screws in the torture chamber; they could commission delegates to apply torture. It was by warrant that they transferred their own immunity to their delegates. Without immunity the use of torture would have exposed the torturer to liability for civil and criminal trespass, and we have seen that the commissions that conducted torture usually contained a lawyer who knew well why he and his fellow commissioners might need immunity. Thus, there appears repeatedly in the warrants some phrase such as: "And this shall be your sufficient warrant for your proceedings . . . ." "This shall be as well to you as to [the other commissioners] sufficient warrant and discharge."[12]

Although the warrants usually contain advice or instructions for the particular examination under torture, they sometimes leave the instructions to be conveyed otherwise. In such cases the warrants are so terse that their only remaining function must have been to confer immunity. For example, in William Monke's case (Case 80, 1626) the warrant is noted in the Privy Council register in its entirety thus:

> A warrant to Sir Allen Apsley, knight, Lieutenant of the Tower, Mr. Serjeant Ashley, Mr. Trumbull and Mr. Mewtas [Meautys] or any two of them to take into examination William Monke, close prisoner in the Tower, upon such interrogatories as should be directed by the Lord Chief Justice of the King's Bench and to use the manacles to the said Monke if in their discretions they shall think it fit and thereupon to certify the Board what they find.

The subsequent course of Monke's case illustrates the effect of sovereign immunity. The Council learned that it had been mistaken in ordering Monke tortured. A thorough job had been done: Monke was under suspicion of high treason, and he was "tortured upon the rack and was thereby utterly disabled to maintain himself, his wife and nine children . . . ."[13] The investigation ultimately established that the documents that had cast Monke under suspicion had been maliciously falsified by a married couple named Blackborne. The Blackbornes fled into Ireland, and in 1627 Monke was seeking redress. He petitioned the Council to aid him, apparently inducing it to sequester and appropriate to him the rents and profits of the

Blackbornes' lands in Staffordshire while they remained fugitive. They were apprehended in Ireland and brought before the Council in the summer of 1628. The Council on advice of the Attorney General dissolved the provisional sequestration order and referred the parties to the court of Star Chamber for redress.[14] In common law terms Monke's underlying grievance was battery, trespass to his person, but he did not pursue a common law remedy. The examiners who "utterly disabled" him enjoyed the immunity of their warrant, and the Blackbornes had not participated with the directness required to sustain an action of trespass.

King and Council kept tight control over the use of torture. The warrants designate particular examiners to investigate particular suspects regarding particular matters.[15] Even recurrent examiners such as the law officers of the crown required fresh authority in each case. The power to torture was not jurisdictionalized in England, in contrast to the pattern in Continental states. Only for the Council in Wales, the distant alter ego of the English Privy Council, is there evidence of a general grant of authority to use torture without the advance approval of the monarch or the English Council.[16] Holdsworth and others[17] in "a very bad error"[18] adduce no evidence for the contention that the court of Star Chamber used torture. Not one case of the use of torture has yet been found in all the reports, records, and treatises of the court.[19] A recent author supplies no authority for the assertion that the court of High Commission, reconstituted in 1583, "began to use torture to extract confessions."[20] The suggestion that the High Court of Admiralty used torture rests on a frail inference from a source predating the known torture warrants.[21]

These mistaken attributions of torture practice to the English prerogative courts probably have two sources. One is the label "prerogative," popularized by Jardine as the basis of the power to torture. The other is the broad similarity between Roman-canon inquisitorial procedure and some features of the procedures of the English prerogative courts. The similarity did not, however, extend to torture.

The Reception?

Jardine believed that the use of torture in England evidenced a borrowing from Continental practice, a reception of Roman law. This idea was already venerable in Jardine's day: Coke[22] may have invented it, and Blackstone[23] repeated it; Holdsworth[24] and others spread it, pleased to be able to treat this ignoble business as foreign.[25]

Jardine initiated his case for the "Roman origin" of English torture practice with the claim that Roman-canon-trained civil lawyers predominated in the commissions that conducted examinations under torture. Indeed, he continued, "in the earlier instances . . . it seems to have been considered necessary that one of the Masters of Requests should be present at examinations by torture . . . in order that the rules prescribed by the civil law for the management of such examinations should be duly observed."[26]

These assertions constitute an inexplicable lapse from Jardine's customary regard to the sources. In truth, only four of the named examiners over the century 1540–1640 were Masters of Requests; they and an unnamed Master of Requests were designated in a total of eight cases (between 1556 and 1591).[27] Two other[28] members of Doctors' Commons appear in five other cases.[29] Thus professional civilians appear in thirteen of our eighty-one warranted cases.[30] All but one of these cases involved state crime as opposed to ordinary felony.[31] Two of the civilians named in five Elizabethan cases involving Jesuits were undoubtedly selected for their command of theology rather than of jurisprudence.[32]

Jardine thought to buttress in another way the conjecture that civilians were put in the examining commissions in order to ensure observance of the Roman-canon law of torture. He suggested that "the 'vehement suspicion' of guilt constantly recited in the warrants, which seems originally to have been necessary to justify the application of torture in England, . . . corresponds entirely to the *indicia ad torturam* amounting to the '*semiplena probatio*' required by the civil law."[33]

In fact there is nothing in the sources to indicate that the Council at any time adhered to Roman-canon standards in deciding whether it had ground for investigating under torture. The Roman-canon evidentiary standards for final conviction were also irrelevant to the English torture practice. In those cases where the English examiners were being asked to gather evidence, they had to satisfy English juries, not Italian jurists. In most of the twelve cases of state crime in which the English did use civilian examiners, the culprits were already doomed; torture was undertaken as a preventive measure, to detect other conspirators.

No institution or doctrine required the Council to justify anything of its torture practice. The Council could have decided for internal purposes to adhere to the Roman-canon standards conditioning the use of torture, but in fact it did not. The Council did not give the grounds for torture with the consistency of a system of legal rules. Numerous warrants disclose nothing of what is known against the suspect. In many others the stated grounds are mere labels, and we have seen in Chapter 1 that verbiage did not satisfy the Continental law of proof. It is interesting that some of the earlier warrants speak of the "vehement suspicion" against the offender, a term sometimes used in Continental practice to signify that the evidentiary prerequisites for torture had been satisfied.[34] It is plausible that someone familiar with Roman-canon literature launched the term in the Privy Council's warrants. The key point is that the Council's practice denied to the term the meaning it had in European law, if indeed the English term originated there. Hence in the 1630s John Selden remarked that the Council still had not articulated any principles for when it would and would not use torture.[35]

Finally, Jardine was mistaken in supposing that Roman-canon-trained examiners would have brought some special expertise to the torture chamber. In truth, once the decision to use torture had been taken, there would have been no particular reason to name a civilian to the examining commission. We have seen that the ius commune was oriented overwhelmingly to the problems of its system of proof, and that it treated with disdain the mechanics of how to choose and use torture instruments. Once inside the torture chamber, Roman lawyers had nothing to teach the English.

The Roman-canon law of torture had no practical influence on the use of torture in England. The most that can fairly be laid to Roman-canon influence is that in a remote sense the mere existence of the Continental systems helped to legitimate the English practice. For example, in an anonymous tract published in 1583 to defend the English government's torturing of Edmund Campion and other Jesuits, the writer found it convenient to conclude with a comparative aside: "that ... by the more general laws of nations, torture hath been and is lawfully judged to be used in lesser cases, and in sharper manner for inquisition of truth in crimes not so near extend-

ing to public danger, as these ungratious persons have committed . . . ."[36] Even then it was their distance from the Continental law
of torture that the English thought significant.

The End of Torture

Why was there no reception? Once the use of torture was underway
in England, why did it not entrench itself in common law criminal
procedure? By the end of Elizabeth's reign there were some ominous
signs that the use of torture to investigate crime might be taking hold
in England. In the 1580s and 1590s the torture warrants reached their
peak.[37] The contemporary understanding of the scope of the power
to torture is expressed in a so-called "Book of Instructions" prepared for the Council in Wales, dated 1602, and probably compiled
in imitation of the authority of the English Privy Council:

> And her majesty doth by these presents give full power and au-
> thority to the . . . Council . . . upon sufficient ground, matter
> and cause to put any person that shall commit, or shall be vehe-
> mently suspected to have committed any treason, petty treason,
> murder, rape, burglary or other felony, or the accessaries to the
> same to tortures when they in their wisdoms, or discretions shall
> think convenient: and the cause shall apparently require the
> same.[38]

Here was sovereign authority for seemingly routine use of torture in
the criminal process in Wales. In the year 1602 an observer reading
this text and reflecting over recent practice in England might well
have concluded that the use of torture had the future before it in
English criminal procedure. He might have predicted that as the use
of torture became more regular, it would have to be regulated by
rule. And he might have guessed that the highly developed Continental jurisprudence of torture would in time commend itself for that
task.

Yet if we look forward from 1602, we can say that torture was
about to disappear from England. We know of only seven cases from
the reigns of James I and Charles I, and although the Council registers for 1603–1613 are missing we think the inference is good that we
are not missing record of many more cases.[39] All seven cases concerned state crime; the last recorded case of the use of torture to
investigate ordinary felony occurred in 1597. In 1640 Charles issued

the last warrant, to examine under torture one John Archer for the names of his accomplices in an attack on Archbishop Laud's palace at Lambeth.[40] After 1640 torture was never again warranted in England.[41] The 1640 case is itself somewhat exceptional in that the warrant was royal rather than conciliar. After William Monke's case in 1626 the Council never again issued a torture warrant. The seven Stuart cases spread over the thirty-seven years from 1603 invite comparison with the total of fifty-one cases for the preceding thirty-seven years.

At first glance it seems curious that the royal and conciliar power to examine under torture should have fallen from use in just that period of nascent absolutism when the largest claims were being made in behalf of royal and conciliar governance. What is still more odd is that this should have happened without any struggle, indeed even without discussion.[42] In the 1620s when the Council was issuing its last torture warrants, other matters affecting the liberty of the subject were being intensely debated in the movement that culminated in the Petition of Right of 1628.[43] The Petition remonstrated against the King and Council for denial of habeas corpus (that is, for detention without cause shown), and it protested the extension of martial law to civilians. Yet neither in the Petition nor in the published parliamentary diaries[44] of the time is there any mention of the use of torture.

Jardine could not bring himself to concede that the demise of torture was occurring under the early Stuarts. He supposed that there must have been a quantity of unrecorded cases up to the Civil War, and he credited the elimination of torture to what he thought was the benign era in criminal procedure that began with the Interregnum.[45] This invited the suggestion that the privilege against self-incrimination, which began to acquire limited recognition in the common law courts during the Interregnum,[46] had something to do with the disappearance of torture. Wigmore observes that the practice of examining "political offenders [under torture] was absolutely inconsistent with the recognition of a privilege against self-incrimination; and it is highly significant that the last recorded instances of torture . . . and the first instances of the established privilege . . . coincide within about a decade."[47]

We do not think that this fortuity of timing was "highly significant." Of course, the use of torture to make someone talk does indeed disregard or override any claimed right not to talk. Where the privilege against self-incrimination in its developed form is given effect, evidence extracted by torture is excluded. We doubt, however, that the appearance of the privilege against self-incrimination in any sense caused the disappearance of torture. The privilege had no currency in the Jacobean period when the decline in torture set in. Moreover, especially in the seventeenth century cases, torture was not primarily used to gather evidence against the person tortured, but to identify accomplices and to forestall future sedition. Self-incrimination was not in question. Finally, even in a case in which a victim were being tortured for self-incriminating evidence, he would have had no effective means of vindicating his claimed privilege. Supposing him to have said to his examiners as they strapped him on the rack, "What about my privilege against self-incrimination?" he would not have received a very satisfying response. The Council's warrant immunized the examiners, and for decades after the use of torture ceased in England there was no judicial recognition of a right to have evidence of involuntarily uttered statements excluded from the jury.[48]

We are particularly concerned to understand why the use of torture disappeared in cases of ordinary felony, that is, crimes without evident religious or political overtones. These cases appear steadily from the 1550s through the 1590s. In the last of them (Case 71, 1597) the Council was investigating the murder of Richard Anger "a double reader of Gray's Inn." The warrant explains that because it "is so horrible that an ancient gentleman should be murdered in his chamber it is thought meet that the manner of this foul murder should be by all means found out ... and who were [ac]complices and privy to this confederacy ...." The Council ordered Richard Anger, son of the victim, and Edward Ingram, porter of Gray's Inn, put to the manacles, as "there are great presumptions" that they were the murderers. Such cases would never be lacking. Why, then, was this the last to be investigated under torture? Why did the use of torture in cases of ordinary felony, once underway, not entrench itself in common law criminal procedure?

Whereas criminal prosecution was mainly local business in England, the use of torture was exclusively[49] central business. During these years when it appears that torture might have become routinized in English criminal procedure, the Privy Council kept the torture power under careful control and never allowed it to fall into the hands of the regular law enforcement officers. We have pointed

out in Chapter 6 that the Council typically confined its torture practice to London; when it was persuaded to use torture in cases of
ordinary crime, it ordered provincial prisoners sent up to London for
examination. More fundamentally, we have said, the power to torture was never jurisdictionalized: no law enforcement officer, no law
court acquired the power to use torture without special warrant.
Thus, although torture was sometimes used in cases of ordinary
felony, it was never an ordinary procedure.

Indeed, there is some risk that we are being misleading in speaking
of the use of torture in cases of "ordinary" felony. These cases were
ordinary in the sense that they did not involve crimes of state. They
were hardly ordinary criminal proceedings, however, precisely because the Privy Council did intervene in the investigations. Sometimes the initiative for the use of torture seems to have come from the
local law enforcement officers, who procured the Council's warrant.[50] More often it appears that the Council intervened at the behest
of some well-placed complainant, as when torture warrants issued to
investigate "the robbing of the Lady Cheek" (Case 44, 1586), or
"the robbery committed on our very good lord the Lord Willoughby
of his plate" (Case 51, 1589).[51]

Why was torture not jurisdictionalized in England? Why was the
requirement of conciliar warrant not relaxed, in order to extend the
use of investigation under torture to the many cases of robbery and
murder that could not come to the attention of the highest political
authorities? Under Mary and Elizabeth the Council used torture too
often for us to believe that there were yet many qualms about its
unreliability or inhumanity. We think, therefore, that the answer is to
be found in institutional factors. By the time the Council began to
make steady use of torture, the English were already committed to a
prosecutorial system to which they could not entrust the power to
torture.

In the sixteenth century as in the thirteenth, the English were still
operating a nonbureaucratic criminal procedure. As jury trial
changed character and the juries ceased to be self-informing, a prosecutorial system had been grafted on the medieval jury procedure.
There were now official evidence-gatherers, the local justices of the
peace, who reinforced the ongoing system of private prosecution,
binding over victims and witnesses to prosecute, occasionally investigating and leading prosecution evidence to the jury.[52] But they
were unpaid amateurs, and it would have been unthinkable to allow

them to operate torture chambers of their own. The Continental jurisprudence of torture presupposed a judicial bureaucracy.[53] The country gentlemen and urban aldermen who constituted the English prosecutorial corps were men of independent means and stature, not hirelings. They were prone to faction and notoriously difficult for the central authorities to control.[54]

The prosecutorial system that the English patched together in the sixteenth century had many imperfections, but it proved adequate for its basic task. In the bulk of cases it assured a sufficient flow of evidence for the now passive trial jury. To be sure, there were always cases in which investigation under torture might have been useful in gathering evidence for the jury. But they were not numerous enough to entice the English into constructing a costly system of professional prosecution.

The Renaissance English did not develop a professional prosecutorial corps to whom the power to torture could be confided for the same reason that they had not developed a system of judicial torture in the Middle Ages: the jury standard of proof made it unnecessary to provide for extensive and refined evidence-gathering. An English jury could still convict on whatever evidence persuaded it, it could still convict on less evidence than was required as a precondition for investigation under torture on the Continent.

It is considerably harder, although for our purposes less important, to explain why the use of torture subsided and finally ceased in cases of state crime. Certainly a major cause was that, for a variety of reasons,[55] the relevant category of menacing political and religious crimes declined after the first years of the reign of James I. James's coronation put an end to the conniving about royal succession that had troubled English politics since the time of Henry VIII. The Peace of 1604 ended hostilities and largely eliminated the threat of subversion promoted from Spain. The aborted Gunpowder Plot of 1605 discredited the Catholic cause and demoralized the Catholic minority in England, bringing to an end the Elizabethan epoch of domestic Catholic intrigue against the state. The growing Puritan opposition was not linked to hostile foreign powers and did not threaten violent methods.

Torture did not disappear under the early Stuarts as a result of legislation or royal decree, nor did the Council make any formal decision to discontinue its use.[56] In this sense, seventeenth-century England did not experience any counterpart to the eighteenth-century

Continental abolition movement, and we have only the record of the cases themselves from which to tra´ce the ultimate surcease.

Two of the cases of torture under the Stuarts date from early in James's reign and may fairly be grouped with the late Elizabethan sedition cases.[57] The last cases in which the Privy Council[58] ordered torture after the Gunpowder Plot, four in all, are a sorry lot. Peacham's case (Case 77, 1615) seems to have been a vendetta of James's.[59] The suggestion to torture Samuel Peacock (Case 78, 1620), a former schoolmaster alleged to have attempted "to infatuate the King's judgment by sorcery"[60] may have originated in an obsequious letter from Bacon to James.[61] Not much is known about the last Jacobean case, James Crasfield (Case 79, 1622); apparently, he had predicted a rebellion.[62] The one case of torture ordered by the Council under Charles I was that of William Monke (Case 80, 1626), previously discussed, in which the Council found that its torture victim had been framed and was in fact innocent of the suspicion of treason cast upon him. With the level of intrigue having subsided, the Council may have learned from these cases a couple of lessons long familiar on the Continent: that investigation under torture was a dangerous business, and not necessarily a very productive one. In 1628 the Council considered torturing John Felton, the assassin of the Duke of Buckingham, to discover whether he had accomplices, but ultimately decided not to do it.[63]

We can understand, therefore, why the Parliament of 1628, in debating the liberty of the subject, could ignore the use of torture. Torture was falling into desuetude. And since the Tudor precedents amply supported the crown's power to use torture,[64] the whole matter was best left to slumber. The Parliamentarians who promoted the Petition of Right had scant reason to fear the application of torture to themselves and their ilk. Even at its peak the use of torture had been confined to two sorts of victims, neither with any following in the House of Commons: suspected seditionists, especially Jesuits; and some suspected felons, mostly of the lower orders.

For the future of common law criminal procedure, the English experiment with torture left no traces. Torture was never more than a sideline of the Privy Council. So long as the Council was operating a torture chamber to investigate crimes of state, it was sometimes induced to use torture to help clear up the odd case of ordinary felony. There had been no barrier to this parasitic usage, but also nothing to sustain it once the level of state crime subsided.

Abbreviations

Allmann   Jean Marie Allmann, *Ausserordentliche Strafe und Instanzentbindung im Inquisitionsprozesse* (Munich, 1903).

APC   *Acts of the Privy Council of England* (J. R. Dasent, ed.), 32 vols. (London, 1890–1907).

APC (Stuart)   *Acts of the Privy Council of England,* 12 vols. (London, 1921–1938).

Beccaria   Cesare Beccaria, *Of Crimes and Punishments* (1st ed. 1764) (J. Grigson, transl.) (London, 1964).

Blackstone   Sir William Blackstone, *Commentaries on the Laws of England,* 4 vols. (Oxford, 1765–1769).

Carolina   *Constitutio Criminalis Carolina* (1532), partial English translation in Langbein, PCR.

Conrad   Hermann Conrad, *Deutsche Rechtsgeschichte,* 2 vols. (Karlsruhe, 1962, 1966).

Damhouder   Joost Damhouder, *Practique judiciare es causes criminelles* (Antwerp, 1564 ed.).

DNB   *Dictionary of National Biography,* 22 vols. (London, 1937–1938 ed.).

Esmein   Adhémar Esmein, *Histoire de la procédure criminelle en France* (Paris, 1882).

Fiorelli   Piero Fiorelli, *La tortura giudiziaria nel diritto comune,* 2 vols. (Milan, 1953–1954).

Hertz   Eduard Hertz, *Voltaire und die französische Strafrechtspflege im achtzehnten Jahrhundert* (Stuttgart, 1897).

HMC Cecil   Historical Manuscripts Commission, *Calendar of the Manuscripts of the Marquis of Salisbury [Robert Cecil]* (London, 1883 ff).

Holdsworth   Sir William Holdsworth, *A History of English Law,* 16 vols. (London, 1922–1966).

Howell	Thomas B. Howell, *A Complete Collection of State Trials*, 21 vols. (London, 1816 ed.).
Hubert	Eugène Hubert, *La torture aux pays-bas autrichiens pendant le XVIIIe siècle: Son application, ses partisans et ses adversaires, son abolition* (Brussels, 1896–1898).
Isambert	Isambert, Decrusy, and Jourdan, *Recueil général des anciennes lois françaises depuis l'an 420 jusqu'à la révolution de 1789,* 29 vols. (Paris, 1823–1833).
Jardine	David Jardine, *A Reading on the Use of Torture in the Criminal Law of England Previously to the Commonwealth* (London, 1837).
Jousse	Daniel Jousse, *Traité de la justice criminelle de France,* 4 vols. (Paris, 1771).
Langbein, PCR	John H. Langbein, *Prosecuting Crime in the Renaissance* (Cambridge, Mass., 1974).
LP	*Letters and Papers, Foreign and Domestic, of the Reign of Henry VIII* (J. S. Brewer et al. eds.), 21 vols. in 37 parts (London, 1862–1932).
Maitland	Sir Frederick Pollock and Frederic W. Maitland, *The History of English Law,* 2 vols. (2d ed., Cambridge, 1898).
Plucknett	T. F. T. Plucknett, *A Concise History of the Common Law* (5th ed., London, 1956).
Schmidt, Einführung	Eberhard Schmidt, *Einführung in die Geschichte der deutschen Strafrechtspflege* (3d ed., Göttingen, 1965).
Schmidt, Freiheitsstrafe	Eberhard Schmidt, *Entwicklung und Vollzug der Freiheitsstrafe in Brandenburg-Preussen bis zum Ausgang des 18. Jahrhunderts* (Berlin, 1915).
Schmidt, Kriminalpolitik	Eberhard Schmidt, *Die Kirminalpolitik Preussens unter Friedrich Wilhelm I. und Friedrich II.* (Berlin, 1914).
Schnapper, Bordeaux	Bernard Schnapper, "La répression pénale au XVIe siècle: L'exemple du Parlement de Bordeaux (1510–1565)," *Recueil de mémoires et travaux publié par la société d'histoire du droit et des institutions des anciens pays de droit écrit,* 8:1–54 (1971).
Schnapper, Paris	Bernard Schnapper, "La justice criminelle rendue par le Parlement de Paris sous le

règne de François Ier," *Revue historique de droit français et étranger* 52:252–284 (1974).

Schnapper, Peines	Bernard Schnapper, "Les peines arbitraires du XIIIe au XVIIIe siècle: Doctrines savantes et usages français," *Tijdschrift voor Rechtsgeschiedenis* 41:237–277 [cited as I], 42:81–112 [cited as II].
SPD	*Calendar of State Papers, Domestic Series, of the Reigns of Edward VI, Mary, Elizabeth, and James I* (R. Lemon et al. eds.), 12 vols. (London, 1856–1872).
Spedding	*The Letters and the Life of Francis Bacon* (J. Spedding, ed.), 7 vols. (London, 1861–1874).
Stephen	Sir James Fitzjames Stephen, *A History of the Criminal Law of England,* 3 vols. (London, 1883).
Wigmore	John H. Wigmore, *A Treatise on the Anglo-American System of Evidence,* 10 vols. (3d ed., Boston, 1940 ed.).

Notes

Chapter One

1. On the geographical extent and dates of appearance of judicial torture, see R. C. van Caenegem, "La preuve dans le droit du moyen âge occidental," *Recueils de la société Jean Bodin pour l'histoire comparative des institutions* 17:691, 735–739, and map no. 3 bound at 430–431 (1965); cf. Piero Fiorelli, *La tortura giudiziaria nel diritto comune* (Milan, I:1953, II:1954) I:105 [hereafter cited as Fiorelli]. On the dates of disappearance of judicial torture, see id. at II:259–269.

2. Although we shall see in Chapter 3, text at note 88, that contemporaries ultimately found it convenient to emphasize the similarity rather than the difference.

3. "Torture was not a punishment . . . ; it was not a mode of proof, which some writers on criminal law call it; it was a *mode of procedure* which the judge employed to obtain . . . proof. . . ." Edmond Poullet, *Histoire du droit pénal dans le duché de Brabant* (Brussels, 1870) 353 (emphasis original).

4. "Two wholly unimpeachable eyewitnesses, who testify to the truth of the crime without anything to the contrary to weaken their word, constituted full proof." Fiorelli II:38. A large body of doctrine dealt with the qualities that might make witnesses objectionable. Schnapper has shown that these rules of safeguard lost some of their rigor in postmedieval practice, a development which parallels the revolution in the law of proof discussed in Chapter 3. Bernard Schnapper, "Testes inhabiles: Les témoins reprochables dans l'ancien droit pénal," *Tijdschrift voor Rechtsgeschiedenis* 33:575 (1965). On confession as the "queen of proof" (*regina probationum*), see Fiorelli at II:103–104. For the rule forbidding conviction on circumstantial evidence, see id. at II:27. There was an undercurrent of dissatisfaction with the strictness of the rule forbidding conviction on circumstantial evidence, and some writers urged an exception for cases of "indubitable indicia." See Fiorelli II:27; cf. Eduard Hertz, *Voltaire und die französische Strafrechtspflege im achtzehnten Jahrhundert* (Stuttgart, 1897) 62–63 [hereafter cited as Hertz].

In modern times as the dangers of identification evidence have become understood and scientific techniques for generating and evaluating many types of circumstantial evidence have appeared, circumstantial evidence has come to be regarded as more reliable than eyewitness testimony. See, e.g., Note, "Weaknesses of Testimonial Proof," in John M. Maguire, et al., *Cases and Materials on Evidence* (6th ed., Mineola, N.Y., 1973) 223–228; Glanville Williams, *Proof of Guilt: A Study of the English Criminal Trial* (2d ed., London, 1958) 99 ff; quite recent English developments are discussed in Robert Thoresby, "A Turnaround in the Use of Identification Evidence," *American Bar Association Journal* 62:1343 (1976). (I owe this point to Professor Lloyd Weinreb.)

5. Carolina Article 54. *Constitutio Criminalis Carolina* (1532) [hereafter cited as Carolina] discussed in text at note 34, partial English translation in John H. Langbein, *Prosecuting Crime in the Renaissance: England, Germany, France* (Cambridge, Mass., 1974) 261–308 [hereafter cited as Langbein, PCR]; see id. at 259–260 for discussion of German editions of the Carolina.

6. Carolina Articles 56, 54.

7. Fiorelli I:8; R. C. van Caenegem, "The Law of Evidence in the Twelfth Century: European Perspectives and Intellectual Background," in *Proceedings of the Second International Congress of Medieval Canon Law* (Vatican City, 1965) 297; R. C. van Caenegem, *The Birth of the English Common Law* (Cambridge, 1973) 62–73; cf. John W. Baldwin, "The Intellectual Preparation for the Canon of 1215 against Ordeals," *Speculum* 36:613 (1961); Sir Frederick Pollock and Frederic W. Maitland, *The History of English Law* (2d ed., Cambridge, 1898) II:598–599 [hereafter cited as Maitland]; S. F. C. Milsom, *Historical Foundations of the Common Law* (London, 1969) 359; T. F. T. Plucknett, *A Concise History of the Common Law* (5th ed., London, 1956) 113–119 [hereafter cited as Plucknett].

8. Noted, e.g., in Bernard Schnapper, "La répression pénale au XVIᵉ siècle: L'exemple du Parlement de Bordeaux (1510–1565)," *Recueil de mémoires et travaux publié par la société d'histoire du droit et des institutions des anciens pays de droit écrit* 8:1, 15 (1971) [hereafter cited as Schnapper, Bordeaux].

9. In civil procedure, despite important distinctions, the solution was similar although more complex. See generally Knut W. Nörr, *Zur Stellung des Richters im gelehrten Prozess der Frühzeit* (Munich, 1967); Jean-Philippe Lévy, *La hiérarchie des preuves dans le droit savant du moyen-âge depuis la renaissance du droit romain jusqu'à la fin du XIVᵉ siècle* (Paris, 1939); A. Engelmann & R. W. Millar, *A History of Continental Civil Procedure* (Continental Legal History Series) (Boston, 1927).

10. Maitland II:660.

11. Van Caenegem, supra note 1, at 735–739; Fiorelli I:131; see Gandinus' chapter *"De questionibus et tormentis,"* *Tractatus de maleficiis,* in Hermann Kantorowicz, *Albertus Gandinus und das Strafrecht der Scholastik* (Berlin, 1926) II:155.

12.   An overtone of the supernatural survived in the law of torture in the jurists' occasional suggestion of "divine intervention: God will give the innocent the strength to resist the pain." J. Gilissen, "La preuve en Europe du XVIᵉ au début du XIXᵉ siècle," *Recueils de la société Jean Bodin pour l'histoire comparative des institutions* 17:755, 788 & n.3. Compare Jacob Döpler, *Theatrum poenarum* ... *Oder Schau-Platz derer Leibes und Lebens-Straffen* (Sondershausen, I:1693; Leipzig, II:1697) I:347, 350–351, recommending that suspected witches be tortured much more severely than other accuseds, since the devil fortifies them against the pain and makes it feel like a soft bed to them.

13.   See Langbein, *PCR* 179–183, for an account of the *Indizienlehre* in the Carolina. The jurists admitted that some discretion at this stage was unavoidable. "It was manifestly impossible to determine *a priori* the evidence sufficient to permit the use of torture. The judge possessed on this point a discretionary power, although regulated by the law (*le droit*) and doctrine." Poullet, supra note 3, at 356. Cf. Eugène Hubert, *La torture aux pays-bas autrichiens pendant le XVIIIᵉ siècle: Son application, ses partisans et ses adversaires, son abolition* (Brussels, 1896–1898) 38 [hereafter cited as Hubert].

14.   Fiorelli I:3. A civil servant in India remarked to Stephen in 1872 that laziness encouraged the native police officers to use torture. "It is far pleasanter to sit comfortably in the shade rubbing red pepper into a poor devil's eyes than to go about in the sun hunting up evidence." Sir James Fitzjames Stephen, *A History of the Criminal Law of England* (London, 1883) I:442 n.1 [hereafter cited as Stephen].

15.   Especially *Digest* 48.18. Modern authority rejects the suggestion that the imperial Roman law of torture continued in uninterrupted force into the medieval ius commune: van Caenegem, supra note 1, at 735–736; cf. Fiorelli I:71–74.

16.   Eberhard Schmidt, *Inquisitionsprozess und Rezeption* (Leipzig, 1940), discussed in Langbein, PCR 142, 146–150.

17.   See Note II, "Torturing the Convicted," infra text at note 56–61.

18.   At Malines a group of arsonists denounced as an accomplice a police serjeant of the city. As they were about to be executed, they withdrew the accusation. Asked why they had falsely accused the serjeant, they replied that when they were being tortured the judge had asked them whether the serjeant was not one of them. Hubert 45 n.2.

Most of the abuses and shortcomings of judicial torture mentioned in this and the next paragraph are illustrated in Manzoni's classic account of a criminal proceeding in which innocent men were condemned for spreading the plague in Milan in 1630. Alessandro Manzoni, The Column of Infamy (1st ed., 1842) (K. Foster, transl.) (London, 1964).

19.   Eberhard Schmidt, *Lehrkommentar zur Strafprozessordnung und Gerichtsverfassungsgesetz* (Teil I) (2d ed., 1964) 197; cf. Fiorelli II:141–

142; van Caenegem, *Proceedings,* supra note 7, at 300. A French judge who wrote a little book denouncing the use of torture in witchcraft trials remarks from experience that the law of torture developed by the doctors "in abstract" and "calm" has to be administered by a judge who can get caught up in the prosecutorial role of trying to convict the prisoner. Augustin Nicolas, *Si la torture est un moyen seur a verifier les crimes secrets* (Amsterdam, 1682) 32. "In this situation the judge is not exempt from passion," and he does not want to get a reputation for being outwitted by criminals. Id. at 32–33.

20.   Joost Damhouder, *Practique judiciaire es causes criminelles* (Antwerp, 1564 ed.) ch. 39, at 44 [hereafter cited as Damhouder]. The work first appeared in Latin as *Praxis rerum criminalium* (Louvain, 1554). Over thirty editions were published in Latin, French, Dutch, and German, the last in 1693. See René Dekkers, *Bibliotheca Belgica juridica* 44 (Brussels, 1951).

21.   Christian Thomasius, *Über die Folter* (dissertation, 1705) (R. Lieberwirth, ed. & transl.) (Weimar, 1960). The attribution of the work is persuasively challenged in Wolfgang Ebner, "Christian Thomasius und die Abschaffung der Folter," *Ius Commune* 4:72 (1972). In general celebration of Thomasius, see Erik Wolf, *Grosse Rechtsdenker der deutschen Geistesgeschichte* (4th ed., Tübingen, 1963) 371–423.

22.   Cesare Beccaria, *Of Crimes and Punishments* (1st ed., 1764) (J. Grigson, transl.) (London, 1964) ch. 12, at 31–37 [hereafter cited as Beccaria] (published with the translation of Manzoni, supra note 18). See generally Cesare Cantù, *Beccaria e il diritto penale* (Florence, 1862); Marcello Maestro, *Voltaire and Beccaria as Reformers of Criminal Law* (New York, 1942).

23.   See the chapters on torture in the essays, *Commentaire sur le livre des délits et des peines* (1766), and *Prix de la justice et le l'humanité* (1777), in [François-Marie Voltaire,] *Œuvres complètes de Voltaire* (Paris, 1835 ed.) V:411, 441–442. See generally Maestro, supra note 22; Hertz; Peter Gay, *Voltaire's Politics* (Princeton, 1959) 273–308.

24.   E.g., Digest 48.18.1.23.

25.   Despite the rules of probable cause, "many bloodthirsty judges . . . subject the accused to torture only on the basis of rumor or bad reputation . . . which the Lords of the Council [of the Spanish Netherlands] correct, when complaints about it come to their attention." Damhouder, ch. 35, at 34ᵛ.

26.   Sir John Fortescue, *De Laudibus Legum Anglie* (S. B. Chrimes, ed.) (Cambridge, 1942) ch. 22, at 46–53.

27.   See the summary in Hubert 61ff. The leading eighteenth-century French treatise on criminal procedure recounts "numerous examples" from

ancient to recent times "of persons who, on account of torture, have confessed to crimes that they never committed." Daniel Jousse, *Traité de la justice
criminelle de France* (Paris, 1771) I:690 & n.b; cf. id. at II:475 n.b [hereaf-
ter cited as Jousse].

28. [Michel de Montaigne,] *The Essays of Montaigne* (George B. Ives,
transl.) (Cambridge, Mass., 1925) II:87; Nicolas, supra note 19, at 169,
178–180.

29. See van Caenegem, supra note 1, at 728–731 and map no. 3 bound
at 430–431.

The example of Scotland is particularly instructive. Although much of the
rest of the medieval Roman-canon law was received there, the criminal jury
system was not displaced. See generally Ian Willock, *The Origins and
Development of the Jury in Scotland* (Stair Society) (Edinburgh, 1966).
Hence, although the Scots were aware that their sources authorized torture,
their criminal procedure had no need of it. George Mackenzie, *The Laws and
Customs of Scotland, in Matters Criminal* (Edinburgh, 1699) 272–273.
Hume believed that in Scotland (as in England) only the Privy Council had
used torture, and infrequently. David Hume, *Commentaries on the Law of
Scotland, Respecting Crimes* (2d ed., Edinburgh, 1819) II:314–315.

30. Maitland made this point prominent. Maitland II:659–661. The
same insight occurred to Bentham. In a tract only recently edited for publication, he wrote: "There are few if any cases in which a man can be put to the
torture under the Roman law, upon less evidence than would be sufficient to
convict him by the English." W. L. and P. E. Twining, "Bentham on
Torture," *Northern Ireland Legal Quarterly* 24:305, 333 (1973).

31. Fiorelli I:243–248.

32. Gilissen, supra note 12, at 797–799; Fiorelli II:259–269;
C. J. A. Mittermaier, *Das deutsche Strafverfahren* (3d ed., Heidelberg,
1839) I:397 n.36.

33. Gilissen, supra note 12, at 787, 829ff.

34. The primary sources are discussed in Fiorelli's narrative bibliography, I:114–179. Editions of the Carolina and Damhouder are cited supra
notes 5, 20. On the influence of the Carolina, see Langbein, PCR 140–141.
On the influence of Damhouder, see Gilissen, supra note 12, at 769; Hermann Conrad, *Deutsche Rechtsgeschichte* (Karlsruhe, 1966) II:419 [hereaf-
ter cited as Conrad].

35. Supra note 31.

36. Damhouder, ch. 35, at 34–34^v.

37. Fiorelli II:9; Damhouder, ch. 35, at 34–34^v.

38. Fiorelli I:276–326; Damhouder, ch. 41, at 45–45^v.

39. Rondel v. Worsley, [1967] 1 Q.B. 443.

40. Remarked in Jean Imbert, *La practique judiciaire* (Paris, 1609 ed.)

bk. III, ch. 14, 3, at 722; cf. Poullet, supra note 3, at 357; Hubert 40. There also developed in the ancien régime a status-based exception of an opposite character. In some jurisdictions torture was authorized more liberally to investigate the doings of so-called vagabonds. "Less [evidence] is needed to employ torture against a vagabond than to employ it against a domiciliary...." Robert J. Pothier, *Traité de la procédure criminelle,* in *Oeuvres de Pothier* (Bugnet, ed.) (Paris, 1848 ed.) X:474 (V.III.144.3); cf. Hubert 34–35. See infra Chapter 2, note 49 and text at notes 60ff.

41. Fiorelli II:84.

42. Döpler, supra note 12, at I:264, 345; Fiorelli II:3–4; Poullet, supra note 3, at 356.

43. Langbein, PCR 179–183; Fiorelli II:10ff.

44. Id. at II:60–62; Carolina Article 46; Hubert 44; Damhouder, ch. 35, at 34–35ᵛ.

45. Fiorelli I:192–209; Damhouder, ch. 37, at 37ᵛ; Poullet, supra note 3, at 358; Carolina Article 58; Döpler, supra note 12, at 279–313; Anonymous, *Umständliche ... Einleitung über den Criminal-Process* (Frankfurt & Leipzig, 1738) 203–218; Hertz 15–18; Charles Berriat-Saint-Prix, *Des tribunaux et de la procédure du grand criminel au XVIIᵉ siècle* (Paris, 1859) 74ff. Paul Parfouru, *La torture et les exécutions en Bretagne au XVIIᵉ et XVIIIᵉ siècles* (Rennes, 1896).

46. Anonymous, *Procès-verbal des conférences tenues ... pour l'examen des articles ... de l'ordonnance criminelle* (Paris, 1740 ed.) II:224, noted in Adhémar Esmein, *Histoire de la procédure criminelle en France et spécialement de la procédure inquisitoire depuis le XIIIᵉ siècle jusqu'à nos jours* (Paris, 1882) 241 [hereafter cited as Esmein]; Hertz 15–16; Fiorelli I:193.

47. Strappado was the *regina tormentorum,* id. at II:103 n.1; cf. Damhouder, ch. 37, at 37ᵛ.

48. Fiorelli II:60; Carolina Article 56.

49. Fiorelli II:67; Carolina Article 56; Hubert 45.

50. Carolina Articles 54, 60; Döpler, supra note 12, at I:379–380.

51. Fiorelli II:143–154; Döpler, supra note 12, at I:382; Schnapper, Bordeaux 22. Van Caenegem reports cases in which torture was repeated seven and nine times. Van Caenegem, "La preuve dans l'ancien droit belge des origines à la fin du XVIIIᵉ siècle," *Recueils de la société Jean Bodin pour l'histoire comparative des institutions* 17:375, 422–423 (1965).

52. Damhouder, ch. 54, at 54ᵛ; Fiorelli II:117–124; Hubert 54–55; Poullet, supra note 3, at 360–362.

53. E.g., the victims in Manzoni, supra note 18.

54. Carolina Article 57; Ordonnance ... du stil general (1570), Article 40, in Bavius Voorda, *De Crimineele Ordonnantien van Koning Philips van Spanje* 64 (Leiden, 1792).

55. Damhouder, ch. 38, at 42–42^v; Ordinance of Blois (1498), Article 114, in Isambert, Decrusy and Jourdan, *Receuil général des anciennes lois françaises* (Paris, 1823–1833) 11:366 [hereafter cited as Isambert].

56. Schnapper, Bordeaux 27, is persuasive that torture préalable was still exceptional in France in the first half of the sixteenth century, although it became widespread thereafter; cf. Damhouder, ch. 38, at 43. For the equivalent practice elsewhere see e.g., *Friedrich Wilhelms Königes in Preussen verbessertes Land-Recht* (Königsberg, 1721) 60 (bk. 6, tit. 3, art. 11, §6) (Prussia); Goswin de Fierlant, "Observations sur la torture," in Eugène Hubert, *Un chapitre de l'histoire du droit criminel dans les Pays-Bas autrichiens au XVIIIe siècle: Les mémoires de Goswin de Fierlant,* Compte rendu des séances de la commission royale d'histoire (5th ser.) (Brussels, 1894) 4:154, 171, at 188ff (Belgium). Remarkably, the equivalent practice was formally authorized in colonial Massachusetts, where the English jury system had forestalled the growth of ordinary judicial torture. The Body of Liberties of 1641 provides: "No man shall be forced by Torture to confess any Crime against himself nor any other unless it be in some Capital case, where he is first fully convicted by clear and sufficient evidence to be guilty, After which if the cause be of that nature, That it is very apparent there be other conspirators, or confederates with him, Then he may be tortured, yet not with such Tortures as be Barbarous and inhumane." Edwin Powers, *Crime and Punishment in Early Massachusetts 1620–1692* (Boston, 1966) 538. (I owe this reference to Mrs. Barbara Black.)

57. Title 19, Article 3, in Isambert 18:412: "By the death sentence it can be ordered that the convict be first [*préalablement*] put to torture in order to discover his accomplices."

58. See Chapter 4, text at note 54.

59. Isambert 26:373; 28:526; see Chapter 4, text at note 42.

60. Van Caenegem, supra note 51, at 419; Hubert 25ff; Poullet, supra note 3, at 354; de Fierlant, supra note 56, at 175ff.

61. Damhouder, ch. 38, at 43.

Chapter Two

This chapter was previously published in a slightly different version as "The Historical Origins of the Sanction of Imprisonment for Serious Crime," *The Journal of Legal Studies* 5:35–60 (1976). References supplied by Paul Bamford, Julius Kirshner, Donald McCloskey, Norval Morris, and Lawrence Towner are gratefully acknowledged.

1. Eberhard Schmidt, *Die Kriminalpolitik Preussens unter Friedrich Wilhelm I. und Friedrich II.* (Berlin, 1914) 65–66 [hereafter cited as Schmidt, Kriminalpolitik].

2. John Howard, *The State of the Prisons* (Everyman's Lib. ed., London & New York, 1929) 63.

3. Voltaire was not in fact an abolitionist. He thought it appropriate to execute the worst offenders, whom he likened to mad dogs. Marcello Maestro, *Voltaire and Beccaria as Reformers of Criminal Law* (New York, 1942) 121.

4. Maitland II:452.

5. Carolina Articles 190–198 collect the sanctions. For particular offenses, see Articles 124 (treason), 131 (child murder), 137 (murder), 159 (burglary). Articles 176 and 195 contemplate a scheme of perpetual preventive detention of someone who is found dangerous and who lacks surety; it seems to have had no practical currency.

6. Conrad II:410; cf. Jousse I:36–73; Schnapper, Bordeaux 28–34; Stephen I:457ff, esp. 475–478, 489–490; Leon Radzinowicz, *A History of English Criminal Law and Its Administration* (London, 1948) I:206ff. See generally the remarkable compilation in Jacob Döpler, *Theatrum poenarum ... Oder Schau-Platz derer Leibes und Lebens-Straffen* (Sondershausen, 1693) I.

7. *Riforma della legislazione criminale del 30 novembre del 1786* (Florence, 1786), described as a "bibliographic rarity" in Stanislaw Salmonowicz, "Leopoldina: Il codice penale toscano dell'anno 1786," *Revista Italiana per le Scienze Giuridiche* (3d ser.) 13:173, 179 n.16 (1969) (citing Italian and French editions). The Italian text was published in England together with an anonymous English translation as *Edict of the Grand Duke of Tuscany for the Reform of Criminal Law in His Dominions* (Warrington, 1789). A German edition of 1787 is cited in Conrad II:449. Article 55 catalogs the sanctions.

8. Leopoldina, supra note 7, Articles 51, 53. A few weeks later Leopold's brother, the Emperor Joseph II, promulgated a criminal code for Austria that preserved the death penalty only for martial law and confirmed the substitution of imprisonment as the ultimate penal sanction: "Patent vom 13ten Januar 1787, für alle Länder §§20–21," in *Joseph des Zweiten römischen Kaisers Gesetze und Verfassungen im Justiz-Fache 1786–1787* (Vienna, 1817) 7, 9. An anonymous contemporary English translation appeared in the same year, from which (with one correction shown in square brackets) we reprint the two sections:

§20. No person shall be punished with death, except in cases in which it shall be pronounced according to law in a court martial. It is resolved that in case of such court-martial, hanging shall be the only punishment by death that can be inflicted ....

§21. The other punishments are [imprisonment in chains], imprisonment with hard labor on the public works, imprisonment only, corporal punishment with whip, rod, or stick, and the pillory.

The Emperor's New Code of Criminal Laws: Published at Vienna, the 15th [sic] *of January, 1787: Translated from the German by an Officer* (London, 1787) 10. See generally Herrmann Conrad, "Zu den geistigen Grundlagen der Strafrechtsreform Josephs II. (1780–1788)," in *Festschrift für Hellmuth von Weber* (Bonn, 1963) 56.

9. Carolina Articles 11, 218.

10. Ralph B. Pugh, *Imprisonment in Medieval England* (Cambridge, 1968) 3–5. The principal English criminal trial court, that of gaol delivery, took its name from the gaols which held prisoners until trial.

11. Annik Porteau-Bitker, "L'emprisonnement dans le droit laïque du Moyen Age," *Revue historique de droit français et étranger* 46:211 (1968); Roger Grand, "La prison et la notion d'emprisonnement dans l'ancien droit," *Revue historique de droit français et étranger* 19/20:58, 58–59 (1940–1941).

12. Pugh, supra note 10, at 5ff; Porteau-Bitker, supra note 11, at 211; Grand, supra note 11, at 58–59; Gotthold Bohne, *Die Freiheitsstrafe in den italienischen Stadtrechten des 12.–16. Jahrhunderts* (Leipzig, I:1922, II:1925) I:34ff.

13. Pugh, supra note 10, at 16ff; Porteau-Bitker, supra note 11, at 211; Grand, supra note 11, at 58–59; Bohne, supra note 12, at I:51ff.

14. Henry Charles Lea, *A History of the Inquisition of the Middle Ages* (New York, 1888) I:534.

15. Bohne, supra note 12, at I:232ff; Porteau-Bitker, supra note 11, at 390–391; Pugh, supra note 10, at 17–18; Lea, supra note 14, at I:484–494.

16. Bohne, supra note 12, at I:57–58; Porteau-Bitker, supra note 11, at 402–403.

17. Porteau-Bitker, supra note 11, at 396–397.

18. Bohne, supra note 12, at I:54–67, 80–90, 98ff; Eberhard Schmidt, *Einführung in die Geschichte der deutschen Strafrechtspflege* (3d ed., Göttingen, 1965) 64–65, 193–194 [hereafter cited as Schmidt, Einführung]; Porteau-Bitker, supra note 11, at 395ff; Pugh, supra note 10, at 26ff.

19. Damhouder, ch. 16, at 16ᵛ–17.

20. P. Frauenstädt, "Zur Geschichte der Galeerenstrafe in Deutschland," *Zeitschrift für die gesamte Strafrechtswissenschaft* 16:518, 519 (1896); compare Bohne, supra note 12, at II:302–303.

21. Paul W. Bamford, *Fighting Ships and Prisons: The Mediterranean Galleys of France in the Age of Louis XIV* (Minneapolis, 1973) 12–18, 272ff.

22. Described in the classic work by Paul Masson, "Les galères de France," *Annales de la faculté des lettres d'Aix* 20:7, 72ff (1937).

23. Bamford, supra note 21, at 138ff.

24. Of course the use of captives in the galleys had been known in antiquity, and may have been a more or less continuous practice in the

Eastern Mediterranean into the Renaissance. See Masson, supra note 22, at 8–10.

25.   See I. A. A. Thompson, "A Map of Crime in Sixteenth-Century Spain," *Economic History Review* (2d ser.) 21:244 (1968).

26.   Bohne, supra note 12, at II:302, 320ff.

27.   The French galley fleet began to be built up in the fifteenth century when Provence was joined to the monarchy and France became involved in the Italian wars. Masson, supra note 22, at 15. The use of convict labor on the galleys was suggested as early as 1443, id. at 80–81. As early as 1490 instructions were issued in the name of the king to the royal and seignorial courts to spare capital convicts for the galleys, and to sentence vagabonds there as well. Id. at 83; cf. infra note 48. Schnapper found the galley sentence in use in the Parlement of Bordeaux in the 1520s. Schnapper, Bordeaux 33.

28.   Thorsten Sellin, *Pioneering in Penology: The Amsterdam Houses of Correction in the Sixteenth and Seventeenth Centuries* (Philadelphia, 1944) 8.

29.   Damhouder added a lengthy chapter to his treatise on Belgian practice to take account of this *"nouvelle punition criminelle."* Damhouder, ch. 151, at 203ᵛ. The earliest ordinance he cites is from 1554. Id. at 204. Elsewhere it is said that convicts were being used on galleys at Antwerp in the middle of the fifteenth century. Louis Stroobant, *Notes sur le système pénal des villes flamandes du XVᵉ au XVIIᵉ siècle* (Malines, 1897) 57.

30.   Frauenstädt, supra note 20, at 522.

31.   Schnapper, Bordeaux 33.

32.   Damhouder, ch. 151, at 204.

33.   Frauenstädt, supra note 20, at 522–524, 539–541.

34.   See Schnapper, Bordeaux 34–35.

35.   Ernest Lavisse, "Sur les galères du roi," *La Revue de Paris* 4:225, 236 (1897).

36.   Jean-Baptiste Colbert, *Lettres instructions et mémoires* (Pierre Clément, ed.) (Paris, 1864) III (pt. 1):1; cf. G. B. Depping, *Correspondance administrative sous le règne de Louis XIV* (Paris, 1851) II:879, 880, 940.

37.   Frauenstädt, supra note 20, at 522–539. In the sixteenth and seventeenth centuries several Italian states, France and Spain contacted the landlocked Swiss and south German states to obtain convicts for the Mediterranean galleys. Louis Carlen, "Die Galeerenstrafe in der Schweiz," *Zeitschrift für die gesamte Strafrechtswissenschaft* 88:557, 558–560 (1976).

38.   Friedrich von Maasburg, *Die Galeerenstrafe in den deutschen und böhmischen Erbländern Oesterreichs* (Vienna, 1885) 7.

39.   Id. at 10–11.

40.   Id. at 14–15.

41. Frauenstädt, supra note 20, at 523, 540–541.
42. Damhouder, ch. 151, at 208^v.
43. Frauenstädt, supra note 20, at 524, 540–541.
44. Id. at 523–524, 540.
45. Isambert 19:465 (1684).
46. Id. at 176.
47. See generally on the conditions of galley life Bamford, supra note 21, at 200ff.
48. For the Spanish Netherlands see the decree of 1561, probably based on one of 1554, authorizing galley sentences of not less than six years for convicts whose offenses do not merit death: Damhouder, ch. 151, at 213^v. Damhouder explains that these ordinances meant to prevent judges from imposing galley sentences of two, three, or four years for such offenders as they had formerly been doing. Id., ch. 151, at 203^v–204. For seventeenth-century Italian city-state sources substituting galley service for the former sanctions of fine, imprisonment, and corporal punishment for lesser crimes see 2 Bohne, supra note 12, at 321ff; for eighteenth-century Austria see von Maasburg, supra note 38, at 7, 10. For seventeenth- and eighteenth-century Switzerland see Carlen, supra note 37, at 565–566.

Schnapper found galley sentences of five and ten years being imposed in the 1520s in the Parliament of Bordeaux. Schnapper, Bordeaux 34–35. By Jousse's day, the sanction of "galères à temps" was being imposed "for a great number of crimes; as for forgery, repeated petty theft, . . . altering boundary markers, theft from churches, highway robbery, etcetera. It is also used against beggars . . . [and] vagabonds." Jousse I:61. Recently published data from the 1748 register of French galley convicts bear out Jousse's account. Of four thousand men, 40 per cent had been sentenced for theft, swindling and forgery; 25 per cent for infractions against the salt and tobacco monopolies, five per cent as vagabonds. André Zysberg, "La société des galériens au milieu du XVIIIe siècle," *Annales Economies Sociétés Civilisations* 30:43–49 (1975). Bamford shows that in the seventeenth century convicts sentenced to determinate terms might be kept in galley service much longer. Bamford, supra note 21, at 250–253.

49. The use of so-called vagabonds as galley conscripts is evidenced from the inception of the galley system in the fifteenth century to its demise in the eighteenth century. Damhouder introduces his account of the galley sentence as "that manner of punishment by which worthless people (*gens de nulle valeur*), vagabonds, living without established reputation or habitation, . . . pests of the republic are condemned to naval prisons, vulgarly called galleys. . . ." Damhouder, ch. 151, at 203^v. As early as 1456 there appear in the French ordinances *lettres de marque* complaining of the influx of vagabonds, their dangerousness and their potential for criminality, and authorizing the authorities to punish them summarily, inter alia, by sending

them to the galleys. Isambert 9:302–303. On the many shades of meaning and the complex causes of vagabondage, see text at notes 60ff.

Proceedings to punish vagabonds, says Damhouder, are "summary and without formal judgment. . . ." Damhouder, ch. 151, at 204ᵛ. For Switzerland compare Carlen, supra note 37, at 563. The high evidentiary standards of the Roman-canon law of proof did not apply: capital sanctions were not in question, and vagabondage was a status crime that did not necessarily raise issues turning on proof of conduct. Vagabonds were considered as outsiders, and the community that felt threatened by vagabonds saw little reason to extend to them the safeguards of the regular criminal law, which were meant for citizens. It is possible that the galley sentence developed first against vagabonds, and was then extended to the ordinary criminal law when experience familiarized the authorities with its utility. (For a parallel in the development of inquisitorial criminal procedure in medieval Germany, see Langbein, PCR 145–151.)

Of course, the use of the galley sentence against vagabonds had a dual aspect: it put the vagabond out of harm's way, and it made his labor available for the navy. The sources suggest that, depending upon the circumstances, one or the other motive might predominate in a particular wave of vagabond repression. When it was the latter, the Continental authorities rounding up vagabonds for the galleys resemble the English of the day impressing sailors, with the difference that the Europeans were casting a wider net. See Colbert, supra note 36, at III (pt. 1):502; cf. Bamford, supra note 21, at 180–181; Masson, supra note 22, at 263, 271–273; R. G. Usher, "Royal Navy Impressment during the American Revolution," *Mississippi Valley Historical Review* 37:673 (1951).

50. Schnapper, Bordeaux 33; Frauenstädt, supra note 20, at 523–524. It would therefore be surprising if Thompson were correct in his wholly undocumented assumption that in Spain "[t]he galleys . . . probably contained the great majority of serious offenders convicted in Spain, for commutation to galley service was the likely punishment for even the most heinous of crimes." Thompson, supra note 25, at 246. Compare Henry Kamen, "Galley Service and Crime in Sixteenth-Century Spain," *Economic History Review* (2d ser.) 22:304 (1969), criticizing Thompson for assuming that figures for galley convicts can be treated as indexes of crime.

51. See the account in Bamford, supra note 21, at 191ff; cf. von Maasburg, supra note 38, at 8–10.

52. Bamford, supra note 21, at 68ff.

53. Bamford, "The Procurement of Oarsmen for French Galleys: 1660–1748," *American Historical Review* 65:31, 47 (1959); cf. Bohne, supra note 12, at II:318.

54. Bamford, supra note 53, at 47.

55. Von Maasburg, supra note 38, at 10–11.

56. Bamford, supra note 21, at 27.
57. Id. at 203.
58. Id. at 225–226.
59. Id. at 234–245, 276–277, 282; Jousse I:48–50, 62.
60. Schnapper, Bordeaux 33.
61. Sellin, supra note 28, at 9.
62. But see page 40.
63. E. M. Leonard, *The Early History of English Poor Relief* (Cambridge, 1900) 11.
64. Fernand Braudel, *The Mediterranean and the Mediterranean World in the Age of Philip II* S. Reynolds, (transl.) (New York, 1973) II:743.
65. Leonard, supra note 63, at 14.
66. Id. at 15.
67. Id. at 15; Isambert 12:216, 218–221; Damhouder, ch. 151, at 205^v.
68. Leonard, supra note 63, at 15–16; Sellin, supra note 28, at 9.
69. Leonard, supra note 63, at 17.
70. Id. at 16; Sellin, supra note 28, at 9–10.
71. Sellin, supra note 28, at 10.
72. Id. Compare Brian Tierney, *Medieval Poor Law: A Sketch of Canonical Theory and Its Application in England* (Berkeley & Los Angeles, 1959) 80ff, 109ff.
73. Leonard, supra note 63, at 18.
74. Infra pages 35–38.
75. Paul A. Slack, "Vagrants and Vagrancy in England 1598–1664," *Economic History Review* (2d ser.) 27:360, 362 (1974); cf. A. L. Beier, "Vagrants and the Social Order in Elizabethan England," *Past & Present* (No. 64) 3 (Aug. 1974).
76. Laslett thinks "that at all times before the beginnings of industrialization a good half of all those living were judged by their contemporaries to be poor...." Peter Laslett, *The World We Have Lost* (New York, 1965) 45. Still others, artisans and craftsmen, "were in poverty at certain times of their lives, or in bad seasons, or for some weeks even in good seasons, but not perpetually dependent in the way that laborers, cottagers, paupers and the common soldiery were." Id. at 45 n.40. Hence: "Begging was universal, as it is today in some of the countries of Asia.... Men sometimes took fright at [the] numbers, especially in Tudor times, and the savage laws against sturdy vagabonds became notorious in the textbooks.... Yet crowds of destitute people were not typical of poverty in the old world in quite the way that queues of unemployed are typical of industrial poverty. The trouble then, as we have hinted, was not so much unemployment, as under-employment, as it is now called, and once more the comparison is with the countries of Asia in our own century." Id. at 31.
77. Damhouder, ch. 151, at 205^v.

78.   Braudel, supra note 64, at II:741.
79.   See generally Leonard, supra note 63; Sellin, supra note 28; Laslett, supra note 76; Sidney and Beatrice Webb, *English Poor Law History: The Old Poor Law* (London, 1927); F. R. Salter, ed., *Some Early Tracts on Poor Relief* (London, 1926); W. K. Jordan, *Philanthropy in England: 1480–1660* (London, 1959).
80.   Leonard, supra note 63, at 62.
81.   Id. at 35–39; E. G. O'Donoghue, *Bridewell Hospital: Palace, Prison, Schools* (London, I:1923, II:1929) I:193ff. See the proposal for the Bridewell workhouse of 1552 in R. H. Tawney and Eileen Power, *Tudor Economic Documents* (London, 1924) II:306ff, taken from Thomas Bowen, *Extracts from the Records and Court Books of Bridewell Hospital* (London, 1798).
82.   Leonard, supra note 63, at 101; see id. at 110–114 for other English municipal houses of correction built before 1597; cf. S. A. Peyton, "The Houses of Correction at Maidstone and Westminster," *English Historical Review* 42:251 (1927). The statute of 18 Eliz. c. 3, §§4–6 (1576) ("An Act for the Setting of the Poor on Work, and for the Avoiding of Idleness") prescribed workhouses for every city, town and county. For an order of the Suffolk Quarter Sessions of 1589 regulating their workhouse, see C. J. Ribton-Turner, *A History of Vagrants and Vagrancy and Beggars and Begging* (London, 1887) 116–119.
83.   Leonard, supra note 63, at 93–98, 101–107.
84.   Id. at 98, 107.
85.   Id. at 99, quoting the London order.
86.   Id. at 313, quoting the Norwich order.
87.   Id. at 312.
88.   Id. at 99.
89.   Robert von Hippel, "Beiträge zur Geschichte der Freiheitsstrafe," *Zeitschrift für die gesamte Strafrechtswissenschaft* 18:419, 437ff, 608 (1898).
90.   Sellin, supra note 28.
91.   The work by O'Donoghue, supra note 81, is amateurish. It is odd that despite a decade of concern in American and British academic circles with the plight of the contemporary poor, social and political historians have not renewed an interest in the phenomenon of vagabondage and its control in Tudor England. Miss Leonard has had not only the first but the latest word. For a recent bibliography collecting related economic history, see John Pound, *Poverty and Vagrancy in Tudor England* (London, 1971) 113–117.
92.   Sellin, supra note 28, at 20–21.
93.   E.g., Schmidt, Einführung 188; see Sellin, supra note 28, at 21 and sources cited id. at 21 nn.29–30. Compare von Hippel, supra note 89, at 648–649.
94.   Sellin, supra note 28, at 21–22.
95.   Id. at 41–43 (footnotes omitted).

96. Id. at 18–19.

97. Banishment was often coupled with branding in Europe, in order that those who returned could be identified. It was a capital offense to return in violation of a decree of banishment. See von Maasburg, supra note 38, at 4–7 &nn.4, 7; cf. Stroobant, supra note 29. Sellin, supra note 28, at 15 n.10, quotes the famous Swedish Judges' Rules of Olavus Petri, lamenting that "those who have stolen . . . stand on the scaffold, lose their ears and are banished from the community; if such persons go to other lands where no one knows them and wish to reform and conduct themselves well, they are never trusted. The punishment is a hindrance to him who is punished and he becomes desperate and worse than before. It might have been better for him to lose his life immediately.'' See generally Gerhard Schmidt, *Die Richterregeln des Olavus Petri* (Göttingen, 1966).

98. Eberhard Schmidt, *Entwicklung und Vollzug der Freiheitsstrafe in Brandenburg-Preussen bis zum Ausgang des 18. Jahrhunderts* (Berlin, 1915) 3 [hereafter cited as Schmidt, Freiheitsstrafe].

99. Supra text at note 18.

100. Supra text at note 87.

101. Leonard, supra note 63, at 100.

102. Sellin, supra note 28, at 49, 53–54, 93.

103. Id. at 56.

104. Id. at 58. Readers of Bamford's detailed account of the economics of galley service, supra note 21, esp. 200–249, will notice remarkable parallels to the system of incentives in the workhouses of the North.

105. Many of the early workhouses were physical outgrowths of former shelters or hospitals for the poor—London (Bridewell), Norwich, Amsterdam, Paris, Lübeck.

106. Sellin, supra note 28, at 46.

107. Paul Bonenfant, *Le problème du paupérisme en Belgique à la fin de l'ancien régime* (Brussels, 1934) 89–91; Sellin, supra note 28, at 102–103; Louis Stroobant, "Le Rasphuys de Gand: Recherches sur la répression du vagabondage et sur le système pénitentiaire établi en Flandre au XVIIe au XVIIIe siècle," *Annales de la société d'histoire et d'archéologie de Gand* 3:191 (1900).

108. Christain Paultre, *De la répression de la mendicité et du vagabondage en France sous l'ancien régime* (Paris, 1906) 137ff, esp. 160.

109. Von Hippel, supra note 89, at 608ff.

110. Id. at 612–647.

111. Schmidt, Einführung 190.

112. Id. For a relatively early perception of the similarity of the workhouse movement in England, the Netherlands and the German states, see Döpler, supra note 6, at I:716–725.

Late in the development one German writer complained that the workhouses were proving expensive to build and maintain, and that the profit from convict labor was not enough to offset these costs. Gallus A. C. von Klein-schrod, *Systematische Entwicklung der Grundbegriffe und Grundwahrheiten des peinlichen Rechts* III:51–52 (2d ed., Erlangen, 1799). It has not been possible to locate another work ascribed to this author, *Über die Strafen der öffentlichen Arbeiten* (Würzburg, 1789).

113. Von Hippel, supra note 89, at 610 n.9.

114. Sellin, supra note 28, at 44.

115. Von Hippel, supra note 89, at 641.

116. Id. at 641; cf. id. at 630 for Lübeck.

117. Schmidt, Freiheitsstrafe 13–14; cf. id. at 57–58, 75.

118. Schmidt, Einführung 186; August Hegler, *Die praktische Thätig-keit der Juristenfakultäten des 17. und 18. Jahrhunderts* (Freiburg, 1899) 87–88.

119. Von Maasburg, supra note 38, at 4 n.2. The variety of penal servitude prescribed in the Territorial Courts Ordinance (*Landgerichtsord-nung*) of Dec. 30, 1656, issued by King Ferdinand III for Lower Austria, is summarized in Hugo Hoegal, *Freiheitsstrafe und Gefängniswesen in Öster-reich von der Theresiana bis zur Gegenwart* 2 (Vienna & Graz, 1916). Criminals could be sent to forced labor on the military settlements along the Hungarian-Turkish border; put to work on the moats or streets of Vienna or in chain gangs; imprisoned, sometimes on a diet of bread and water; or made to tend the ill in institutions.

120. Döpler, supra note 6, at I:791; cf. Schmidt, Freiheitsstrafe 8; Schmidt, Einführung 186.

121. Hegler, supra note 118, at 88 n.2.

122. Id. at 88ff.

123. Schmidt, Freiheitsstrafe 8–9; Schmidt, Einführung 192.

124. An express concern of Frederick the Great, see Schmidt, Kriminal-politik 56–57.

125. Schmidt, Einführung 192–193; Schmidt, Freiheitsstrafe 6–9; Hegler, supra note 118, at 87.

126. Id. at 94ff; Schmidt, Kriminalpolitik 29–32.

127. Hegler, supra note 118, at 87–88; Bohne, supra note 12, at II:278–279. Banishment, too, was converted into imprisonment; see, e.g., Schmidt, Kriminalpolitik 53; Bernard Schnapper, "La justice criminelle rendue par le Parlement de Paris sous le règne de François Ier," *Revue historique de droit français et étranger* 52:252, 266 (1974) [hereafter cited as Schnapper, Paris].

128. Theodor Hampe, *Die Nürnberger Malefizbücher als Quellen der reichstädtischen Sittengeschichte* (Bamberg, 1927) 81.

129. Schmidt, Kriminalpolitik 65.

130. Ernest Kwiatkowski, *Die Constitutio Criminalis Theresiana: Ein Beitrag zur Theresianischen Reichs- und Rechtsgeschichte* (Innsbruck, 1903) 40–41. For France, see Schnapper, Paris, 266ff, esp. 270; and Schnapper, Bordeaux 4–5. Other recent archive studies (cited id. at 5 n.11) hint that

capital punishment was becoming relatively infrequent from the late sixteenth century: Bernadette Boutelet, "Etude par sondage de la criminalité dans le bailliage du Pont-de-l'Arche," *Annales de Normandie* 12:235, 242–245, 247 n.22 (1962); Jean-Claude Gégot, "Etude par sondage de la criminalité dans le bailliage de Falaise," *Annales de Normandie* 16:103, 115–118 (1966). See also Noël Laveau, "La criminalité à Bordeaux au XVIIe siècle: Etude par sondages," *Receuil de mémoires et travaux publié par la société d'histoire du droit et des institutions des anciens pays de droit écrit* 8:85, 99–103 (1971). Compare for Tuscany Salmonowicz, supra note 7, at 176: "in practice, already in the years before the penal reform of 1786, the death penalty came to be not much executed in the territory. . . ."

Further archive study is much to be desired, but it is hardly likely to contradict the conclusion of Hegler, supra note 118, at 84–85: "The slow, fundamental transformation of the system of punishments . . . of the [Carolina] . . . belongs among the most remarkable events in the development of criminal law in the seventeenth and eighteenth centuries."

131. See generally R. S. E. Hinde, *The British Penal System: 1773–1950* (London, 1951); H. B. Simpson, "Penal Servitude: Its Past and Its Future," *Law Quarterly Review* 15:33 (1899).

132. The eighteenth-century Continental writers whose esteem for English criminal procedure was expressed in the campaigns to abolish judicial torture and to introduce the jury system in Europe were not admirers of English substantive criminal law. On the notorious severity of the English criminal statutes, see generally Radzinowicz, supra note 6, at I; on the disdain of the philosophes, see id. at I:719ff; Maestro, supra note 3, at 128ff.

133. Stephen I:468.

134. The evidence thus far brought to light is thin. "In 1596 Edward Hext, a Somersetshire Justice, wrote a letter to one of the members of the Privy Council. . . . He encloses in it the calendar of the Somerset assizes for that year, showing that forty felons had been executed. . . ." Frank Aydelotte, *Elizabethan Rogues and Vagabonds* (Oxford, 1913) 73; see id. at 167–173 for the text of Hext's letter. Cockburn's figures for Devonshire for twenty-eight years over a forty-year period (1598–1639) work out to 22.1 executions per year. J. S. Cockburn, *A History of English Assizes: 1558–1714* (Cambridge, 1972) 94–96. Stephen was estimating as average twenty executions per year in forty counties.

135. Radzinowicz, supra note 6, at I:160 n.52.

136. Id. at I:141–142. Jeaffreson's seventeenth-century data is from Middlesex alone; he arbitrarily doubled his figures on the assumption, endorsed by Radzinowicz, that the incidence of crime and of punishment was at least as high in the city as in the environs of Middlesex. Id. at I:141, citing J. C. Jeaffreson, *Middlesex County Records* (London, 1886–1892) II:xvii–xxi, III:xvii–xxii.

137. Id. at III:xx.

138. Radzinowicz, supra note 6, at I:91ff; Stephen I:459–471; Abbot E. Smith, "The Transportation of Convicts to the American Colonies in the Seventeenth Century," *American Historical Review* 39:232, at 248 (1934): "no accurate idea of the criminal processes of the seventeenth century can be gained without a study of the system of pardons."

139. 39 Eliz. c. 4 (1597).

140. Jordan, supra note 79, at 91.

141. A. H. A. Hamilton, *Quarter Sessions from Queen Elizabeth to Queen Anne* (London, 1878) 31; Cockburn, supra note 134, at 129. See also a record of letters issued by the Privy Council on June 19, 1602 "to all the Justices of Assize . . . for the reprieving of such felons as shall be condemned in their several Circuits to serve in the galleys (if they be not condemned for rape, burglary or other notorious offenses). . . ." *Acts of the Privy Council of England* (J. R. Dascent, ed.) (London, 1907) 32:489. The second paragraph of the document restates the exclusion "that none shall be sent to the galleys that are condemned for murder, rape or burglary, &c." Id. The order probably contemplated petty thieves rather than capital convicts, since it conditioned the granting of reprieves on the convicts' "friends [giving] 3 pounds by the year towards their maintenance in the galleys if they be able, or otherwise that the country [i.e., the locality] be moved to contribute so much because by this means they shall be freed from such unprofitable members that would do more mischief to the country than so much money would make good . . . ." Id. Quaere whether the word "galley" was being used metaphorically for other naval vessels.

There is an even earlier source foreshadowing these turn-of-the-century stirrings. In April 1586 Secretary of State Francis Walsingham wrote to Thomas Egerton, then Solicitor General, instructing him to arrange for reprieving convicts from execution for labor on the galleys. The letter says that one galley "is already built, and more are meant to be built . . . ." *The Egerton Papers* (J. P. Collier, ed.) (Camden Society) (London, 1840) 116, cited by Cockburn, supra note 134, at 129.

142. Printed in Thomas Rymer, *Foedera, conventiones, literae, et cujuscunque generis acta publica inter reges angliae VII* (pt. 2):36 (3d ed., The Hague, 1742). See Daines Barrington, *Observations on the More Ancient Statutes* (4th ed., London, 1775) 93 n.c.

143. Partially transcribed in Abbot E. Smith, *Colonists in Bondage: White Servitude and Convict Labor in America: 1607–1776* (Chapel Hill, 1947) 92–93.

144. Smith, supra note 138, largely incorporated in Smith, supra note 143.

145. Smith, supra note 143, at 94–95.

146. Id. at 96.

147. Id at 96–98.

148. Id. at 104.
149. Smith, supra note 138, at 243.
150. Id.
151. Id. Compare French practice in directing galley convicts into the opposing army for the same war; Bamford, supra note 21, at 258.
152. Smith, supra note 143, at 110ff.
153. 4 Geo. I c. 11 (1717).
154. See Plucknett 440.
155. Smith, supra note 143, at 113.
156. Id. at 117, 119.
There is also considerable evidence of the use of penal servitude in lieu of the former sanctions for serious crime in the colonial legal systems in the seventeenth and eighteenth centuries. See Richard B. Morris, *Government and Labor in Early America* (New York, 1946) 345ff and sources there cited.
157. Smith, supra note 143, at 117 & n.23, citing an unpublished London University Ph.D. Thesis: Wilfrid Oldham, "The Administration of the System of Transportation of British Convicts: 1763–1793" (1933) 35.
158. A. L. Shaw, *Convicts and the Colonies: A Study of Penal Transportation from Great Britain and Ireland to Australia and other Parts of the British Empire* (London, 1966) 43.
159. Id. at 48–57.
160. Bernard Mandeville, *An Enquiry into the Causes of the Frequent Executions at Tyburn* (London, 1725).
161. Id. at 53.
162. Id. at 47ff. Mandeville foresaw as the principal drawback to his scheme the concern that some of the repatriated English sailors might have fallen into apostasy during captivity. "Amongst our Seafaring Men, the Practice of Piety is very scarce.... There are not many that are well grounded in the Principles of their Religion, or would be capable of maintaining it against an Adversary of the least Ability; and we are not certain, that under great Temptations, they would remain steadfast to the Christian Faith." Id. at 48–49.
163. Depping, supra note 36, at II:245. The French did experiment with transporting aged and invalid galley convicts. See Bamford, supra note 21, at 255, 260.
164. A. E. Smith, supra note 143, at 107.
165. Considerable differences persisted among nations, of course. We have seen that the British figures were many times the Prussian. A flamboyant French abolitionist tract suggested in 1770 that the penal death rate was higher in France than elsewhere, although the proposition is unsupported: "The Sicilians put their criminals to work in the quarries; the Portuguese employ them in those discoveries that have extended for us the limits

of the world; the Russians in populating their deserts; the English in developing their colonies; the Germans make them roll their wheelbarrows [in]
galères de terre; the Africans exchange them for goods; are we alone in
wringing the life out of them in public, in order to send them [i.e., the rotting
corpses] from there to infect our highways?'' Philopon de la Madeleine,
''Discours sur la nécessité et les moyens de supprimer les peines capitales,
Lu dans la séance publique tenue par l'Académie des sciences, belles-lettres
& arts de Besançon, le 15 décembre 1770,'' in *Bibliothèque philosophique
du législateur* (J. P. Brissot de Warville, ed.) (Berlin, Paris & Lyon, 1782)
IV:63.

    166. Hegler, supra note 118, at 87; George L. Beer, *The Origins of the
British Colonial System: 1578–1660* (New York, 1908) 32–52, esp. 34.

Chapter Three

    1. See generally Bernard Schnapper, ''Les peines arbitraires du XIIIe
au XVIIIe siècle: Doctrines savantes et usages français,'' *Tijdschrift voor
Rechtsgeschiedenis* 41:237, 42:81 (1973, 1974) [hereafter cited as Schnapper, Peines I & II]. See id. at I:258ff on the Roman law texts out of which the
Glossators spun the doctrine.

    The word ''arbitrary'' has a modern connotation of ''capricious'' or
''tyrannical'' that ought not to be read into the ''arbitraria'' of Roman-canon
law, which meant simply the judge's power of appreciation or evaluation.
Schnapper, Peines I:237.

    2. Conrad II:412ff; Robert von Hippel, *Deutsches Strafrecht* (Berlin,
1925) I:235–240; Schnapper, Bordeaux 28 (the period 1510–1565 ''is that
which implanted in French law the principle of the *peines arbitraires.*'');
Schnapper, Peines II:89ff.

    3. Damhouder, ch. 55, at 55^v.

    4. Because the so-called general part of the criminal law was as yet
underdeveloped, defensive matters such as incapacity or self-defense were
often treated as moderating the sentence rather than negativing liability itself. See Schnapper, Peines I:268ff.

    5. Jousse II:594; cf. id. at I:38, II:599; Philippe Bornier, *Conferences
des ordonnances de Louis XIV* (Paris, 1719 ed.) II:359–360. Contrast the
Belgian ordinance of 1570, which recognizes judicial discretion in sentencing when no fixed penalty is prescribed (Article 58), but forbids the courts
''to set themselves up as judges of the equity or inequity of [statutory
penalties]'' (Article 56). Ordonnance . . . de la justice criminelle, in Bavius
Voorda, *De Crimineele Ordonnantien van Koning Philips van Spanje*
(Leiden, 1792) 27–28. Compare Article 41 of the companion Ordonnance . . . du stil general, id. at 64–65, apparently authorizing the imposition
of poena extraordinaria after unsuccessful application of judicial torture, the
practice discussed elsewhere in this chapter. Damhouder's treatise, written a

few years before the ordinance, does not know this usage. See Jean Marie Allmann, *Ausserordentliche Strafe und Instanzentbindung im Inquisitionsprozesse* (Munich, 1903) 35 [hereafter cited as Allmann].

6. E.g., Jousse II:600ff; Gottfried Boldt, *Johann Samuel Friedrich von Böhmer und die gemeinrechtliche Strafrechtswissenschaft* (Berlin & Leipzig, 1936) 78ff, esp. 84ff; cf. August Hegler, *Die praktische Thätigkeit der Juristenfakultäten des 17. und 18. Jahrhunderts* (Freiburg, 1899) 105ff; von Hippel, supra note 2, at I:236ff.

Blackstone, who thought that the penal sanctions of English law, though "[d]isgusting," nevertheless "do honor to the English law" when compared to "the shocking apparatus of death and torment" in European law, also thought the English system superior for the fixity of its sanctions. "[T]he nature, though not always the quantity or degree, of punishment is *ascertained* for every offense. . . ." Sir William Blackstone, *Commentaries on the Laws of England* (London, 1769) IV:370–371 (italics original) [hereafter cited as Blackstone]. Both propositions are dubious. The English did not have quite the Europeans' variety of death and maiming sanctions, but the differences were relatively slight. See Stephen I:457ff, esp. 475–478, 489–490; Sir Leon Radzinowicz, *A History of English Criminal Law and Its Administration* (London, 1948) I:206ff. Likewise, although the English common law lacked the doctrinal base of poena extraordinaria on which to erect a system of individuated sentencing, it achieved a similar result by judicial manipulation of the royal powers of conditional and absolute pardon. Radzinowicz, id. at I:114ff, summarizes the factors that the English judges relied upon in recommending or opposing royal pardon; they bear a striking resemblance to the mitigating and aggravating factors cataloged in the Continental treatises on poena extraordinaria.

7. See Schnapper, Peines I:255ff; Boldt, supra note 6, at 32ff, 69ff, 78.

8. Id. at 54–58.

9. Schnapper, Peines I:272–273; II:85–86, 94–96.

10. Jousse I:41.

11. Compare the medieval practice of abandoning the convict to the pleasure of his lord, Schnapper, Peines I:240ff; cf. Maitland II:460–462.

12. Modern American law exhibits a similar contrast: elaborate and rigid rules of guilt determination followed by expansive judicial discretion in sentencing. See Marvin E. Frankel, *Criminal Sentences: Law without Order* (New York, 1973).

13. Imprisonment and forced labor schemes, often characterized as *opera publica* in the sources, were everywhere reckoned as poena extraordinaria. See Thorsten Sellin, *Pioneering in Penology: The Amsterdam Houses of Correction in the Sixteenth and Seventeenth Centuries* (Philadelphia, 1944) 43–44; Hegler, supra note 6, at 87ff; Schmidt, Freiheitsstrafe 15–17; Schmidt, Einführung 190; Friedrich von Maasburg, *Die Galeerenstrafe in den deutschen und böhmischen Erbländern Oesterreichs*

(Vienna, 1885) 4 n.2; Gotthold Bohne, *Die Freiheitsstrafe in den italienischen Stadtrechten des 12.–16. Jahrhunderts* (Leipzig, 1925) II:320–321.

14. This rule is not to be confused with the asserted rule, supra text at note 9, that in cases of full proof the courts could not impose a death penalty not prescribed by statute.

15. This distinction was reflected in Amsterdam practice in a curious manner. The city registers of the seventeenth century show that suspects put to torture were seldom acquitted if they did not confess, but were banished or sent to prison. This is the variety of poena extraordinaria we shall examine shortly in France, where it was called *torture avec réserve des preuves*. However, "this disposition was not worded in the form of a sentence, but as a marginal footnote in the register of interrogatories." Hubert 60 n.2.

Late in the development Jousse recommends against preserving the distinction, as is sometimes done in cases of serious crime for which full proof is lacking, when the sentence recites that the accused is "'violently suspect' of the crime for which he is being punished....'" Jousse II:651.

16. The word is sometimes spelled with a single "s," e.g., in Allmann; von Hippel, supra note 2. For the two-"s" spelling used in text, see, e.g., Walter Sax, "Zur Anwendbarkeit des Satzes *'in dubio pro reo'* im strafprozessualen Bereich," in *Studien zur Strafrechtswissenschaft: Festschrift für Ulrich Stock* (Würzburg, 1966) 143.

17. E.g., the nineteenth-century German writer, H. A. Zachariae, who defined as a poena extraordinaria a punishment "imposed against someone on the mere suspicion (*auf den blossen Verdacht*) that he committed a crime," as opposed to an ordinary punishment imposed "against a fully convicted criminal." Quoted in Allmann 2n. For similar treatment of the French *torture avec réserve des preuves*, see Esmein 282–283.

Even writers who recognized that the Verdachtsstrafe was being applied to punish persons thought guilty on the basis of circumstantial evidence understated or overlooked the enormous significance of that change in the law of proof. See, e.g., von Hippel, supra note 2, at I:229–230; Carl L. von Bar, *A History of Continental Criminal Law* (Continental Legal History Series) (Boston, 1916) 239–240 (translated from *Geschichte des deutschen Strafrechts und der Strafrechtstheorien*, 1882). Von Hippel, in an inexplicable passage, managed to conclude that "the field for application of torture was substantially expanded" on account of the development of poena extraordinaria for cases of incomplete proof. Von Hippel, supra note 2, at 230.

One recent historical account does squarely reject the notion of the Verdachtsstrafe as punishment for suspicion. The article by Sax, supra note 16, at 153, calls the term an "unjust and incorrect" epithet, and remarks, id. at 153–154 n.43, that it conceals what was in fact punishment for guilt perceived subjectively rather than guilt determined objectively according to the Roman-canon law of proof. Sax comes to the point in the course of a

devastating critique of a book by Peter Holtappels, *Die Entwicklungsgeschichte des Grundsatzes "in dubio pro reo"* (Hamburg, 1965). Holtappels
seeks to trace back into antiquity the career of the maxim that in criminal
cases doubts are to be resolved in favor of the accused. He deems the
Verdachtsstrafe the antithesis of the rule. Sax replies, supra note 16, at 147,
that the very notion of doubt presumes the subjective theory of proof, so that
it is nonsense to look for the maxim within the sphere of the Roman-canon
law of proof. Sax is not, however, the only writer to point out that conviction
upon incomplete proof need not be conviction upon mere suspicion. See
Jarke, "Bemerkungen über die Lehre vom unvollständigen Beweise, vor-
nehmlich in Bezug auf die ausserordentlichen Strafen," *Neues Archiv des
Criminalrechts* 8:97, 97–98, 116ff (1826); J. Carmignani, "Historisch-
juristische Darstellung der Criminal-Prozessgesetzgebung Peter Leopolds II,
Grossherzog von Toscana," *Kritische Zeitschrift* 1:350, 360 (1829).

The *Ungehorsamstrafe*, literally the punishment for insubordination, has
a similar reputation in the literature. E.g., J. Gilissen, "La preuve en Europe
du XVIᵉ au début du XIXᵉ siècle," *Receuils de la société Jean Bodin pour
l'histoire comparative des institutions* 17:755, 788; H. A. Zachariae, *Die
Gebrechen und die Reform des deutschen Strafverfahrens* (Göttingen, 1846)
71, 107ff. Whether it, like the Verdachtsstrafe, was generally a punishment
for persuasive circumstantial evidence is not always clear. One unmistakable
case: "A certain Jean Baillu who had killed his wife was tortured for 24
hours at Ghent on September 4, 1780. He underwent the torture coura-
geously, without confessing. He was condemned to 30 years in prison for his
lack of respect towards the judges...." R. C. van Caenegem, "La preuve
dans l'ancien droit belge des origins à la fin du XVIIIᵉ siècle," *Receuils de
la société Jean Bodin pour l'histoire comparative des institutions* 17:375,
421. Closely related to the Ungehorsamstrafe was the *Lügenstrafe*, a
punishment ostensibly imposed for not telling the truth to the court. See
C. J. A. Mittermaier, *Das deutsche Strafverfahren* (3d ed., Heidelberg,
1839) I:400 nn.18–19, for citation to German and Swiss statutes perpetuat-
ing the Ungehorsamstrafe and the Lügenstrafe into the early nineteenth century.

18.   On medieval practice see Schnapper, Peines I:274–276; Sax, supra
note 16, at 149–150. On the Italian writers of the fifteenth and sixteenth
centuries see Allmann 12–29. On the "prodigious success in the sixteenth
century" of the practice of imposing a lesser sanction for incomplete proof
see Schnapper, Peines II:88, citing case law and juristic literature of the
Italian states, Belgium, Spain and France. For sixteenth-century German
authority see Sax, supra note 16, at 154–156. On the influence of Carpzov in
establishing the practice in the German states see Allmann 38ff; Holtappels,
supra note 17, at 46ff.

19.   See Allmann 20–22 & n.40, noticing that in the Italian practice of

the sixteenth century poena extraordinaria is extended from mere money fine
to other punishments, including flogging and galley serivce (*tiremes*). She
cites Julius Clarus' account of someone accused of homicide and sentenced
in Milan in 1557 to ten years galley service on the basis of "indubitable
circumstantial evidence." Id. at 21–22n.; cf. Schnapper, Peines II:88 n.286;
Allmann 26.

20. Supra Chapter 1, text at notes 35–36. The connection between
poena extraordinaria on circumstantial evidence for serious crimes and the
lower standard of proof for delicta levia is implicit in Carpzov, whose
account of poena extraordinaria is followed by the observation: "An accused
who is accused of a lesser offense and against whom there is violent suspicion
and hence half proof, may also, even if he denies his guilt, be punished
according to the discretion (*arbitro*) of the judge.... [T]his rule ... has
effect only for delicta levia for which the punishment is either imprisonment,
banishment or money fine." Quoted in Holtappels, supra note 17, at 48. See
also Klaus Bollmann, Die Stellung des Inquisiten bei Carpzov (Marburg
diss., 1963) 211–212; Allmann 39.

21. Carolina Article 22, translated in Langbein, PCR 273:

> It is further to be noticed that no one shall be definitely sentenced to
> penal sanction on the basis of any indication of a suspicious sign or
> upon suspicion, rather on that basis there may only be examination
> under torture; when the indications are sufficient (as will be found be-
> low), then the person shall be finally condemned to penal sanction;
> however, that must take place upon the basis of his own confession or a
> witness proof procedure (*beweisung*) (as will be found plainly elsewhere
> in this ordinance), and not on the basis of presumption or indication.

22. Carolina Articles 62 and 67, id. at 284:

> (62) Where the accused will not confess, and the complainant wishes to
> prove the crime complained of, he shall be allowed that according to the
> law ....

> (67) When a crime is proved with at least two or three credible good
> witnesses, who testify from a true knowledge, then there shall be pro-
> cess and judgment of penal law according to the nature of the case.

23. Ordinance of Villers-Cotterets, Article 164, translated id. at 313.

> And if through interrogation or torture nothing can be gained against the
> accused, so that there is no basis for condemning him: we wish that he,
> upon being absolved, be done justice as regards the partie civile for
> reparation of the calumnious accusation: and to that end the parties shall
> have a hearing of their *conclusions,* the one against the other, and to be
> disposed of in ordinary procedure, if need be, and if the judges consider
> it appropriate to the case.

24. *Constitutio Criminalis Theresiana* (Vienna, 1769). See generally
Conrad II:426–428; Hermann Conrad, "Zu den geistigen Grundlagen der

Strafrechtsreform Joseph II. (1780–1788),'' in *Festschrift für Hellmuth von
Weber* (Bonn, 1963) 56, 56–57; Allmann 55–57; Ernest Kwiatkowski, *Die
Constitutio Criminalis Theresiana: Ein Beitrag zur Theresianischen Reichs-
und Rechtsgeschichte* (Innsbruck, 1903).

25. Constitutio Criminalis Theresiana (Vienna, 1769) Article 34, Sections 1–3, 17:

§1. There has hitherto been a not insignificant doubt whether, in addition to confession and to conviction (*Ueberweisung*) by means of competent witnesses, some other means of proof are to be allowed, namely:
first, unmistakable indicia (*Anzeigungen*).... Because particular prudence is to be used in this important matter, we therefore wish to have
the following guideline prescribed for general observance. Viz:

§2. Regarding the aforementioned first means of proof, we confirm for
the future in our hereditary domains the hitherto established principle, to
wit that in criminal cases which concern life and limb, or which impose
a penalty equivalent to death, no one may be condemned to death or to
a punishment regarded as equivalent to death solely on suspicions
(*Vermuthungen*) and indicia (*Anzeigungen*), no matter how strong and
vehement. However, such a case may be proceeded with according to
the circumstances by torture, or when the circumstances do not allow that,
by an extraordinary penal sentence (*ausserordentlichen Strafferkannt-
nuss*).

§3. On the other hand in pettier crimes carrying no penalty of death or
severe corporal punishment (where in any event such an exact conviction is seldom needed) we of course remit to the considered discretion
of the criminal courts the judgment whether the circumstances and indicia are so indubitable, unmistakable and convincing that the ordinary
punishment propounded by the law (*Gesetz*) may be inflicted against the
suspect with firm ground....

§17. If complete legal proof according to our rules above is lacking, the
converse follows, that in this event no one may be condemned to the
ordinary punishment prescribed by law. However, since greater or lesser suspicions and inculpating circumstances may pertain against the
accused, the judge has to weigh carefully all the circumstances in such a
case, and it depends on his considered discretion whether, acccording to
the state of the matter, either provisionally to release the suspect from
arrest until further indicia appear, or according to the circumstances to
order him to take the oath, of purgation; or when, according to our
elsewhere[-prescribed] rule, sufficient indicia are found for examination
under torture, to impose it; or finally, when the accused was charged
with severe suspicions, but on account of legal grounds torture could
not be used, to proceed to an arbitrary punishment.

Id. Article 38, Section 29:

§29. Nevertheless, there may be condemned to an extraordinary
punishment not only someone who persists in denial, having withstood

the torture regarding the main crime with stubborn denial, in the case in which he has confessed other crimes, or some punishable circumstances and misdemeanors regarding the main crime, or their legal elements have been proven; but also a suspect who confesses and then recants after completion of torture, in the case in which his disavowal is found to be wholly improbable and malicious; or in case he is a very suspicious and dangerous person, he may be removed from the affected district, or indeed if he is a foreigner, he may be banished from our entire hereditary domains as a man dangerous to the country, also notwithstanding that he confessed or was convicted of nothing.

26. Id. Article 34, Sections 1–2. However, for delicta levia there may be conviction on circumstantial evidence. Id. Article 34, Section 3.

27. Id. Article 34, Section 2, last lines.

28. Id. Article 38, Section 29.

29. Id. Article 34, Section 1.

30. The requirement of adherence to the Roman-canon law of proof "was made almost illusory" in the codifying Landrecht of 1721. Allmann 51. Book 6, Title 3, Article 12, Section 1 of the statute makes sweeping provision for poena extraordinaria short of full proof: "For crimes which merit death or bodily punishment, and the indications (Anzeigungen) [that is, circumstantial evidence] are not so substantial [as to warrant investigation under torture, the statute authorizes] a poena extraordinaria either of a bodily [including imprisonment] or monetary sort according to the character of the crime or the circumstances of its gravity . . . ." Friedrich Wilhelms Königes in Preussen verbessertes Land-Recht (Königsberg, 1721) 61. Likewise, when torture is authorized but successfully resisted, a poena extraordinaria short of the blood sanctions is approved. Id. at 59–60 (bk. 6, tit. 3, art. 11, §§4–5). See chapter 4, text at notes 2–8.

Schmidt noticed numerous cases in the Magdeburg records of this period, especially involving women accused of child murder, in which defendants who would have been sentenced to death on full proof were instead confined to the Zuchthaus. Schmidt, Freiheitsstrafe 18 & n.3. Schmidt attributes, id. at 18 & n.4, to Carl E. Wächter, Über Zuchthäuser und Zuchthausstrafen (Stuttgart, 1786) 51, the observation that this practice had "beeinträchtigt" torture, that is, encroached upon its sphere. (It has not been possible to locate a copy of this work.)

31. In Bremen in 1696 a man accused of theft who did not confess under torture was ordered confined to the Zuchthaus for one year and thereafter banished in perpetuity. Robert von Hippel, "Beiträge zur Geschichte der Freiheitsstrafe," Zeitschrift für die gesamte Strafrechtswissenschaft 18:608, 610 n.9. See id. at 647 on the deliberations in Danzig in 1690 on the need for a special prison for those persons who are sentenced to a poena extraordinaria because they cannot be capitally convicted.

The Codex juris bavarici criminalis of 1751 (Munich, 1771 ed.) (pt.1, ch. 12, §11), at 38, provides: "The suspicion (*Verdacht*) to the extent that it is based upon a sufficiently proven *Indicio proximo* [that is, a compelling piece of circumstantial evidence], or also upon several connected *Indiciis remotis* [that is, items of circumstantial evidence more remote from the probandum] . . . shall in the end always be punished only with extraordinary and arbitrary, but never with the ordinary penalty." See Allmann 52–55.

For Saxony in the early seventeenth century there is the evidence from Carpzov's practice, e.g., a case in 1625 of a woman accused of child murder who resisted confession under torture and was sentenced to three or four years banishment. Holtappels, supra note 17, at 49. Holtappels also reports cases from the late eighteenth-century opinions of C. F. G. Meister where long prison terms were imposed against accused murderers against whom full proof was lacking. Id. at 60.

32.   In Lausanne in 1736 an accused rustler named Des Vaux, against whom there was considerable circumstantial evidence, confessed the theft of four cows, but then recanted in order to avoid capital punishment. He resisted confession thereafter, despite repeated torture. Since he could not be put to death on the evidence available, he was instead condemned to the public works. S.D.C. [Gabriel Seigneux de Correvon], *Essai sur l'usage, l'abus et les inconveniens de la torture dans la procédure criminelle* (Lausanne, 1768) 52–54.

33.   See Article 41 of the Ordonnance . . . du stil general, cited supra note 5; Article 44 is the counterpart to the French *plus amplement informé*, discussed text at note 44ff; cf. Damhouder, ch. 40, at 44^v; Hubert 56–57. See also the eighteenth-century case described by van Caenegem, supra note 17.

34.   Supra note 15.

35.   See Clarus' case in Milan in 1557, supra note 19. The Leopoldina (Tuscany, 1786), discussed supra Chapter 2, text at note 7, provides in Article 110 for poena extraordinaria of banishment or imprisonment when full proof is lacking where there is "a concurrence of the most urgent [i.e., persuasive] circumstantial evidence (*indizi*) . . . ." Articles 111 and 113 hint at something like the French *plus amplement informé*.

For Sardinia see *Leggi e costitzioni di sua maesta* (Turin, 1770) (Italian and French texts) II:150 (bk. 4, tit. 19, §2): in cases where, although full proof is lacking, guilt can be inferred from circumstantial evidence, "our superior judges shall have the authority to impose a poena extraordinaria according to the circumstances of the case, and they can even extend the penalty to that of determinate galley sentence if it shall appear appropriate to them." This provision is derived from Title 25, Article 13 of the French ordinance of 1670, discussed text at note 90; a provision for *torture avec réserve des preuves* (bk. 4, tit. 19, §2) is derived from Title 19, Article 2 of the French ordinance, discussed text at note 37ff.

36.   On the origins of the ordinance, see Esmein 175ff. Minutes of the

draftsmen's deliberations were published in several editions; citation in the present work is to Anon., *Procès-verbal des conférencs tenues . . . pour l'examen des articles . . . de l'ordonnance criminelle* (Paris, 1740 ed.). On the treatise writers, see Esmein 212 n.1, 346–347.

The most comprehensive and prestigious of the treatises is the 4-volume work by Jousse. The other writer who is most widely cited, Pierre-François Muyart de Vouglans, wrote three different works, each of which went through various editions. For the present study we cite *Institutes au droit criminel* (Paris, 1768 ed.); *Instruction criminelle* (Paris, 1767 ed.); *Les loix criminelles de France dans leur ordre naturel* (Paris, 1780 ed.).

Others of the treatises cited in this chapter are Bornier, supra note 5, at II; François Lange, *La nouvelle pratique civile, criminelle et beneficiale* (5th ed., Paris, 1692); Robert J. Pothier, *Traité de la procédure criminelle,* in *Oeuvres de Pothier* (Bugnet, ed.) (Paris, 1848 ed.) X (posthumously published; Pothier died in 1772); Augustin Marie Poullain du Parc, *Principes du droit françois, suivant les maximes de Bretagne* (Rennes, 1771) XI & XII; Guy du Rousseaud de la Combe, *Traité des matières criminelles, suivant l'ordonnance du mois d'Août 1670* (Paris, 1756 ed.); Jacques-Antoine Salle, *L'esprit des ordonnances de Louis XIV* (Paris, 1758) II; François Serpillon, *Code criminel, ou commentaire sur l'ordonnance de 1670* (Lyon, 1784 ed.).

One of the Enlightenment reformers made a contemptuous assessment of the treatises that is largely accurate: "If you have read one of the French writers on the criminal law, you have read them all. Their works seem to come from the same mold." Jacques Pierre Brissot de Warville, *Théorie des loix criminelles* (Berlin, 1781) 105 n.200. Many of the treatises are commentaries on the ordinance of 1670 and follow its organization. The writers borrow from one another, and not always with proper disclosure; cf. Schnapper, Peines II:97 n.346.

37.   Isambert 18:412.

38.   Guillaume François Letrosne, "Vues sur la justice criminelle," in *Bibliotheque philosophique du législateur* (Jacques Pierre Brissot de Warville, ed.) (Berlin & Paris, 1782) II:227, 295n. Letrosne was, inter alia, "avocat du roi au présidial d'Orléans." Id. at 227.

39.   Jousse II:587; see also id. at II:478.

40.   Bornier, supra note 5, at II:318.

41.   Schnapper, Bordeaux 26–27; Schnapper, Paris 264. See also Jean Imbert, *La practique judiciaire* (Paris, 1609 ed.) bk. III, ch. 14, §2, at 722, cited by Esmein, 283 & n.1, and by Schnapper, Bordeaux 26 n.93 (to other editions).

42.   Jousse I:47, 50. Serpillon, supra note 36, at II:176: "Perpetual or determinate galley service or banishment are the usual punishments to which accused persons who have confessed nothing are sentenced when the proofs have been reserved, *and when the judges find that they* [the proofs] *are sufficient to pronounce these punishments.*" (Italics supplied.)

43.   Jousse II:604. Writers unaware of the significance of such a sentence mistake it for condemnation on mere suspicion, e.g., Hertz 67–68, discussing Jousse's case of Barberousse. Compare Paul W. Bamford, *Fighting Ships and Prisons: The Mediterranean Galleys of France in the Age of Louis XIV* (Minneapolis, 1973) 180: "some unfortunates [were] sent off to the oar when merely 'suspected' or 'accused' of some crime. Examples in the registers demonstrate that vague suspicions and unproved charges could send men to the oar." It seems likely that Bamford's sources are evidencing cases of poena extraordinaria, and that the charges were "unproved" only in the sense that they did not meet the standard of Roman-canon full proof. Cf. Paul Masson, "Les galères de France," *Annales de la faculté des lettres d'Aix* 20:7, 84–85 (1937) (persons merely "accused" of capital crime ordered to the galleys).

44.   Muyart de Vouglans, Institutes, supra note 36, at 289; cf. id. at 208; Muyart de Vouglans, Instruction, supra note 36, at 459; Jousse, quoted supra text at note 39; Rousseaud de la Combe, supra note 36, at 323.

45.   Jousse II:603; see text at note 91 and note 91.

46.   Schnapper, Bordeaux 16–18; Schnapper, Paris 260–262; Jousse II:559.

47.   Procès-verbal, supra note 36, at II:232, cited by Muyart de Vouglans, Institutes, supra note 36, at 259; Muyart de Vouglans, Loix, supra note 36, at I:79.

48.   Muyart de Vouglans, Institutes, supra note 36, at 259. This sort of defensive remark may have been meant to counter criticism such as that of the reform writer Servan, that the plus amplement informé "is not founded on any statute (*loi*): only judicial practice (*usage*) gave it birth and life, which is already a major defect...." Servan, "Réflexions sur quelques points de nos loix," in *Bibliotheque philosophique du législateur* (Jacques Pierre Brissot de Warville, ed.) (Berlin & Paris, 1782) VII:153, 216.

49.   Jousse II:558. Servan found it convenient to emphasize the label rather than the ordinary function, in order to depict the practice unfavorably:

It appears to me that the plus amplement informé requires the concurrence of two reasons.

One, that there is a great likelihood that the accused is guilty; the other, that there is a great likelihood that he will be convicted by new evidence (*preuves*).

Insufficient attention is paid to this last reason. Often the judge pronounces a plus amplement informé without having in his mind the least reasonable hope of obtaining new evidence....

Servan, supra note 48, at VII:221.

50.   Muyart de Vouglans wrote a tract to refute Beccaria, reprinted as an appendix to volume II of his Loix, supra note 36; cf. id. at I:60.

51.   Id. at I:79.

52.   When the evidence was skimpy or the investigation just commenc-

ing, a plus amplement informé à temps could be pronounced that did not order the accused to be imprisoned. This was a genuinely interlocutory order, without penal character. Id. at I:78–79. The practice resembles the contemporary English binding over to appear at sessions or assizes.

53. Jousse I:834.

54. Id. at II:585; Pothier, supra note 36, at X:475 (V.IV.149).

55. Muyart de Vouglans, Loix, supra note 36, at I:78. Servan, supra note 48, at 218–219, thinks this a corruption as well. He contends that only the perpeutal variety of plus amplement informé, discussed infra, is supposed to import infamy, although in practice the plus amplement informé à temps does too.

56. Rousseaud de la Combe, supra note 36, at 323.

57. Pothier, supra note 36, at X:476 (V.V.150); Jousse II:556, 585; Schnapper, Bordeaux 14–16.

58. Jousse I:835; cf. id. at II:558.

59. Id. at II:585.

60. Id. at I:835 cf. id. at II:558.

61. Id. at II:558.

62. Muyart de Vouglans, Institutes, supra note 36, at 259–260. If the accused has been put to torture without reserving the evidence, Pothier thinks that the court cannot thereafter order a plus amplement informé against him, because it "should be based upon the evidence (*preuves et indices*) that subsist against him. But they no longer subsist, the torture having purged them...." Pothier, supra note 36, at X:475 (V.III.147).

63. Id. at 296; cf. id. at 286; Muyart de Vouglans, Instruction, supra note 36, at 523; Muyart de Vouglans, Loix, supra note 36, at I:78.

64. Robert J. Pothier, *Traité des personnes et des choses*, in *Oeuvres de Pothier* (Bugnet ed.) (Paris, 1848 ed.) IX:44 (I.III.III.110–111); see generally François Richer, *Traité de la mort civile* (Paris, 1755).

65. Rousseaud de la Combe, supra note 36, at 323–324; Muyart de Vouglans, Loix, supra note 36, at I:78.

66. Schnapper, Bordeaux 19.

67. Procès-verbal, supra note 36, at II:224.

68. Id.

69. Isambert 26:373–375. As printed at 26:373, the decree refers to Title 9, a misprint for Title 19.

70. See R. C. van Caenegem, "The Law of Evidence in the Twelfth Century: European Perspective and Intellectual Background," in *Proceedings of the Second International Congress of Medieval Canon Law* (Vatican City, 1965) 297.

71. The great themes of Eberhard Schmidt's writing on *Inquisitionsprozess*, summarized in Langbein, PCR 129ff.

72. Says Schnapper, Peines I:237, of the developed system of poena

extraordinaria: "Only a society that respects its judges . . . can permit such a system."

73. See generally John P. Dawson, *A History of Lay Judges* (Cambridge, Mass., 1960) 60ff; John P. Dawson, *The Oracles of the Law* (Ann Arbor, 1968) 191ff. There are few subjects of comparable importance in European legal history on which so little research has yet been done as the restructuring of the courts and the judiciary in the ancien régime.

74. See Esmein 212–221. Schnapper, Peines II:89, remarks on the "double movement" in France in the epoch of Louis XIV by which criminal justice was being liberated from local law while the judiciary was being confined in a more centralized hierarchy.

75. Ernst Boehm, "Der Schöppenstuhl zu Leipzig und der sächsiche Inquisitionsprozess im Barockzeitalter," *Zeitschrift für die gesamte Strafrechtswissenschaft* 59:371, 620; 60:155; 61:300 (1940–1942), esp. 59:388, noted by Dawson, Oracles, supra note 73, at 203–204. With Schnapper's observation, supra note 72, compare Boehm's comment on the imposition of a Verdachtsstrafe in a case lacking full proof: "one sees in this example the impossibility of allowing this sort of judgment [to be imposed by] the numerous little courts in the countryside that were possessed of high jurisdiction." Boehm, op. cit., at 59:400. For similar concern expressed by a contemporary see Josef von Sonnenfels, *Ueber die Abschaffung der Tortur* (Zurich, 1775 ed.) 85ff.

76. See Langbein, PCR 175–177, 191–192, 198–202.

77. Adolf Stölzel, *Die Entwicklung des gelehrten Richtertums in deutschen Territorien* (Stuttgart, 1872) I:349, 355ff.

78. On Aktenversendung see Dawson, Oracles, supra note 73, at 200ff; Langbein, PCR 198–202.

79. See Boehm, supra note 75, at 61:345–365.

80. Hegler, supra note 6, at 1–4; Adolf Stölzel, *Brandenburg-Preussens Rechtsverwaltung und Rechtsverfassung* (Berlin, 1888) I:337–338, 340n., 377–378; Stölzel, supra note 77, at 349–385; Eduard Kern, *Geschichte des Gerichtsverfassungsrechts* (Munich & Berlin, 1954) 38ff.

81. E.g., Lange's seventeenth-century treatise, supra note 36, at 174, remarking on the difficulty of knowing if the evidence is sufficient for torture "because the Doctors' opinions differ concerning the force of the circumstances (*indices*), the quality of the evidence (*preuve*) that results, and what more should be added." See Hertz 64–65.

82. See Boldt, supra note 6, at 139.

83. Chancellor d'Aguesseau remarked in 1742 that "experience shows that the severest punishments are not always the most useful, because their natural repugnance at pronouncing the death penalty inclines the judges to seek a pretext either in form or in substance for not finding the proof complete, or for diminishing the seriousness of the crime . . . ." [Henri François

d'Aguesseau,] *Oeuvres de M. le chancelier d'Aguesseau* (Paris, 1774 ed.) 8:159–160.

84. Hegler, supra note 6, at 87ff.

85. "There was a stiffening of repression in the first third of the sixteenth century, in Italy above all, which increased bit by bit." Schnapper, Peines II:88. Compare Fiorelli II:140: "The infliction of the poena extraordinaria, supported with greater frequency by the jurists of the second half of the sixteenth century and of the following century, was responding to a political exigency that the absolutist state felt much more intensely than [past governments] . . . . The more important legislation of the last epoch of torture sanctioned the new tendency . . . ."

86. For example, the criminal procedure ordinance enacted for Lower Austria in 1656 authorized the court to impose a poena extraordinaria such as imprisonment in cases in which there was a technically unobjectionable confession that the court nevertheless distrusted, perhaps for the reasons that often made tortured confessions untrustworthy. Allmann 49. Likewise, it has been pointed out that a lesser sanction was occasionally imposed as a poena extraordinaria in cases in which tortured confessions were not verified or not verifiable. Sax, supra note 16, at 154–155.

87. E.g., Damhouder, ch. 35, at 34^v, forbidding torture for "petty crimes or delicts, on which neither body nor member depends." Similar logic underlies the rule of modern American law that permits the use of deadly force against fleeing felons, but not misdemeanants.

88. "The punishments (*peines*) are the various penalties (*punitions*) that criminals are made to suffer in order to correct them or to chastise them and to keep them from recidivism. However, there are some punishments (*peines*) that are employed not to punish the crime, but only in order to get better evidence (*preuve*) of it . . . ; such is torture." Jousse I:36. Article 61 of the Carolina, translated in Langbein, PCR 283–284, grants a civil remedy to the innocent accused who is examined under torture in violation of the requirement that there be sufficient incriminating evidence against him, but not to the innocent accused who is lawfully examined under torture, because in the latter case the evidence "gave reason and excuse for the examination which took place; for the law says that one should keep oneself not only from the committing of crime, but also from all appearance of evil, of the sort that can cause ill repute or indication of crime, and he who does not do that has himself in this way caused his own complaint."

89. "Although the ordinance makes mention only of these, there are several other corporal punishments that are equally recognized in our practice." Muyart de Vouglans, Institutes, supra note 36, at 286; id. at 294ff for illustrations; cf. Salle, supra note 36, at 303.

90. Isambert 18:417; on the *amende honorable,* see von Bar, supra note 17, at 274–275.

91. Poullain du Parc, supra note 36, at XI:115, cited by Esmein 277 n.3. Lange cites a judgment of the Parlement of Paris from 1609 holding that "when the judges are divided in their opinions [in a case], some favoring condemnation to the galleys, the others favoring torture," the accused should be sentenced to the galleys on the ground that that is the lighter punishment, because the man put to torture is in danger of losing his life if he confesses. Lange, supra note 36, at 172.

Chapter Four

1. Reinhold Koser, "Die Abschaffung der Tortur durch Friedrich den Grossen," *Forschungen zur Brandenburgischen und Preussischen Geschichte* 6 (pt.2):233, 236 & n.5 (1893). Frederick William I had previously decreed that all sentences imposing judicial torture in witchcraft cases "be submitted to us for confirmation before the execution." Edict of Dec. 13, 1714, in *Des Corporis Constitutionum Marchicarum* 2:cols. 57–58 (Berlin & Halle, 1736). See infra note 43 for other instances in which the abolition of torture was preceded by a scheme of royal approval of torture sentences.

2. *Friedrich Wilhelms Königes in Preussen verbessertes Land-Recht* (Königsberg, 1721). All citations are to Book 6, Title 3.

3. Id., Articles 2–11, at 40–60.

4. Id., Article 2, §3, at 41.

5. Id., Article 3, §4, at 44.

6. Allmann 51, noted supra Chapter 3, note 30.

7. Land-Recht, supra note 2, Article 12, §1, at 61.

8. Id., Article 11, §§4–5, at 59–60.

9. Ferdinand Willenbücher, *Die strafrechtsphilosophischen Anschauungen Friedrichs des Grossen* (Breslau, 1904) 51.

10. Quoted id.

11. See Koser, supra note 1, at 236.

12. Id. at 237; cf. id. at 237 n.3.

13. Id. at 237.

14. Id.

15. The decrees are reproduced in Willenbücher, supra note 9, at 51–53 nn.

16. Decree of Jun. 27, 1754, id. at 51n.

17. Decree of Aug. 4, 1754, id. at 52n, substantially repeated in one of Aug. 8, 1754, id. at 53n.

18. Elsewhere in these decrees Frederick extended the new law of proof into the sphere that the jurists and judges had been so reluctant to enter, the death penalty. He authorized the courts to sentence a culprit to death when

his guilt was established "through clear circumstantial evidence (*indicia*) or else witnesses and other wholly clear . . . circumstances (*Umstände*). . . ." Decree of Jun. 27, 1754, id. at 51n.

19. The system of poena extraordinaria for less than full proof was codified in the so-called Criminal-Ordnung of 1805. *Allgemeines Criminalrecht für die Preussischen Staaten* (pt. 1) (Berlin, 1806) §400–408, at 145–147. See Allmann 66–69; Conrad II:447. Explicit freie Beweiswürdigung was enacted in 1846. Allmann 78.

20. Benedict Carpzov, *Practica nova Imperialis Saxonicae rerum criminalium* (1st ed. 1635), discussed in Allmann 38–42.

21. *Codex Saxonicus: Chronologische Sammlung der gesammten practisch-gültigen königlich Sächsischen* Gesetze (Leipzig, 1842), I:990.

22. Id. at 990–991, severely abridged; we follow Allmann 59–60, who had a proper edition of the text of the instruction. Cf. Ernst Boehm, "Der Schöppenstuhl zu Leipzig und der sächsische Inquisitionsprozess im Barockzeitalter," *Zeitschrift für die gesamte Strafrechtswissenschaft* 59:371, 398ff (1940).

23. Supra Chapter 3, text at notes 23–29 & note 24.

24. See the chronology in Conrad II:441, 443.

25. Josef von Sonnenfels, *Ueber die Abschaffung der Tortur* (Zurich, 1775 ed.). Sonnenfels had to defend himself in disciplinary proceedings against the charge that he had breached his sworn duty of confidentiality in allowing the work to be published. He claimed that it was published without his consent. Wilhelm Emil Wahlberg, "Zur Geschichte der Aufhebung der Tortur in Oesterreich," in *Gesammelte kleinere Schriften und Bruchstücke über Strafrecht, Strafprozess* . . . II:265, 265–268 (Vienna, 1877).

26. Sonnenfels, supra note 25, at 48; cf. id. at 89–90.

27. Conrad II:441, 443. In Croatia torture was abolished in April 1776, according to Professor Mirjan Damaska, who cites *Acta Consilii Regii Croatici*, No. 90 ex A. 1776. Letter to the author, June 21, 1976.

28. *Joseph des Zweyten Römischen Kaisers Gesetze und Verfassungen im Justizfache* . . . *in dem achten Jahre seiner Regierung* (Prague & Vienna, 1789) §§143, 148, at 120, 122.

29. Hubert 118–119.

30. "Edit de l'Empereur pour la réformation de la justice aux Pays-Bas, Article 63," in *Recueil des ordonnances des Pays-Bas autrichiens 1700–1794* (3d ser.) (M. P. Verhaegen, ed.) (Brussels, 1914) 3:34, at 43.

31. Hubert 118–121.

32. R. C. van Caenegem, "La preuve dans l'ancien droit belge des origines à la fin du XVIIIe siècle," *Recueils de la société Jean Bodin pour l'histoire comparative des institutions* 17:375, 425–426; Hubert 96–100. For background see Eugène Hubert, "Joseph II," in *The Cambridge Modern History* (New York, 1925 ed.) 6:626, 648ff.

33. Hubert 118 n.2.
34. Règlement provisionnel pour la procédure criminelle dans les Pays-Bas autrichiens (Brussels, 1787) ch. 22, §243.
35. Hubert 121–132.
36. Isambert 26:373.
37. Supra Chapter 3, text at note 69.
38. E.g., Christian Thomasius, *Über die Folter* (dissertation, 1705) (R. Lieberwirth, ed. & transl.) (Weimar, 1960) 156/157–164/165; Beccaria, ch. 12, at 33–34. Voltaire, as always, said it sharply: "The law (*loi*) does not convict them, yet it inflicts on them, on account of the uncertainty whether it is their crime, a punishment more frightful than the death that is given them when it is certain that they deserve it." "Commentaire sur le livre des délits et des peines (1766)," in [François-Marie Voltaire,] *Oeuvres complètes de Voltaire* (Paris, 1835 ed.) 5:403, 411.
39. Goswin de Fierlant, "Observations sur la torture," in Eugène Hubert, "Un chapitre de l'histoire du droit criminel dans les Pays-Bas autrichiens au XVIIIᵉ siècle: Les mémoires de Goswin de Fierlant," *Compte rendu des séances de la commission royale d'histoire* (5th ser.) (Brussels, 1894) 4:154, 171, at 228; cf. id. at 224–225 for a summary of de Fierlant's critique of torture, which resembles in all respects those cited supra note 38.
40. Sonnenfels, supra note 25, at 69–73.
41. Supra note 26. Other abolitionist writers nibble at the theme, but none make it a major argument. The Swiss writer Seigneux de Correvon stops tantalizingly short of realizing the implications of his own argument when he derides the "'jargon'" that a suspect who resists confession under torture purges the evidence (*indices*) against him. S.D.C. [Gabriel Seigneux de Correvon], *Essai sur l'usage, l'abus et les inconveniens de la torture, dans la procédure criminelle* (Lausanne, 1768) 75. If the torture victim is guilty, he gets off too lightly. If he is innocent, he has been made to suffer unfairly. Id. at 76. "Notice that even those who contend that Torture [undergone without confession] purges the evidence (*indices*) of the crime establish that it does not destroy the effect of the evidence (*preuves*) that incriminates (*condamnent*) him: it exempts only the ordinary punishment (*peine ordinaire*), imposing a lesser punishment on the guilty person than he would have suffered had he confessed . . . ." Id. at 77.

Another writer who gropes toward the new law of proof without understanding its implications is de Fierlant. When "the investigation presents a case where torture could have been used . . . the proofs not being complete, it is certainly correct to say that there is insufficient proof at law that the accused is guilty, but it is equally correct to say that it has been established that this man is vehemently suspect . . . ." De Fierlant, supra note 39, at 232–233. Accepting that society cannot punish the accused because he has not been found guilty (according to the Roman-canon standard of full proof), de Fierlant argues that the accused may nevertheless be banished as a preventive measure. Id. at 233–234.

42. Isambert 28:526, 529. Like the Belgian abolition decree of 1787, this order was part of a larger reform measure that the superior courts (the Parlements) resisted. The decree was not implemented; the Revolutionary Declaration of Oct. 8/9, 1789, finally abolished torture préalable. See Hertz 498–506; Hubert 82–83.

43. Noticed for Prussia, supra text at note 1, and for Belgium, supra text at note 29; cf. Fiorelli II:172–173.

44. Koser, supra note 1, at 236.

45. Willenbücher, supra note 9, at 53n. This requirement is odd because Frederick had boasted of the abolition of torture in his *Dissertation sur les raisons d'établir ou d'abroger les lois* (1749), presented to the Academy of Berlin in 1750. Koser, supra note 1, at 237. Apparently it was thought that potential criminals would be more given to reading published legislation than the proceedings of the Academy. A decree of Nov. 18, 1756, reiterating the prohibition of torture, was contemporaneously published. *Novum Corpus Constitutionum Prussico-Brandenburgensium* (Berlin, 1756–1760) II: cols 185/186–187/188.

46. Wahlberg, supra note 25, at 2:270.

47. Hubert 118.

48. Lieberwirth, Introduction to Thomasius, supra note 38, at 112.

49. See the works cited in Wolfgang Ebner, "Christian Thomasius und die Abschaffung der Folter," *Ius Commune* 4:72, 73 n.3 (1972); Peter Holtappels, *Die Entwicklungsgeschichte des Grundsatzes "in dubio pro reo"* (Hamburg, 1965) 64. See also the little work by Kurt Mehring, *Inwieweit ist praktischer Einfluss Montesquieus und Voltaires auf die strafrechtliche Tätigkeit Friedrichs des Grossen anzunehmen bezw. nachzuweisen?* (Breslau, 1927), showing that Frederick the Great formed his views on criminal justice in advance of the publication of Montesquieu's *L'esprit des Lois* (1748), and that Voltaire's interest in criminal justice developed much later. Id. at 38–57 passim. Neither writer deserves any credit for inspiring Frederick's reforms.

50. Except for confusing torture with the ancient ordeals. Beccaria, ch. 12, at 32.

51. Beccaria, ch. 6, at 20. Beccaria takes it as a first principle, id., ch. 3, at 15, "that the laws alone can decree punishments for crime, and this authority can reside only in the legislator who represents society as a whole united by a social contract. No magistrate (himself a part of society) may with justice ordain punishments for another member of the same society. A punishment increased beyond the limit fixed by the laws is another punishment added to the just one; it follows that a magistrate cannot, on whatever pretext of zeal or the public good, increase the punishment decreed [by the

legislator] against an offending citizen.'' Beccaria does not talk about the propriety of the judge reducing the prescribed penalty, the primary use of poena extraordinaria and the one which underlay the revolution in the law of proof, but his argument cuts against all judicial discretion. The theme of subordinating the judges to "the legislator" was an important component of eighteenth-century positivist thought leading to the codification movement.

52. Beccaria had no theory of proof. The treatise divides the judicial function into interpretation and application of the law. He insists, id., ch. 4, at 16, "that authority to interpret penal laws cannot rest with criminal judges, precisely because they are not makers of law." The sovereign should interpret the law, Beccaria says mysteriously. "Nothing is more dangerous than the common axiom that [the judge] should 'consult the spirit of the law' . . . [because that will] depend upon the good or bad logic of the judge, upon his good or bad digestion . . . ." Id., ch. 4, at 17. By contrast, in the application of the law Beccaria sees that the requisite "moral certitude in the matter of proof is one more easily felt than exactly defined. For that reason I believe the best law to be one which assigns to the chief judge a jury chosen by lot rather than selected; ignorance, which judges by feeling, being in this case more dependable than knowledge which judges by opinion." Id., ch. 7, at 23. Interpretation may not be left to turn upon good or bad digestion, but application may. Yet even that illogical program is inconsistently pursued. In the next paragraph Beccaria announces: "It is an important point in all good legislation to determine exactly the credibility of witnesses and the proofs of guilt." Id., ch. 8, at 24. That, of course, is what the Roman-canon law had tried to do, in contradistinction to a law of proof based on achieving "moral certainty" in the mind of the trier.

Beccaria simply did not understand the irreconcilable contest between objective and subjective standards of proof. Hence he vacillated between them, criticizing and endorsing both, and at one point pretending that the future law of proof would meet the standard of the old: "moral certitude, strictly speaking, can be no more than a probability—but one of such a kind as to be called a certainty . . . ." Id., ch. 7, at 22.

53.   Voltaire, supra note 38.

54.   Id. at 5:422.

55.   Id. at 11:386 (*Dictionnaire Philosophique*, entry for "crimes").

56.   Id.

57.   John Gilissen, "La preuve en Europe du XVIe au début du XIXe siècle," *Recueils de la société Jean Bodin pour l'histoire comparative des institutions* 17:755, 797 (1965).

58.   Thomasius, supra note 38, at 182/183; Charles Louis de Montesquieu, *The Spirit of the Laws* (T. Nugent, transl.) (New York & London, 1949 ed.) bk. 6, §17, at 91. Thomasius also points to Holland, although torture was not abolished there until 1798. Jan Willem Bosch, "La preuve

dans l'ancien droit néerlandais," *Recueils de la société Jean Bodin pour l'histoire comparative des institutions* 17:453, 469 (1965). On seventeenth- and eighteenth-century Dutch abolitionist writing see Hubert 90–93.

59. Beccaria, ch. 12, at 36.

60. Voltaire, supra note 38, at 5:441–442.

61. Sonnenfels, supra note 25, at 75.

62. Quoted by Hubert, supra note 39, at 162 n.1.

63. De Fierlant, supra note 39, at 229–230; Seigneux de Correvon, supra note 41, at 110–111.

Chapter Five

1. See generally T. F. T. Plucknett, "The Relations between Roman Law and English Common Law," *University of Toronto Law Journal* 3:24 (1939); R. C. van Caenegem, "L'histoire du droit et la chronologie: Reflexions sur la formation du 'Common Law' et la procédure Romano-canonique," in *Études d'histoire du droit canonique dédiées à Gabriel Le Bras* (Paris, 1965) II:1459; Langbein, PCR 211–212.

2. Eberhard Schmidt, *Inquisitionsprozess und Rezeption* (Leipzig, 1940), discussed in Langbein, PCR 140ff.

3. Stephen I:222.

4. Sir John Fortescue, *De Laudibus Legem Anglie* (S. B. Chrimes, ed.) (Cambridge, 1942) 46, 47.

5. Sir Thomas Smith, *De Republica Anglorum* (L. Alston, ed.) (Cambridge, 1906) 105 (bk. 2, ch. 24).

6. Sir Edward Coke, *The Third Part of the Institutes of the Laws of England* (London, 1797 ed.) *35. Unlike Fortescue and Smith, Coke did not pretend that torture was unused; he was arguing that it lacked juridical basis. "[T]here is no law to warrant tortures in this land, nor can they be justified by any prescription being so lately brought in." Id.

7. As were many other important common law figures of the age: Bacon, Bromley, Crooke, Dyer, Egerton, Montagu, Popham, Yelverton. See the case references in the Index of Named Commissioners to Torture, Chapter 6, pages 125–127.

8. David Jardine, A Reading on the Use of Torture in the Criminal Law of England Previously to the Commonwealth (London, 1837) [hereafter cited as Jardine].

9. In an appendix to his book, id. at 71–109, Jardine transcribed and numbered the warrants he had found, except for the curious omission of the one in Guy Fawkes' case, which he discussed id. at 47–48. We show Jardine's numbers in parentheses following our own numbers in the "Case Number" column in the table following Chapter 6.

10. Jardine 13–14, 16, 52–53.

11. E.g., Sir William Holdsworth, *A History of English Law* (London, 1922–1966) V:185 [hereafter cited as Holdsworth].

12. E.g., L. A. Parry, *The History of Torture in England* (London, 1933) 104; R. D. Melville, "The Use and Forms of Judicial Torture in England and Scotland," *Scottish Historical Review* 2:225, at 230–231 (1905).

The British have no monopoly on this genre; compare Rudolf Quanter, *Die Folter in der deutschen Rechtspflege sonst und jetzt* (Dresden, 1900); Alec Mellor, *La torture: Son histoire, son abolition, sa réapparition au XXe siècle* (Paris, 1961 ed.); Daniel P. Mannix, *The History of Torture* (New York, 1964). The most ambitious of the lot is Franz Helbing & Max Bauer, *Die Tortur: Geschichte der Folter im Kriminalverfahren aller Zeiten und Völker* (Berlin, 1926 ed.), which mixes judicial torture not only with the ordeals and the afflictive punishments, but also with "self-torture" by religious fanatics (at 68–73) and sadistic sexual practices, ranging from those of Caligula down to the activities of a twentieth-century harem proprietor, one Sultan Abdul Hamid II (at 74–85).

13. 12 Geo. III c. 20 (1772); 7 & 8 Geo. IV c. 28 (1827).

14. See Frederic W. Maitland, Introduction, *Pleas of the Crown for the County of Gloucester* (London, 1884) xxxviiiff; Plucknett, 118–126; James Bradley Thayer, *A Preliminary Treatise on Evidence at the Common Law* (Boston, 1898) 70–74.

15. See Stephen I:297–300; Thayer, supra note 14, at 74–81.

16. "This death some strong and stout hearted man doth choose, for being not condemned of felony, his blood is not corrupted, [nor] his lands nor goods confiscate to the Prince...." Smith, supra note 5, at 97 (bk. 2, ch. 23).

17. See Daines Barrington, *Observations on the More Ancient Statutes* (4th ed., London, 1775) 85.

18. Thomas B. Howell, A Complete Collection of State Trials (London, 1816 ed.) 2:911, 914 [hereafter cited as Howell; the work is paginated by column rather than page] [in citation to other English law reports we follow the forms prescribed in Harvard Law Review Association, *A Uniform System of Citation* (11th ed., Cambridge, Mass., 1967)]. Coke's formulation of the sentence to peine forte et dure was fairly standard; see William Staunford, *Les Plees del Coron* (London, 1567 ed.) 150–151.

Kelyng reports a case at Newgate Sessions in October 1662 in which a man who refused to plead to an indictment for robbery had "his two Thumbs ... tied together with Whipcord, that the Pain of that might compel him to plead...." It did. Thorley's Case, Kel. J. 27, 84 Eng. Rep. 1066 (1662). Kelyng adds: "And this was said to be the constant Practice at Newgate." Id. at 28, 84 Eng. Rep. at 1066.

19. Howell 2:922–923.

20. The essential similarity is that in the course of displacing the or-deals both the Roman-canon law of proof and the English common law granted to criminal defendants an overbroad procedural right—the two-eyewitness rule on the Continent, the right to refuse jury trial in England. From the thirteenth century to the eighteenth, both systems effectively with-drew these overbroad rights by coercing defendants to waive them. Neither system permitted unrestrained coercion; each required a finding of probable cause as a precondition for the use of coercion (the half-proof of Roman-canon law, the indictment of the English jury of accusation). The key differ-ence is that the English were forcing consent to a less central matter: not to the merits, but to the mode of proof. Whereas judicial torture on the Conti-nent was designed to overcome the established standard of proof, the peine forte et dure was meant to bring into operation the established standard of proof. We are about to remark, text at notes 25–31, that it was precisely this standard of proof, the jury standard, that spared England from a true system of judicial torture.

Another instructive parallel between the Continental practice of torture and the English peine forte et dure is that neither applied to petty crime; in both systems the overbroad procedural right governed cases of capital crime only. We have seen in Chapter 1 that the two-eyewitness rule did not pertain to so-called delicta levia. Likewise, the English recognized no right of re-fusal to plead in cases of misdemeanor. See Blackstone IV:320; Sir Matthew Hale, *The History of the Pleas of the Crown* (S. Emlyn, ed.) (London, 1736; posthumous first ed., Hale died in 1676) II:320. We have shown in Chapter 3 that when the Europeans rid themselves of judicial torture by undermining the two-eyewitness rule, they did it by extending the lower standard of proof that had always pertained to delicta levia. Likewise, when the English abolished the peine forte et dure in 1772, they extended to felony the rule that they had always followed for misdemeanor: willful refusal to plead became equivalent to conviction. See Blackstone, supra; 12 Geo. III c. 20 (1772). The modern rule, treating refusal to plead as though it were a plea of not guilty, was enacted by 7 & 8 Geo. IV c. 28 (1827).

21. Sonnenfels' famous abolitionist tract, discussed supra Chapter 4, makes the point that the English peine forte et dure is really a mode of punishment, not of torture. Josef von Sonnenfels, *Ueber die Abschaffung der Tortur* (Zurich, 1775 ed.) 13 & n.

22. E.g., Parry, supra note 12, at 88.

23. The Unitarians Bartholomew Legatt and Edward Wightman, exe-cuted in 1612, were the last heretics to be burnt alive. See Howell 2:727; G. P. V. Akrigg, Jacobean Pageant (New York, Atheneum ed., 1967) 311. For the traitors' deaths of the Gunpowder Plotters see Howell 2:215–218.

24. The systematic infliction of pain, be it torture or punishment, in criminal procedure seems inconsistent with our conception of the vaunted

humanism of the Renaissance. How, we wonder, could Francis Bacon (Chapter 6, text at note 31; cf. Chapter 7, text at note 60) be an eager participant in investigation under torture? It may be that the tortures and punishments of the age seemed less cruel to contemporaries. We must bear in mind that no aspect of the human condition has changed so greatly in the twentieth century as our tolerance of pain. The common pain-killers and anesthesia have largely eliminated the experience of pain from our lives. In disease, childbirth, surgery, and dentistry, our ancestors were acclimated to levels of suffering we find incomprehensible. Cf. Ernst Boehm, "Der Schöppenstuhl zu Leipzig und der sächsische Inquisitionsprozess im Barockzeitalter," *Zeitschrift für die gesamte Strafrechtswissenschaft*, 61:300, 378–380 (1941).

25. Maitland II:659.

26. Id. at II:660.

27. "Like the ordeals, the jury also was inscrutable." T. F. T. Plucknett, *Edward I and Criminal Law* (Cambridge, 1960) 75.

28. Maitland II:660.

29. Id. at II:660–661.

30. Id. at II:659–660.

31. Howell 2:1, 18. English law experimented with a two-witness rule for treason, and Raleigh was trying to invoke it. During the Marian-Elizabethan period when most of the English torture cases occurred, the two-witness rule was treated as having been repealed by the statute of 1& 2 P. & M. c. 10 (1554–1555). John H. Wigmore, *A Treatise on the Anglo-American System of Evidence* (Boston, 1940 ed.) VII:§2036, at 263–268, esp. 263 n.3 [hereafter cited as Wigmore].

It is an instructive coincidence that Warburton's example of a murderer caught exiting with a bloody sword was precisely the case urged among some Roman-canon jurists to support an exception to the general two-eyewitness rule in cases of especially cogent circumstantial evidence. See supra Chapter 1, note 4.

Wigmore believed that there was a "conflict of the common law and the ecclesiastical system" in the sixteenth and seventeenth centuries by which England risked adopting the Roman-canon system of quantitative proofs. Wigmore VII:§2032, at 247. His evidence is very slender and it appears that he was misled by "Professor F. W. Maitland's enlightening essay, English Law and the Renaissance ([Cambridge,] 1901)." Wigmore VII:§2032, at 248 n.18. Wigmore seems not to have known of Holdsworth's convincing refutation of Maitland's thesis. Holdsworth IV:217–293; see also Samuel E. Thorne, "English Law and the Renaissance," in *Atti del primo congresso internazionale della società italiana di storia del diritto* (Florence, 1966) 437–445.

32. Thayer, supra note 14, at 90.

33. See Maitland II:622–625. "Indeed it is the duty of the jurors, so soon as they have been summoned, to make inquiries about the facts of which they will have to speak when they come before the court." Id. at II:624–625.

34. See Langbein, PCR 118–124.

35. Langbein, "The Origins of Public Prosecution at Common Law," *American Journal of Legal History* 17:313 (1973); Langbein, PCR 1–125, 202–209, 248–251.

36. See Langbein, Origins, supra note 35, at 315–317. It is remarkable how little is known about the emergence and the activities of the law officers of the crown in Tudor-Stuart times. See generally Holdsworth VI:457–472; J. L. J. Edwards, *The Law Officers of the Crown* (London, 1964).

37. Sources cited supra note 35.

The proposition is there developed that the English elaborated a prosecutorial system operated by the justices of the peace (JPs) on the basis of the statutes of 1 & 2 Philip & Mary c. 13 (1554–55) and 2 & 3 Philip & Mary c. 10 (1555). This analysis has been widely endorsed by reviewers of Langbein, PCR, although Dr. J. H. Baker has resisted it on what amounts to a definitional ground. Reviewing the book in *English Historical Review* 91:192, 193 (1976), Dr. Baker takes exception to the view expressed in the book that the JPs "orchestrated" prosecution at trial. Dr. Baker has explained (in correspondence with the author) that he believes that the book understates the role of the clerks of quarter sessions and assizes in processing routine cases at trial.

Dr. Baker's point is well taken, and although it should have been implicit from the book, it was certainly not explicit. By 1660, for example, when the *Clerk of Assize* manual gives us good narrative evidence, it was routine for the examining JP to surrender his pretrial depositions to a clerk in advance of the trial, "and if it be Evidence for the King, [the Clerk] readeth it to the Jury." T. W., *The Clerk of Assize . . .* (London, 1660) 14.

The book emphasizes that the central concern of the Marian legislation was to develop the pretrial prosecutorial role of the JP. In the ongoing system of citizen prosecution at trial, it would ordinarily suffice for the JP to bind over the citizen accusers and any other witnesses whom the JP may have located in more active investigation. E.g., Langbein, PCR 39. "In this way the Marian scheme was making the JPs into back-up prosecutors. Private citizens, now bound by recognizance as required by the Marian statute, would continue to prosecute most cases." Langbein, Origins, supra note 35, at 323.

Although "[t]he JP's forensic role at trial was exceptional," Langbein, PCR 51, it is manifest in the sources there discussed and has not been controverted. Dr. Baker, now seconded by J. S. Cockburn, "Early-Modern

Assize Records as Historical Evidence," *Journal of the Society of Archivists* 5:215, 226–27 (1975), is emphasizing the corollary—that in the ordinary cases in which the JP's prosecutorial work did not require him to take up a forensic role at trial, a clerk could work from the JP's pretrial documents in the courtroom and call citizen prosecutors to give their evidence without the participation of the JP.

38. See, e.g., C. L'Estrange Ewen, *Witch Hunting and Witch Trials* (London, 1929) 98–111 (indictments contrasted with convictions and executions in witchcraft cases, 1558–1736); Joel Samaha, *Law and Order in Historical Perspective* (New York & London, 1974) 120–133 (acquittal figures for Elizabethan Essex).

39. Case 26. Case numbers are discussed at page 91.

Chapter Six

1. For 1540–1542: *Proceedings and Ordinances of the Privy Council of England* (H. Nicolas, ed.) (London, 1837) VII. For 1542–1602: *Acts of the Privy Council of England* (J. R. Dasent, ed.) (London, 1890–1907) [hereafter cited as APC]. For 1613–1629: *Acts of the Privy Council of England* (London, 1921–1958) [hereafter cited as APC (Stuart)]. For 1631–1637 (unpublished): *Privy Council Registers* (microcard edition) (London, 1962). For 1637–1645: *Privy Council Registers Preserved in the Public Record Office: Reproduced in Facsimile* (London, 1967–1968).

2. For 1509–1547: *Letters and Papers, Foreign and Domestic, of the Reign of Henry VIII* (J. S. Brewer et al., eds.) (London, 1862–1932) [hereafter cited as LP]. For 1547–1625: *Calendar of State Papers, Domestic Series, of the Reigns of Edward VI, Mary, Elizabeth, and James I* (R. Lemon et al., eds.) (London, 1856–1872) [hereafter cited as SPD]. For 1625–1649: *Calendar of State Papers, Domestic Series, of the Reign of Charles I* (J. Bruce, et al., eds.) (London, 1858–1897).

3. The first entry is dated August 10; Cromwell was executed on July 28. In the 1530s he directed much of the investigatory activity that later fell to the Council. See generally G. R. Elton, *The Tudor Revolution in Government* (Cambridge, 1953); G. R. Elton, *Policy and Police: The Enforcement of the Reformation in the Age of Thomas Cromwell* (Cambridge, 1972); G. R. Elton, "Why the History of the Early-Tudor Council Remains Unwritten," *Annali della fondazione italiana per la storia amministrativa* (Milan, 1964) I:268, 290ff.

4. Infra notes 8–9.

5. The legend was current in Coke's time that the rack was first brought to the Tower of London by John Holland, the Duke of Exeter, who was constable of the Tower in the reign of Henry VI (1422–1461). Sir Edward

Coke, *The Third Part of the Institutes of the Laws of England* (London, 1797 ed.) *35.

Jardine was probably following Barrington in inferring from the preamble to the Statute of Pirates, 27 Hen. VIII c. 4 (1535–1536), 28 Hen. VIII c. 15 (1536), that torture had theretofore been in use in the English admiralty courts. Jardine 14; compare Daines Barrington, *Observations on the More Ancient Statutes* (4th ed., London, 1775) 495. The inference seems dubious. The Act provides for the introduction in Admiralty of common law criminal procedure (including indictment by grand jury and verdict by petty jury) in place of "the civil Laws, the nature whereof is that before judgment of death can be given against the offenders either they must plainly confess their offenses (which they will never do without torture or pains) or else their offenses be so plainly and directly proved by Witnesses indifferent such as saw their offenses committed, which cannot be gotten but by chance at few times, because such offenders commit their offenses upon the Sea and at many times murder and kill such persons being in the ship or boat where they commit their offenses which should bear witness against them in that behalf." The complaint is that pirates have been killing off the witnesses required for conviction under the Roman-canon law of proof. The statute does not say that torture has been used in Admiralty, but rather that the confession evidence permitted by Roman-canon law cannot be had without torture, hence the adoption of jury procedure under the Act.

The Statute of Pirates is the only occasion in which the English ever faced a clear-cut choice between the indigenous and the Roman-canon systems of proof; and in this ancient civilian jurisdiction, they substituted jury procedure.

6. E.g., Case 53.

7. As reported in the prefaces to the published series, registers are missing or imperfect for the following periods: Jul. 22, 1543–May 10, 1545; Jun. 15, 1553–Jul. 19, 1553; May 12, 1559–May 28, 1562; Sept. 6, 1562–c. Jan. 10, 1563; Jan. 23, 1563–Aug. 10, 1563; Aug. 10, 1563–Apr. 12, 1564; May 28, 1564–Nov. 4, 1564; Dec. 31, 1565–Oct. 8, 1566; May 3, 1567–May 24, 1570; Jun. 26, 1582–c. Feb. 19, 1586; Aug. 26, 1593–Oct. 1, 1595; Apr. 21, 1599–Jan. 23, 1600; Jan. 1, 1602–Apr. 30, 1613. APC 1:viii; 4:vii–viii; 7:vii–viii; 13:xxxvi; 25:vii; 29:vii; 32:viii; APC (Stuart) 1:v.

8. Listed by date with name or description of person probably ordered tortured:

1539: an unnamed Irish monk, LP 14(pt. 1):209.

1540: Gendon, LP 15:180.

1544: Octavian Bos, LP 19(pt. 1):340, 359, 365, 367, 577.

1569: Thomas Wood, SPD 1:348.

1583: Francis Throckmorton, SPD 2:130, 188.

1584: William Shelley and Jervais Pierpont, SPD 2:159.

9. Listed as in note 8:

1538: three unnamed thieves, LP 13(pt. 1):286–287.

1538: Anthony Browne, LP 13(pt. 2):12.

1546: Anne Askew, a legendary case, doubted by Jardine, at 65–66; compare *Dictionary of National Biography* (London, 1937–1938 ed.) I:662, 663 [hereafter cited as DNB].

1556: William Stanton, SPD 1:81.

Elton thinks he has identified other cases involving Cromwell's use of torture, although he does not report warrants. Elton, Policy and Police, supra note 3, at 145 n.4, 384 n.4. The evidence in one: a suspect "was twice interrogated . . . ; his second signature is much more shaky than the first, which suggests that torture was used on him." Id. at 145 n.4.

10. E.g., Case 42.

11. Cases 13–14, 34–35.

12. Discussed supra Chapter 2, text at note 127. For the same reason, the decision was made not to undertake for purposes of the present study an extensive search for further warrants in uncalendared or poorly calendared English manuscript collections. The printed sources allow us to determine the approximate dimensions of English torture practice; no amount of archive work would enable us to perfect the data base, or even materially to improve it.

13. John Gerard, *The Autobiography of a Hunted Priest* (P. Caraman, transl.) (New York, 1952 ed.). The book was written in Latin about 1609. Id. at xvii. This edition has been meticulously annotated to extrinsic sources.

14. APC 27:38.

15. See the "Venue" column in the table at the end of this Chapter (pp. 94–123).

16. Case 51. Since the warrant instructs the examiner to "use towards him the torture of the House," we suppose that torture in Bridewell precedes our record of it.

17. Case 55 in 1591 and Case 69 (Gerard) in 1597 are the exceptions.

18. Dr. Alan Borg, Assistant Keeper of the Armouries, suggests "that perhaps, with the Spanish War at its height, the issue and receipt of arms at the Tower made it an inconvenient place to use. State prisoners were of course still kept there." Letter to the author, Sept. 20, 1973.

19. See generally Alan Borg, *Torture and Punishment: Treasures of the Tower* (London, 1975).

20. Maitland I:49 (Pollock's chapter; his context was the punishment of slaves among the Anglo-Saxons).

21. E.g., Cases 2, 4, 12, 30, 31, 32, 36.

22. Case 46.

23. Supra note 16.

24. John Popham, Lord Chief Justice, was replaced with William

Waad, Clerk of the Council. On Jardine's misconstruction of this substitution, see Chapter 7, note 25.

25.   See Gerard, supra note 13, at 107–115, for his account of suffering the manacles.

26.   Also ordered in Case 7. See Borg, supra note 19, at 2.

In one of the parliamentary privilege disputes, the House of Commons directed the Lieutenant of the Tower to confine John Trenche, the Warden of the Fleet, in Little Ease to force him to honor its writ of habeas corpus to release a jailed member of Commons. *Journals of the House of Commons* I:207 (entry for May 11, 1604). The warden was resisting because he feared liability to the member's creditor; see Spedding's account in *The Letters and the Life of Francis Bacon* (J. Spedding, ed.) (London, 1868) III:172–176 [hereafter cited as Spedding]. The House also appointed a committee of inspection to visit the Tower "to inform themselves whether the Warden of the Fleet were committed Prisoner to the Place called Little Ease, according to his Judgment; and to make Report. . . ." Journals, supra, at I:208 (entry for May 11, 1604). At the next sitting of the House the committee reported that the Lieutenant had not confined the warden to Little Ease. The Lieutenant then uttered some justification of himself, apparently (in the language of a subsequent motion) that he had not had adequate time to "make clean and ready the Place called Little Ease (being reported to be very loathsome, unclean, and not used a long Time, either for Prison, or other cleanly Purpose). . . ." Id. at I:209 (entry for May 14, 1604). Commons nevertheless insisted that the warden be committed to Little Ease, id. at I:210. Two days later the Commons resolved to continue the warden's confinement in Little Ease, id. at I:211. The warden's letter of submission to the House is dated "From *Little Ease* in the Tower, 16 *May,* 1604," id. at I:213 (italics original); cf. id. at I:215.

Jardine's brief account of these proceedings, at 15 n.1, is misleading. He reports only the language about Little Ease being loathsome and unclean and attributes it to a committee of inquiry. He does not disclose that the House was trying to employ the dungeon. He leaves the impression that the House was disapproving of conditions in Little Ease.

Of course, we do not include this incident in our list of 81 torture cases, because the House of Commons was not using coercion to gather evidence or information.

27.   Discussed in the note to Case 41; cf. Borg, supra note 19, at 2–3, 8.

28.   Case 76. This famous manuscript is photographically reproduced in part in Borg, supra note 19, at 7.

29.   Cases 18, 21.

30.   The recordership was a waystation to the common law bench throughout the century 1540–1640. There is an authoritative list of the recorders and their terms of office: *Recorders of the City of London 1298–1850:*

Printed by Direction of the Court of Aldermen (London, 1850). We have
used this compilation to identify the incumbents by name in the table, as the
warrants usually commission the recorder by title of office alone. On the
judicial position of the recorder see infra Chapter 7, note 25.

    31. See infra Chapter 7, note 25.

    32. For Norton, see DNB 14:666–670; see also infra note 35. For
Topcliffe, see DNB 19:979–980. Young, although more ubiquitous in the
torture warrants, is less well known. He is identified in some volumes of the
APC as·a customs officer; cf. the warrant in Case 52. He is referred to as
"Mr. Justice Young" in the warrant in Case 54. A number of recognizances
taken by Young as JP for Middlesex, the earliest from Aug. 1582, appear in
Middlesex County Records (J. C. Jeaffreson, ed.) (London, 1886) I:133.

    The warrant in Case 58 lends implicit support to the view that Topcliffe
and Young were thought to be torture specialists. It authorizes the Attorney
General and the Solicitor General alone to examine the suspect Thomas
Clinton. But "if he shall not deal plainly and truly in declaring the truth of
those things ... , then you shall send for Mr. Topcliffe and Mr. Young,
esquires, and cause him to be by them removed unto Bridewell and there to
be put to the manacles and such torture as is there used...."

    33. Gerard, supra note 13, at 106; SPD 4:389.

    34. Jardine 64.

    35. The warrants occasionally display their unease about the use of
torture, reciting that suspects are being put to torture because they could not
be got to talk "by fair means." Case 47; cf. Case 62. When the use of torture
against Edmund Campion unsettled the Catholic community, a government
tract was produced asserting that torture had been applied mildly, to discover
plots and not on matters of conscience, and with probable cause. Anon., *A
Declaration of the Favourable Dealing of Her Majesties Commissioners,
Appointed for the Examination of Certaine Traytours, and of Tortures Un-
justly Reported to be Done upon Them for Matter of Religion* (London,
1583), reprinted in *A Collection of Scarce and Valuable Tracts ... Selected
from ... Libraries; Particularly That of the Late Lord [John] Somers*
(W. Scott, ed.) (2d ed., London, 1809) I:209.

    The tract has traditionally been attributed to William Cecil, Lord Burgh-
ley. "The only ground for ascribing [it] to Cecil seems to be that it was
joined with [another undoubtedly by him] in a Latin translation published in
1584. It was probably written by Thomas Norton, one of the commissioners
who examined Campion. Norton had been imprisoned in the Tower late in
the spring of 1581, because of indiscreet manifestations of puritanism in and
out of parliament. While in prison he was employed by Walsingham to write
an account of the torturing of Campion. He sent this to Walsingham on 27
March 1582. The argument in the [tract attributed to Cecil] followed this
account closely." Conyers Read, "William Cecil and Elizabethan Public

Relations,'' in *Elizabethan Government and Society: Essays Presented to Sir John Neale* (S. T. Bindoff et al., eds.) (London, 1961) 21, 37 (footnotes omitted). (I owe this reference to Professor G. R. Elton.) Norton's draft is reprinted in William D. Cooper, "Further Particulars of Thomas Norton," *Archaeologia* 36:105, 116 (1855).

36.   Cases 6, 11, 15, 21, 24, 34, 35.

37.   Murder: Cases 8, 16, 29, 36, 71; robbery, burglary and theft: Cases 5, 12, 13, 14, 18, 22, 25, 32, 37, 44, 51, 54, 65; counterfeiting: Cases 10, 20; and in Case 19 the "riot and disorder ... upon the goods and corn of Jane Stourton."

38.   We reckon among the state crimes several arguable cases, including four of theft touching royal interests: Cases 2, 9, 17, 70; also Case 4, which seems to have involved a search for plate forfeit to the crown; and Case 66, an investigation of the activities of a Gypsy band.

Five of the six apparently authoritative cases of torture for which evidence of warrants does not survive, supra note 8, also involved state crime.

39.   Gerard, supra note 13, at 65.

40.   27 Eliz. c. 2 (1584–1585).

41.   Gerard, supra note 13, at 107. See also Philip Caraman, *Henry Garnet (1555–1606) and the Gunpowder Plot* (London, 1964) 230ff.

42.   Spedding V:90–94. The results of the examination, as reported by Sir Ralph Winwood, one of the commissioners: "Upon these interrogatories, Peacham this day was examined before torture, in torture, between tortures, and after torture. Notwithstanding, nothing could be drawn from him, he still persisting in his obstinate and insensible denials, and former answers." Id. at 94; see generally DNB 15:576–578.

43.   Cro. Car. 125, 79 Eng. Rep. 711 (1615).

44.   Spedding 3:114.

45.   Raleigh tried it, Howell 2:1, 22 [1603]; so did Thomas Tonge, Howell 6:225, 259 [1662], cited by Wigmore III:§818, at 295 n.7.

46.   The only treason acquittal in the State Trials for the century 1540–1640 is Nicholas Throckmorton's case, Howell 1:869 [1544]. The ease with which a case could be trumped up, for example, against Campion or Raleigh, shows how well the crown could manipulate the ordinary criminal procedure without need of evidence gathered under torture.

Notes to the Table (pages 94–123)

Case 1.   Warrant: Proceedings, etc. (H. Nicolas, ed.), cited supra Chapter 6, note 1, at 7:83; cf. id. at 7:81, 194. Thwaytes is identified as "servant unto [blank] Shrington, page of the King's wardrobe of robes ...." He had already confessed the words charged against him and was being ordered tortured to reveal "of whom he had heard the things confessed." A later entry, dated May 25, 1541, records that he was released, "having a good lesson given him to use his tongue with more discretion hereafter." Id. at 194.

Case 2.   Warrant: LP 16:588. The document is a report from the Council in London to the Council with the King, reporting proceedings undoubtedly warranted by the former.

Case 3.   Warrant: LP 18(pt. 1):157; cf. id. at 18(pt. 1):35–36, 115, 134, 137–138.

Case 4.   Warrant: APC 3:106; cf. id. at 3:99. The examiners were searching for money supposedly hidden in Fowlkes' house. Fowlkes is reported accused by "one William Haldesworthe, lately executed at York," which suggests that the concealed trove may have been forfeit to the crown. The two examiners are listed as JPs for Norfolk as of 1547. *Calendar of the Patent Rolls 1547–1548* (London, 1924) 87.

Case 5.   Warrant: APC 3:230. Torture is only conditionally authorized. Hungerforde is directed to "proceed against [Reede] by the law, unless he be afraid of bearing in that behalf [*i.e.*, unless he doubts he has sufficient evidence to induce a jury to convict]; in which case he shall advertise and order shall be given that [Reede] may be sent up hither to be put to torment." We reckon Hungerforde as the commissioner to torture with hesitation; it seems he might not have been meant to conduct the examination under torture, but to decide whether to have it ordered.

Case 6.   Warrant: APC 3:407.

Case 7. Warrant: APC 4:171; cf. id. at 4:143, 154, 155, 336. The warrant does not disclose Holland's offense, but he appears to have been involved with one Thomas Thurland, who was being investigated "for certain seditious reports." Id. at 4:143.

Case 8.   Warrant: APC 4:201.

Case 9.   Warrant: APC 4:284; cf. id. at 4:287. Because the two men "obstinately refuse to confess the truth of their doings," they are ordered sent up "to the end [that] they may be here further examined and put to the torture, if need be, to the example of other[s]." It is not clear whether the Council thinks that the use of torture will serve a general deterrent purpose, in which case that fact would have had to be publicized; or whether it is the ultimate conviction of the men that will be "to the example of other[s]."

Case 10.   Warrant: APC 5:93. This is one of the few cases in which local officers are authorized to examine under torture locally. It seems quite improbable that the city of Bristol had its own rack, hence the term may already have become a metaphor for any mode of torture. The mayor is identified in William Adams, *Chronicle of Bristol* (Bristol, 1910 ed.) 103. It is there recorded that on April 4, 1555, "four men were hanged, drawn and quartered in Bristol for coining of money, viz: John Walton, Robert Haddy, Gilbert Sheath and John White."

Case 11.   Warrant: APC 5:145. North and others, as commissioners of gaol delivery for London, were instructed by the Council a few months earlier "to take pains in the examination of such offenders as are already committed to any prisons in London or thereabouts for Felony, and to make search for such as they shall suspect to be faulty herein . . . ." Id. at 5:103. If the warrant in Case 11 refers to that group of gaol delivery commissioners, it is a very ominous grant of general authority to torture in cases of ordinary felony. The text of the warrant in full: "A letter to the Lord North and the rest of the Commissioners for the examination of prisoners to bring such obstinate persons, as will not confess points wherein they are touched, to the tortures, and there to order them to their discretions. A letter to the Lieutenant of the Tower for the same purpose."

Case 12.   Warrant: APC 5:198. Mulcaster is identified as "servant to Dr. Canis, vehemently suspect for robbing his master . . . ." In Cases 12–15 we infer that the Tower was the venue because of the presence of Bedingfield, the Lieutenant, in the commission.

Case 13.   Warrant: APC 5:202. Curate was "vehemently suspected of robbing Mr. Kelleawaie," and was to be examined "according to such interrogatories as the said Mr. Kelleaway [sic] shall deliver unto [the commissioners] for that purpose . . . ."

Case 14.   Warrant: APC 5:202. The warrant appears immediately following that in Case 13, and reads in its entirety: "A like letter for to bring one Hugh of Warwick, suspected for horse stealing, to the rack and to do *ut supra*."

Case 15.   Warrant: APC 5:235–236.

Case 16.   Warrant: APC 5:289; cf. id. at 5:291. The second entry is dated June 23, two days after the torture warrant, and directs that Gill be "conveyed to Dorset where he committed the murder, to be there further ordered according to justice."

Case 17.   Warrant: APC 5:316; cf. id. at 6:7. The register entry notes that "the Keeper of the said prison is likewise written unto in that matter." That language is not clear enough for us to deem him a member of the examining commission. The warrant records that Taverner "will by no means hitherto declare where the [loot] is . . . , notwithstanding the matter is already confessed against him by two others . . . ." He was released in October 1556.

Case 18.   Warrant: APC 6:124; cf. id. at 6:127–128, 129, 135, 151–152, 251–252. Among those suspected, according to the later documents, were Edward Vaughn and one Bayneham, and they may have been tortured pursuant to the warrant. Warner, a former Lieutenant of the Tower who was later reappointed to the office under Elizabeth (DNB 20:849–850), was the robbery victim. Quaere whether the same grievance and the same Edward Vaughn are before the Council in 1565 in APC 7:149, 154, 156, 195.

Case 19.   Warrant: APC 6:130. St. John is not identified as Lord

Lieutenant in the warrant, but because it seems to have been directed to him in that capacity, we have interpolated the title on the table. The same document continues on to give him instructions on an unrelated matter—how to handle some Frenchmen who have settled in the county. The warrant is further discussed infra Chapter 7, note 19.

Case 20. Warrant A: APC 6:187; Warrant B: APC 6:193; cf. id. at 6:209–210, 247–248, 253–254, 258, 310–311. Warrant B directs the commissioners to examine Newporte as well as the servant, but it authorizes torture to be used only against the servant. In May 1558 the Council sent a letter "to the Lord Chief Justice and other the [sic] Justices of the King's Bench, remitting unto them one Edward Newporte, gent., remaining presently in the Tower, to be ordered in such sort as the laws will, for whose examinations taken since his imprisonment they be willed to call upon the Queen's Attorney [General] and Solicitor [General]." Two servants of Newporte's are mentioned in some of the later entries, Humfrey Hardeman and Roger Hall, but it is not discernible whether either was the servant referred to in the torture warrants.

Case 21. Warrant: APC 6:314; cf. id. at 6:323–324.

Case 22. Warrant: APC 7:66–67. The robbery was committed against "a widow called Bate in St. Ellyn's in London . . . ."

Case 23. Warrant: APC 7:222. The Council wanted Heath tortured to "declare the full truth why he wandereth abroad . . . ." Because the Council was involved it is likely that something more than vagabondage was at stake.

Case 24. Warrant: APC 7:319–320.

Case 25. Warrant: APC 7:324. Rice is described as a bucklermaker.

Case 26. Warrant: APC 7:367–368; cf. id. at 8:67–68. Andrews was suspected of the robbery and murder of Thomas Stover, his wife and family in Somerset. The warrant records that he "is vehemently suspected, and will hitherto confess nothing;" the second entry, dated February 1572, records that Andrews has confessed the crime. The case is further discussed supra Chapter 5, text at note 39.

Case 27. Warrant: APC 7:373; cf. SPD 1:385; 7:321, 356; Historical Manuscripts Commission, Calendar of the Manuscripts of the Marquis of Salisbury [Robert Cecil] (London, 1883ff) 1:473 [hereafter cited as HMC Cecil]. Felton was accused of "having of the printed Bull [excommunicating Elizabeth and deposing her as Queen] and speech [i.e., speaking] also with the Spanish Ambassador . . . ." The rack is not explicitly ordered, but Felton was to be "brought to the place of torture and so put in fear thereof," and if he remained "obstinate," the examiners were "to spare not to lay him upon it, to the end he may feel [the] smart and pains thereof . . . ." The rack must have been meant.

This John Felton is not to be confused with the assassin of the Duke of Buckingham, see infra Chapter 7, note 63.

Case 28. Warrant A: HMC Cecil 1:496; Warrant B: British Museum

Cotton MS. Caligula C. III, fol. 228ᵛ–229 ("By the Queen"). Jardine did not know the warrant to torture Bailly. Jardine's version of our Warrant B omits Sadler from the examining commission. Jardine 78–79. Jardine took his warrant from a similarly mistaken transcript of the Cotton MS. in *Original Letters, Illustrative of English History* (H. Ellis, ed.) (London, 1825 ed.) II:260–261 (Jardine cites the 1824 edition). Cf. HMC Cecil 1:495–578 passim; APC 8:70, 118, 149–150, 171, 242, 271, 325; SPD 7:54–56, 256, 377, 415, 420–421.

Case 29. Warrant: APC 8:94; cf. id. at 8:91, 92, 96, 105, 121, 142. Browne was "vehemently suspected," id. at 8:91, of the murder of one Saunders, a London merchant. The warrant shows special solicitude for "the brethren and friends of Saunders," who are permitted "to be present at the examination, and to [ad]minister interrogatories . . . ." The warrant is dated April 1; on April 14 the Council sent "for a physician . . . to look unto [Browne] . . . ." Id. at 8:96.

The Council's investigation appears to have elicited the complicity of Saunders' wife, who had been convicted and condemned by May 12 when the Council ordered the sheriffs of London to proceed to her execution. Id. at 8:105.

Case 30. Warrant: APC 8:319; cf. id. at 8:261, 322–323, 340–341; SPD 1:470. The investigation concerned "letters and writings" from Nedeham to the Archbishop of Canterbury. The Council wanted to know "the truth who set him on," for which purpose it authorized the commissioners as "a *post script* to bring him to the rack without stretching his body . . . ."

Case 31. Warrant: APC 8:336. Cicking was "a bookbinder in [St.] Paul's Churchyard, lately committed to the Tower, upon such matter as Mr. Secretary Walsingham was privy of." We infer that the offense concerned affairs of state ("sedition" in the table) because Walsingham was directing the investigation and the suspect was in the printing trades.

Case 32. Warrant: APC 9:222. Wells was "lately apprehended and vehemently suspected of the robbery not long since committed upon the Knight Marshall [Sir George Cary?] as he went to London, which the said Wells denied, although he is found seized with some part of the spoil then taken away . . . ." Some phrase ordering a mode of torture has probably been omitted from the register, which directs the commissioners, "in case he will not confess the deed and who were his partners, they should bring him in fear thereof . . . ."

Case 33. Warrant A: APC 10:94; Warrant B: id. at 10:111; cf. id. at 10:92; SPD 1:655; 7:532. The case originated in a proceeding of the court of High Commission. When "matter of High Treason against her Majesty's person" appeared, the High Commission referred the case to the Council, which called in the Attorney General. The Council wanted the Attorney General "to acquaint the Lord Chief Justice [of Queen's Bench] therewith,

and presently to give order that the said Sherwood be this Term arraigned
and proceeded against according to the laws . . . ." Further investigation was
undertaken only to attempt to identify accomplices. Between the first and the
second warrants Sherwood retracted his former confession, in which he had
"affirmed her Majesty to be an heretic and usurper . . . ." The second warrant to rack him, however, continues to speak only of discovering accomplices.

Case 34. Warrant: APC 10:373; cf. SPD 1:628; HMC Cecil 13:160–
161.

Case 35. Warrant: APC 10:373–374. Cases 34 and 35 are contained in
the same register entry, but appear to deal with unrelated offenders and
offenses. Sanforde is "deeply suspected to be privy to the dealings of John
Prescall," whereas Harding, the culprit in Case 34, is ordered racked "to
confess the truth of those things wherewith he is to be charged . . . ."

Case 36. Warrant: APC 11:157–158; cf. id. at 11:14, 101–102, 185–
186; SPD 1:627. Torture was ordered after "Mr. Browne and other Justices
[i.e., JPs] of Surrey" reported to the Council that their examinations of the
suspects had yielded "nothing of moment . . . that may enforce their condemnation . . . ." The suspects were accused of murdering Richard Mel-
lershe of Dounford, Surrey. They were to be "terrified by showing unto
them the Rack or otherwise, . . . to bring them to confess the fact, that
thereupon (sufficient matter appearing) they may be further proceeded withall, according to law." For other activity of Browne and Levesey as Surrey
JPs see *The Loseley Manuscripts* (A. J. Kempe, ed.) (London, 1836) 249–
250.

Case 37. Warrant: APC 12:275–276. The three examiners were Norfolk JPs. John H. Gleason, *The Justices of the Peace in England 1558–1640*
(Oxford, 1969) 148, So too was Sir Drew Drury, whose house had been
burglarized. The warrant recites that the house "hath of late been robbed by
certain lewd persons with the privity of one Humfrey, a boy dwelling in that
house, who being since committed and examined touching the said robbery,
refuseth to discover the rest of his [ac]complices . . . ." The examiners are
authorized "by some slight kind of torture, such as may not touch the loss of
any limb, as by whipping, [to] wring from him the knowledge of the persons
and the manner of the robbery, that thereupon order may be taken for their
apprehension and punishment according to the laws . . . ."

Case 38. Warrant: APC 12:294–295; cf. SOD 1:691; 2:24, 62, 223,
427. The three suspects had "lately arrived within the realm from Rome and
other places beyond the seas, with intent to pervert and seduce her Majesty's
subjects . . . ." Hart and Bosgrave were Jesuits; see DNB 9:61; 2:882.

Case 39. Warrant: APC 13:37–38; cf. SPD 2:22, 48. Briant, a Jesuit,
was convicted and executed with Campion. DNB 2:1217.

Case 40. Warrant: APC 13:98. The Bishop of Chester reported to the

Council the girl's "two feigned visions . . . put into writing and scattered abroad among the Popish and ignorant people of his Diocese . . . ." In order to discover "the inventors thereof," the Council authorized the Bishop to cause "the maid (in case by fair means she shall not confess the same) to be secretly whipped, and so brought to declare the truth of this imposture . . . ."

Case 41. Warrant APC 13:147; cf. id. at 13:168. Fenton, Secretary of the Council in Ireland, was "appointed . . . for the examining of Thomas Myagh heretofore committed to his charge, and to charge him with such matters as he hath heretofore denied, and now are certified from thence [i.e., Ireland] to be verified by deposition of witnesses . . . ."

Jardine, at 83–85, prints two letters to Walsingham from Hopton, the Lieutenant of the Tower, and Dr. John Hammond (examiner in Cases 39, 42 & 43) dated March 10 and March 17, 1581. Jardine found the letters among the State Papers; they may since have disappeared, as they are not indexed in the SPD (or in the British Museum calendars). In the first, Hopton and Hammond report that they have twice examined him, forbearing to put him to the torture of Skevington's Irons because Walsingham has instructed them to examine him secretly, whereas that mode of torture requires "the presence and aid of one of the jailors all the time . . . ; and besides, we find the man so resolute, as in our opinions little will be wrung out of him but by some sharper torture." The second letter reports that they have put him to Skevington's Irons, "yet can we get from him no further matter . . . ." The warrant in the Council register, dated July 30, orders him racked. Myagh inscribed his fate in verse on the wall of his cell in the Tower: see Jardine 30; Alan Borg, *Torture & Punishment: Treasures of the Tower* 2–3 (London, 1975).

Case 42. Warrant A: APC 13:144–155; Warrant B: id. at 13:171–172; Warrant C: id. at 13:249. Numerous entries in APC 12–13 and SPD 1–2 & 12 concern the investigation of Campion and his associates. See generally Richard Simpson, *Edmund Campion: A Biography* (London, 1867) 218ff.

Case 43. Warrant: APC 13:400–401; cf. SPD 2:57, 153, 243, 249. Owen is styled in the warrant "Mr. Owen of Lincoln's Inn." Alfield, "a Seminary Priest, . . . is supposed [to be] able to discover many matters touching the practices and proceedings of the Jesuits and Seminary Priests within the Realm . . . ." He was convicted and executed three years later for publishing seditious books. DNB 1:282.

Case 44. Warrant A: APC 14:56; Warrant B: id. at 14:62; Warrant C: id. at 14:107–108. Warrant A identifies the crime as "the robbing of the Lady Cheek," and directs the Lieutenant and Messrs. MacWilliams and Young to examine Beaumond under torture "of any robberies by him and others in any sort committed . . . ." We infer that this investigation led to Warrant B a week later to the same commissioners to examine Wakeman. The entry we treat as Warrant C is not a warrant to torture, but an order reciting that torture of the three men had been ordered and conducted, and that they were now to be transferred to Newgate to await trial "according to the quality of their offenses . . . ." We treat this as evidencing an unrecorded warrant to torture the third man, Pynder.

Case 45. Warrant: APC 14:271–272. For earlier and later orders concerning some of these suspects, who may not have been related, see id. at 14:214, 258; 16:207; 17:311–312; 18:356; 19:308–309, 394; SPD 2:35, 83, 242, 346, 350, 351, 373, 484, 544; 12:152.

Case 46. Warrant: APC 15:51; cf. SPD 2:484. The suspect "stood charged with certain matter concerning her Majesty's State and person which he did obstinately refuse to confess . . . ."

Case 47. Warrant: APC 15:330; cf. SPD 2:484. The suspects were "charged with disobedience, misbehavior and practices against the State . . . ."

Case 48. Warrant: APC 15:334–335; cf. SPD 2:399. Torture was authorized upon interrogatories "concerning her Majesty or the State . . . ." Asheton was "a companion . . . greatly trusted by Sir William Stanley," who had betrayed his English command in the Netherlands to the Spanish in 1587. See DNB 18:969, 970–971.

Case 49. Warrant APC 15:365. Stoker had just "come from the enemy out of the Low Countries . . . ; forasmuch as he was known to have been a pensioner of the King of Spain's, and one evil affected to her Majesty and the present State, it was to be probably conjectured that his repair into this Realm was for some secret practice or other notable mischief by him to be wrought . . . ."

Case 50. Warrant: APC 16:273; cf. id. at 18:387. Winslade, apparently an Englishman, had been "taken in one of the Spanish ships [i.e., of the Armada] . . . ." The Council ordered Winslade released five months later, persuaded "that he was brought hither against his will . . . ." Winslade had by then "been often examined . . . also upon the rack . . . ." Id. at 18:387.

Case 51. Warrant: APC 17:310; cf. id. at 17:233. This is the first warrant to direct torture at Bridewell, although the instruction to the examiner to "use towards him the torture of the House" suggests that the practice was not new. The warrant describes the offense being investigated as "the robbery committed on our verie good Lord the Lord Willoughby of his plate . . . ." The crime was in fact burglary; an earlier entry records that the plate was "stolen out of his house," id. at 17:233, not taken from his person.

Case 52. Warrant: APC 18:62; cf. id. at 18:59. Hodgkins and his two assistants were "lately apprehended by the Earl of Derby, near unto Manchester in the county of Lancaster, where they had begun to print a very seditious book penned by him that termeth himself Martin Marprelate . . . ." The warrant runs initially to the first three examiners alone; but "[i]f Mr

Fortescue be not at London then may they call unto them for their assistance in this service Richard Young the Customer.'' If torture at Bridewell is ineffective, the examiners are authorized to adjourn to the Tower, presumably in order to use the rack.

As the Marprelate investigation advanced, different and larger commissions were appointed to examine other suspects. Id. at 18:225–226, 227; 19:292–293. These included the civilians Drs. William Awbrey and William Lewin together with Edmund Anderson, Chief Justice of the Court of Common Pleas and Francis Gawdy, Justice of Queen's Bench. An undated examination of Hodgkins in which Gawdy participated is transcribed in William Pierce, *An Historical Introduction to the Marprelate Tracts* (London, 1908) 333–335. Pierce also reprints, id. at 335–339, an examination of Syms and Thomlyn, dated December 10, 1589, taken by Aubry, Lewin, Anderson and Gawdy, together with, inter alia, Francis Walsingham and John Fortescue. (I owe this reference to E. G. W. Bill, Librarian of Lambeth Palace Library.) In 1591 Hodgkins is recorded among a group of three Puritans ''who are condemned of Felony, [and] whose time of execution as it is now appointed draweth very near . . . .'' APC 21:130. Syms (and therefore probably Thomlyn as well) was released; see Pierce, supra, at 204–205. On Syms' place in the history of printing, see W. Craig Ferguson, *Valentine Simmes: Printer to Drayton, Shakespeare . . . and Other Elizabethans* (Charlottesville, 1968).

Case 53.   Warrant: SPD 2:646; cf. id. at 12:166–167, 174, 314; APC 18: 338, 378. The warrant, issued by the Council, describes Christopher Bayles as ''a seminary priest'' and John Bayles as ''his brother.'' The warrant is not recorded in the Privy Council register, although there is an entry dated the same day to the Attorney and Solicitor General (John Popham and Thomas Egerton) ''signifying that they shall receive from Mr. Topcliffe certain informations against two or three Jesuits or Seminari[an]s, whereof when they shall have considered . . . [and] confer[red] with the Lord Chief Justice of her Majesty's Bench and with the rest of the Justices of that Court, and finding the case of the Jesuits within the compass of the laws, they are required to cause them forthwith to be brought to their trial this Term . . . .'' Christopher Bayles is recorded condemned in an entry dated three weeks later.

Case 54.   Warrant: APC 19:69–70. The warrant is undated; we infer the date on the table from the sequence of the register entry, although a date one day later would also be possible. The warrant is addressed to ''Mr. Justice Young.'' It commends him for ''the paines you have taken in the examining of the four persons lately committed by you unto Newgate upon suspicion of a robbery lately done at Wickham in Kent . . . .'' Torture is authorized at Bridewell because the suspects refuse to confess although ''the proofs are so manifest and evident against them . . . .'' Young is to reexamine them ''with the assistance of some of the Justices" to bring them "to confess the whole truth of that robbery and who were the rest of their [ac]complices . . . ." Torture is especially recommended for Browne, "a butcher, who knoweth the whole society of these wicked disposed persons."

The "Mr. Justice Young" must have been Richard Young, the quasi-professional torturer. He was a JP for Middlesex. See supra Chapter 6, note 32. There was no Young among the common law judges at this time. Nor is there a Young among the Kent JPs in the rosters for 1584 and 1608 published in Gleason, supra note to Case 37, at 16–17, 126–128 (excluding John Young, Bishop of Rochester, who would never be styled merely "Mr. Justice"). The phrase "the Justices" must refer to Richard Young's colleagues in the Middlesex commission of the peace. It is unthinkable that someone like Young would be authorized to beckon common law judges.

It seems likely that the William Browne, butcher, who was ordered tortured in the present case of robbery, was not the same William Browne, yeoman, who together with one Thomas Best, was referred to in a register entry the previous week, April 9, 1590, as having been lately "indicted and condemned for a robbery committed in the county of Middlesex." Id. at 19:38–39. This had happened "at the last Sessions holden at Newgate," i.e., at Quarter Sessions before the JPs. The entry records that a group of five knights and esquires were directed to enquire whether "such as gave evidence against" Browne and Best had perjured themselves. It is thinkable that this investigation, undertaken on behalf of Browne, actually cast him into suspicion of having committed the robbery in Kent referred to in the torture warrant of April 18, 1590. We think, however, that the William Browne of our Case 54 was not the culprit in the earlier case because a further order dated May 3, 1590 was made, looking to the exoneration of the former Browne and his codefendant Best, id. at 19:101; they were pardoned on October 10, 1590; SPD 2:692.

Case 55.   Warrant: APC 20:204; cf. id. at 20:148–149; 21:247. The warrant identifies Beesley as "a Seminary priest" and Humberson as "his familiar companion and confederate . . . . " The examiners were to imprison them in Little Ease if they refuse "to declare the truth of such things as shall be laid to their charge in her Majesty's behalf . . . ." Beesley was sent for trial six months later, June 29, 1591, id. at 21:247. He was executed on July 2, 1591, convicted of violating the statute of 27 Eliz. c. 2 (1584–1585), which made it treason for Jesuits or other Catholic priests to enter or remain in the realm. DNB 2:125. Humberson, styled as a recusant, was still in the Tower in April 1594. SPD 3:484.

Case 56.   Warrant: APC 21:300; cf. id. at 21:293–294, 297 (earlier examinations of Hacket and others), 319, 325–326, 361; SPD 3:75–76. Hacket's case is discussed supra Chapter 6, text at note 44; cf. DNB 8:864.

Case 57.   Warrant: APC 22:39–40; cf. id. at 21:426; 22:15; SPD 2:165. White is described as "a Seminary Priest," Lassy as "a disperser and distributor of letters to papists and other evil affected subjects . . . ."

Case 58.   Warrant: APC 22:41–42. Initially, the Attorney General and the Solicitor General are alone instructed to examine Clinton about matters unrecorded. But "if he shall not deal plainly and truly in declaring the truth of those things . . . , then you shall send for Mr. Topcliffe and Mr. Young, esquires, and cause him to be by them removed unto Bridewell and there to be put to the manacles and such torture as is there used . . . ." The guarded language of the commission and the presence of the two law officers has led us to infer that some sort of sedition was at issue.

Case 59.   Warrant: APC 22:512. Edmondes, an "Irishman, standeth at this present charged very deeply with matters concerning the State and . . . it seemeth there is good proof against him . . . , notwithstanding he obstinately refuses to confess the same."

Case 60.   Warrant: APC 24:56; cf. id. at 24:10, 26–27, 50; SPD 3:534. Urmeston "is a very dangerous person and able to discover much for her Majesty's service . . . ." Bagshaw, "late servant to one Bell, a Seminary priest," and Aysh, "late servant to one Richard Sampson *alias* Gayle, also a Seminary priest," the Council had sent up from Derby for examination.

Case 61.   Warrant: APC 24:187. The mayor had apprehended someone suspected of writing "a lewd and vile ticket or placard set up upon some post in London [urging] the apprentices . . . to attempt some violence on the strangers . . . ." The warrant instructs the mayor to inquire of the suspect "who were any way privy to the same and did give him advice or encouragement . . . ." If "he will not by fair means be brought to utter his knowledge, we think it convenient he shall be punished by torture used in like cases and so compelled to reveal the same." Sir John Spencer is identified as the Lord Mayor in 1593 in [Corporation of the City of London,] *Index to the . . . Remembrancia 1579–1664* (London, 1878) 447 n.1.

Case 62.   Warrant: APC 24:222. Alderman Buckle is identified as Sir Cuthbert Buckle, vintner, in the *Index* cited supra, note to Case 61, at 315 n.1. This case may well be connected to Case 61. It concerns "divers lewd and malicious libels set up within the city of London . . . ." The culprits were unknown; the warrant authorizes the commissioners to search for them, and to use torture on those found "duly to be suspected [who] shall refuse to confess the truth . . . ."

Case 63.   Warrant: APC 25:73; cf. id. at 26:10. Colford, "lately apprehended," had "brought certain seditious books hither from beyond the seas into the realm . . . ." He lodged with Foulkes, a tailor, in Fleet Street "both now and at other times when he came over hither from the parts beyond the seas." Examination under torture is being ordered because "these parties, having been often examined by the Lord Chief Justice of her Majesty's Bench [John Popham], will not by good and fair means be brought to reveal those things within their knowledge concerning her majesty and the State . . . ." Colford was released on bonds seven months later, having revealed nothing of note under torture.

Case 64. Warrant: APC 25:179–180. Hardie, a Frenchman aged twenty, lately apprehended, had "come into the realm for no good purpose, as may be conjectured, for that there have been found about him secretly sowed [i.e., sewn] up in his dublett divers letters and memorials containing matters of great suspicion, which he refuseth to disclose."

Case 65. Warrant: APC 25:251–252; cf. id. at 25:278–279; SPD 4:378. Hodges had committed several burglaries in the royal court and elsewhere, including one on the court chamber of Sir Henry Bagnall, Marshall of Ireland. Although there was already "much matter fit to be prosecuted and punished according to law," torture was ordered to discover "what is become of the hundred pounds hid [in] the ground . . . ." In the second register entry a few days later, the Council was intervening to require the sheriffs of London to abandon their claim to the money and return it to Bagnall.

Case 66. Warrant: APC 26:325. A group of eighty Gypsies gathered in Northamptonshire were apprehended and "some of the ringleaders" sent to London for examination "to bring them to reveal their lewd behavior, practices and ringleaders . . . ." By statute it was a felony for Gypsies to remain in England. 1& 2 P. & M. c. 4 (1554–1555); 5 Eliz. c. 20 (1562–1563).

Case 67. Warrant: APC 26:373–374; cf. id. at 26:364, 365–366, 383, 398, 412–413, 455; SPD 4:296 (wrong date), 316–320, 323–324, 342–345; HMC Cecil 7:49–50. The five men "intended to make a rising" in Oxfordshire. The torture warrant was issued after the plot was detected and the men apprehended by the Lord Lieutenant and other Oxfordshire JPs, whose examinations are calendared in SPD 4:316–320. The torture warrant was meant to discover collaborators. This rising was held treasonable under the statute of 13 Eliz. c. 1 (1571). Pop. 122, 79 Eng. Rep. 1227; 2 And. 66, 123 Eng. Rep. 549 (1597) (cited, Jardine 42 n.1).

Case 68. Warrant: APC 26:457; cf. SPD 3:202–203 (dated 1592); HMC Cecil 7:95–96. Thomson, "lately apprehended," is "a very lewd and dangerous person that is charged to have a purpose to burn her Majesty's ships . . . ." The examiners were to inquire "by whom he hath been moved thereunto and who are privy or partakers to his said intended purposes . . . ."

Case 69. Warrant: APC 27:38; cf. APC 28:455–456; SPD 4:7, 8, 39, 389 (Gerard's examination); 12:410; HMC Cecil 6:311–313. The warrant is reproduced, supra Chapter 6, text at note 14; cf. Chapter 6, note 13.

Case 70. Warrant: APC 28:165. The large panel of examiners is qualified by a quorum clause permitting "any two of them" to conduct the examination, which suggests that the Council simply authorized a number of thinkable examiners without much caring which of them ultimately exercised

the commission. Although "detected for stealing a standish of her Majesty by examination of witnesses, . . . yet [Travers] still persisted in obstinate denial. . . ." He is ordered tortured to "declare the truth . . . ."
Case 71. Warrant: APC 28:187; cf. HMC Cecil 7:392. The case is discussed in Chapter 7, text at notes 48–49.
Case 72. Warrant: APC 28:406–407; cf. id. at 28:417; SPD 5:78, 134–135; 12:408; HMC Cecil 11:137; 15:34–35, 119–120. Thomas, "a lewd fellow" lately apprehended "coming out of Scotland . . . is charged with matters concerning greatly the Estate. . . ." He was put to death under James in 1603.
Case 73. Warrant: APC 29:428. The warrant seems to have been requested by the examiners, who "last night apprehended" the two suspects "that are supposed to be privy unto some dangerous practice against the person of her Majesty and the State. . . ." Torture is authorized "to make them particularly discover and declare the truth of the said practice. . . ."
Case 74. Warrant: APC 31:281. Waad and Fowler are identified as justices of the peace for Middlesex. Howson, "a young stripling" and "servant to a scrivener dwelling in the Strand," had been previously examined regarding "railing [i.e., abusive] and scandalous libels . . . written and dispersed by him. And because it appeareth that his later examinations are contrary to his former confessions, and there is great likelihood that he [had accomplices in] the dispersing of divers seditious libels," torture is authorized to force him to identify them.
Case 75. Warrant A: calendared in SPD 8:4 (no. 30), transcribed in Jardine 103–104; Warrant B: calendared in SPD 8:4 (no. 41), transcribed in Jardine 104–106; cf. SPD 8:6, HMC Cecil 15:53. Warrant B, a day later than Warrant A, substitutes Waad for Popham in the commission and increases the quorum from two to three. May, servant to the Lord Chamberlain, called the new King a Papist, Jardine 46. Both warrants seek a confession; Warrant B says that he ought to be made "not only to confess plainly those heinous speeches he used, but to make true and plain declaration of the cause that moved him to utter the same; of whom he hath heard any such speeches, with whom he hath had any conference touching such matters, and such like questions. . . ." The case is discussed infra Chapter 7, note 25.
Case 76. Warrant: SPD 8:241 ("The King to the Lords Commissioners [for the Plot]"). A portion is photographically reproduced in Borg, supra note to Case 41, at 7. The Lords Commissioners are given in Samuel R. Gardiner, What [the] Gunpowder Plot Was (London, 1897), 24–25. Other documents: SPD 8:239ff, 247 (examination under torture), 291, 292; HMC Cecil 17:479, 502, 514, 527–528. Jardine discussed the case, at 47–50, but did not reproduce the warrant or include it in his numbered series.
Case 77. Warrant: APC (Stuart) 2:17–18; cf. id. at 1:653–654, 660; 2:59, 61–62, 256, 257; SPD 9:263, 269, 270 (the torture warrant whose

issuance is recorded in the Privy Council register), 273, 275, 279, 305, 306, 344, 357. The case is discussed in Chapter 6, text at note 42, and in Chapter 7, text at note 59, where other references are cited.

Case 78. Warrant: APC (Stuart) 5:137; cf. SPD 10:125. The case is discussed in Chapter 7, text at note 60.

Case 79. Warrant: APC (Stuart) 6:113; cf. id. at 112, 113; SPD 10:336. Crasfield, a "base . . . fellow," predicted a rebellion.

Case 80. Warrant: APC (Stuart) 8:452; cf. id. at 434–435, 449, 452; 9:31; 11:146, 320, 488–489; 12:6; SPD 11:517. The case is discussed in Chapter 7, text at note 62.

Case 81. Warrant: *Calendar of State Papers, Domestic Series, of the Reign of Charles I,* supra Chapter 6, note 2, at 16:191–192; cf. id. at 16:161–162, 210; *Privy Council Registers . . . in Facsimile,* supra Chapter 6, note 1, at 10:490. The case is discussed in Chapter 7, text at note 40, where other references appear.

Chapter Seven

1. Warrants in the hands of Elizabeth, James, and Charles survive in Cases 28, 76, 81.

2. Sir Edward Coke, *The Third Part of the Institutes of the Laws of England* (London, 1797 ed.) *35.

3. Blackstone IV:321.

4. But see text at note 38 and note 38 regarding the Council of Wales. In the registers the earlier warrants are often called "letters." We take it this is not a matter of any significance.

5. Jardine 68.

6. *An Exposition of the Kinges Prerogative* (London, 1573 ed.).

7. For a bibliography on the contemporary pamphlet war concerning the torture and trial of Edmund Campion, discussed supra Chapter 6, note 35, see Richard Simpson, *Edmund Campion: A Biography* (London, 1867) 349–353. See supra Chapter 6, note 45, for references to claims of torture made by State Trial defendants. James I advertised in an account published in his lifetime that Guy Fawkes had been threatened with torture when he refused to identify his accomplices. Howell 2:159, 201–202; another contemporary tract is reprinted id. at 2:215. See infra note 35 for Selden's published remark.

8. "Cases of the King's Prerogatives," in *The Works of Francis Bacon* (J. Spedding et al., eds.) VII:775–778.

9. Spedding IV:280.

10. Cases 67, 68, 69, 72, 77. Bacon was also instrumental in instigating the use of torture in Case 78, infra note 61.

11. The principle was formulated both substantively and procedurally:

"The king can do no wrong." Blackstone I:238. "[N]o court can have jurisdiction over him." Id. at I:235.

12. Cases 72, 81.

13. APC 11:320; cf. SPD 11:517.

14. APC 11:488–489. On conspiracy and false accusation as a head of Star Chamber jurisdiction, see William Hudson, *A Treatise on the Court of Star Chamber* [*temp. Chas. I*], printed in *Collectanea Juridica* (F. Hargrave, ed.) (London, 1792) II:104–107. The recently published *List and Index to the Proceedings in Star Chamber for the Reign of James I* (T. G. Barnes, ed.) (Chicago, 1975) does not reach 1628, date of the reference in this case.

15. The draftsmanship of some of the earlier warrants was sloppier; although particular offenders were meant, they were not always precisely described.

16. Text at note 38.

17. Holdsworth V:185; Sir Almeric Fitzroy, *The History of the Privy Council* (London, 1928) 122; James Williams, "Torture," Encyclopedia Britannica (11th ed., New York, 1910–1911) 27:72, 75; Leonard W. Levy, *Origins of the Fifth Amendment* (New York, 1968) 34–35.

18. G. R. Elton, *The Tudor Constitution* (Cambridge, 1965) 170 n.1.

19. See, e.g., Hudson's authoritative treatise on Star Chamber procedure, supra note 14. There may have been instances in which information gathered by torture ultimately figured in Star Chamber proceedings. The warrant in Case 19 (1557) directs Lord St. John, Lord Lieutenant for Dorset, to use torture to identify, apprehend, and indict the persons responsible "for the riot and disorder of late committed upon the goods and corn of Jane Stourton," and also "to signify the same with the examinations he shall take of them into the Star Chamber at the beginning of the next Term," presumably in aid of restitutionary remedies there.

It is crucial to bear in mind that Star Chamber lacked capital jurisdiction, and in England (as on the Continent) torture was used only in capital cases: felony and state crime. The only seeming exception among our eighty-one English cases is this Case 19, and here too the "riot and disorder" may have involved grand larceny or some other common law felony. See Hudson, supra note 14, at 224–225, for a catalog of Star Chamber sanctions, all noncapital. The "jurisdiction [of] this court . . . in punishment," says Coke, "extendeth not to any offense that concerns the life of man or obtruncation of any member, the ears only excepted, and those rarely and in most heinous and detestable offenses." Sir Edward Coke, *The Fourth Part of the Institutes of the Laws of England* (London, 1797 ed.) *66.

20. Anthony Granucci, "'Nor Cruel and Unusual Punishments Inflicted': The Original Meaning," *California Law Review* 57:839, 848. There is evidence that Archbishop John Whitgift employed torture in his

capacity as Vice President of the Council in Wales before he took over the Court of High Commission; see infra note 38.

21. Supra Chapter 6, note 5.

22. The Duke of Exeter "and others, intended to have brought in the civil laws. For a beginning whereof, the duke . . . first brought into the Tower the rack or brake allowed in many cases by the civil law . . . ." Coke, supra note 2, at *35; see supra, Chapter 6, note 5.

23. Blackstone, IV:320–321.

24. Holdsworth V:184–187, 194–195.

25. The prerogative theory and the reception theory are intertwined in the literature (and have been since Coke's *Third Institute*). Both notions put distance between the common law and the torture practice that occurred. Jardine's interpretation wanders indistinctly from prerogative (Jardine 58–64) to reception (id. at 64–67) to prerogative (id. at 67–70).

Jardine was misled by an apparently fortuitous lacuna of his sources to make a wholly spurious argument in support of the prerogative theory; had he known the true state of the matter, he would surely have viewed the entire question of prerogative and reception differently. Although Jardine knew about two-thirds of our eighty-one torture cases, it happens that he identified only two of those in which common law judges were named in the examining commissions. Cases 20, 24, 26, 29, and 36, in which seven judges of the common law courts were in the commissions, Jardine did not know. Either the subsequently published Privy Council registers were not then to hand in manuscript, or he did not read them with care.

Jardine gave great emphasis to the "circumstance" he thought he had detected "that the torture warrants were not directed to the common-law judges . . . ." Jardine 62. He did not take note of the involvement of the Lord Chief Justice in Cases 63, 76 and 80 (see our notes to those cases). Jardine thought to distinguish the two cases in which the warrants expressly named the Lord Chief Justice. In Case 75, he noted, the first warrant was superseded a day later by a second warrant that did not name the Lord Chief Justice. "I think there is reason to believe that [the first] warrant was never actually executed." Id. at 45. That left Case 77, which Jardine dismissed lamely. "I have not been able to discover any evidence of the actual application of torture in the case . . . ." Id. at 52. (Such evidence is always rare; in this case there is some: SPD 10:125).

Jardine also did not ask himself whether he ought to classify the Recorder of London as a species of common law judge. Jardine surely knew that "[t]he *Recorder* of *London*, is one of the Justices of *Oyer* and *Terminer*; and a Justice of Peace of the *Quorum*, for putting the Laws in Execution . . . . And being the Mouth of the said City, he learnedly delivers the Sentences and Judgments of the Courts therein . . . ." Giles Jacob, *A New Law Diction-ary* (4th ed., London, 1739) (unpaginated; see under alphabetical entry

"Recorder") (italics original). See also supra Chapter 6, note 30.

We cannot really fault Jardine for his misreading of the evidence, which was set in motion by a dearth of other evidence for which he was probably not to blame. He would not have drawn such sharp lines between law and prerogative, and between common law and Roman law, had he known that common law judges and recorders sat in a quarter of the identifiable cases (20 of 81). (Curiously, no judge overlapped the recorder in these examining commissions; where the one is named the other is not.)

26. Jardine 64.

27. Case 16, "one of the Masters of Requests"; Cases 17, 21, Thomas Martin; Case 28, Thomas Wilson; Cases 45, 52, Ralph Rokeby; Cases 55, 57, Giles Fletcher. The four named examiners are identified as Masters of Requests in their DNB biographies, respectively 12:1205; 21:603, 604; 17:152; 7:299, 300. See generally regarding the English civilians Brian P. Levack, *The Civil Lawyers in England: 1603–1641* (Oxford, 1973).

28. Of the four named Masters of Requests, supra note 27, Mr. G. D. Squibb has identified three in the register of the members of Doctors' Commons. Cf. supra page 93. Ralph Rokeby appears not to have been a member.

29. Cases 39, 42, 43, John Hammond; Case 77, Julius Caesar; cf. DNB 8:1131; 3:656. Hammond also figures in the torture proceedings in Case 41, discussed supra in the note to Case 41, for which we lack the warrant. Hammond and Caesar appear in the register of Doctors' Commons.

30. Of course there were others with some Roman law training, e.g., Sir Thomas Smith.

31. Case 16 is the exception.

32. Hammond in Cases 39, 42 and 43; and Rokeby, the nonmember of Doctors' Commons, in Cases 45 and 52. See the DNB entries for both, cited supra notes 27, 29.

33. Jardine 64.

34. See Schnapper, Peines I, at 41:249 & n.70.

35. *Table Talk of John Selden* (F. Pollock, ed.) (London, 1927 ed.) 133: "The Rack is used no where as in England. In other Countries 'tis used in Judicature, when there is a *semi-plena probatio,* a half proof against a man, then to see if they can make it full, they rack him to try if he will Confess. But here in England, they take a man & rack him I do not know why, nor when, not in time of Judicature, but when somebody bids."

36. *A Declaration of the Favourable Dealing, etc.,* cited supra Chapter 6, note 35, at I:212.

37. See "Torture Warrants by Year," supra page 128. See also supra Chapter 6, note 7.

38. PRO:SP 46/3, loose document, fol. 5, §10; a title is inscribed on the rear cover in a later hand: "Wales—Instructions given by Queen

Elizabeth to her Council within her Dominion & Principality of
Wales ... 1602." There is another copy of the document in the same box.
This class of "State Papers Domestic: Supplementary" is uncalendared. (I
owe this reference to Professor J. S. Cockburn and Dr. J. A. Guy.) Author-
ity to torture appears in equivalent "Instructions" as early as 1553. Penry
Williams, *The Council in the Marches of Wales under Elizabeth I* (Cardiff,
1958) 56 & n.58; cf. id. at 48–49, 57, 81. See, e.g., the 1574 text in
Documents Connected with the History of Ludlow (London, 1841) 309, 318.

It seems that John Whitgift exercised this authority during his tenure as
Vice President of the Council. He was appointed in 1557; see *A Calendar of
the Register of the Queen's Majesty's Council in the Dominion and Principality of Wales* (R. Flenley, ed.) (London, 1916) 173. In 1585, as Arch-
chbishop of Canterbury, Whitgift was engaged in a bitter fight with Robert
Beale, then Clerk to the Privy Council, over the High Commission's pros-
ecutions of Puritans. Beale, in a tract now lost, accused Whitgift of abuse in
the use of torture. Whitgift expressed his anger to Lord Burghley that Beale
should presume to give "a *caveat* to those in the Marches of Wales, that
execute torture by virtue of instructions under her Majesty's hand, according
to a statute, to look unto it., that their doings be well warranted." Quoted in
John Strype, *The Life and Acts of John Whitgift* (Oxford, 1822 ed.) I:402; cf.
id. at I:168. The statute Whitgift had in mind was 34 & 35 Hen. VIII c. 26
(1542–1543) providing for the maintenance of a President and Council in
Wales "in manner and form as hath heretofore been used and accustomed;
which President and Council shall have power and authority to hear and
determine by their wisdoms and discretions such causes and matters as be or
hereafter shall be assigned to them by the King's Majesty, as heretofore hath
been accustomed and used."

39. The State Papers Domestic are fuller for the Jacobean years, especially by contrast with the early decades of our period 1540–1640. The four
cases known to us from the Privy Council registers after 1613 are also
evidenced as torture cases in the State Papers (see the notes to Cases 77–80).
Hence the inference that the State Papers for 1603–1613 from which we
know Cases 75–76, are moderately comprehensive in this regard, and that if
they were not, the literary sources of the time would warn us.

40. Case 81. In addition to the sources cited in the note to this case, see
H. R. Trevor-Roper, *Archbishop Laud: 1573–1645* (London, 1940) 388;
Samuel R. Gardiner, *History of England from the Accession of James I to
the Outbreak of the Civil War: 1603–1642* (New York, 1965 ed.) IX:141.

41. We exclude happenings in Scotland and Ireland, see sources cited
in Holdsworth V:185 n.11. But see John Kenyon, *The Popish Plot* (London,
1972) 132 (Miles Prance confined to a cell called Little Ease in Newgate [*sic*]
to make him talk; no warrant; December 1678). See also infra note 49.

42. The Continental abolitionist literature has no counterpart in

England. It seems that the closest thing to criticism of torture in the seventeenth century was Selden's little aside, quoted supra note 35.

43. 3 Car. I. c. 1 (1627 [1628]).

44. See Frances H. Relf, *The Petition of Right* (Minneapolis, 1917); for a short bibliography of parliamentary diaries see Margaret A. Judson, *The Crisis of the Constitution* (New York, 1964) ix–xi.

45. Jardine 16, 45, 69–70.

46. See Wigmore VIII:§2250, at 267, 285–292.

47. Id., VIII:§2250, at 287 n.89.

48. Id., III:§817–819, at 291–297 (Chadbourn rev. 1970).

49. We reiterate that coercion inflicted without authority is not for our purposes to be reckoned as torture. There is considerable evidence of brutality in provincial investigations of witchcraft cases in Tudor-Stuart times. See, e.g., C. L'Estrange Ewen, *Witch Hunting and Witch Trials* (London, 1929) 65ff, 314; Wallace Notestein, *A History of Witchcraft in England* (Washington, 1911) 174ff. Mathew Hopkins, "the great witch-finder" (id. at 205) of 1645–46 sometimes obtained confessions by keeping suspects from sleeping for several days. Id. at 167; cf. id. at 175–176. Self-appointed witch-finders employed the ancient swimming ordeal, originally a mode of procuring the judgment of God (see Plucknett 114), as a pretrial experiment for detecting witches. Ewen, supra, at 66–69, 314; Notestein, supra, collects many references in his index ("Water, ordeal of") at 440. Notestein emphasizes that such outbreaks of popular witch-hunting occurred mostly in periods of disorder, like 1645–1646, when central authority was preoccupied or in abeyance. Id. at 199–205; cf. id. at 313ff.

Because the witch-finders lacked conciliar authority for their practices, they were liable to civil and criminal suit. We know of several such suits. "One Joan Bibb of Rushock in Worcestershire was tied and thrown into a pool as a witch to see whether she could swim. And she did bring her action against Mr. Shaw the parson, and recovered £10 damages, 8 March 1661." "Henry Townshend's 'Notes of the office of a Justice of Peace,' 1661–3" (R. D. Hunt, ed.), in *Miscellany II* (Worcestershire Historical Society, 1967) 118 (footnotes omitted); cf. the case of Elizabeth Stile in *Somerset Assize Orders 1629–1640* (T. G. Barnes, ed.) (Frome, 1959) 28. Two men who broke into the house of a suspected witch in Somerset in 1694 and forced her to undergo the water test appear to have been prosecuted for it. "The Records of Quarter Sessions in the County of Wilts.," in *Historical Manuscripts Commission, Report on Manuscripts in Various Collections* (London, 1901) I:65, 160–161, cited by Notestein, supra, at 418. Thomas Colley, a chimney sweep who conducted a witch-swimming in April 1751 at Tring in Hertfordshire during which the woman drowned, "was tried at Hertford Assizes, before Sir William Lee, and having been found guilty of murder, was sent back to the scene of the crime under the large escort of one hundred and eight men, seven officers, and two trumpeters, and was hung on August 24, 1751, at Gubblecote Cross, where his body swung in chains for many years." Lewis Evans, "Witchcraft in Hertfordshire," in *Bygone Hertfordshire* (W. Andrews, ed.) (Hull & London, 1898) 229.

Of course, it did not require witchcraft to incite some investigators to acts of illegal coercion against suspects. See, e.g., Thomas Harman, *A Caveat or Warning for Common Cursitors, Vulgarly Called Vagabonds* [London, 1566], reprinted in *The Elizabethan Underworld* (A. V. Judges, ed.) (New York, 1965 ed.) 61, 91–92 (vagabond, pretending to be dumb, forced to speak by being hoisted over a beam and made to hang by his wrists).

50.   E.g., Case 36.

51.   Other certain instances include Cases 13, 36.

52.   Supra Chapter 5, text at note 37.

53.   The great theme of *Offizialprinzip* in the German scholarship, discussed briefly in Langbein, PCR 131–132, 146–148, 150, 177–178. The classic account is Eberhard Schmidt, *Inquisitionsprozess und Rezeption* (Leipzig, 1940).

54.   See Thomas G. Barnes, "Introduction," *Somerset Assize Orders 1629–1640,* supra note 49, at xxiv–xxv; cf. id. at 12 n.2; A. Hassel Smith, *County and Court: Government and Politics in Norfolk 1558–1603* (Oxford, 1974) 60–61, 75ff, 181–200 passim.

55.   For a concise account of these matters see G. P. V. Akrigg, *Jacobean Pageant* (New York, Atheneum ed., 1967) 1–17, 60–62, 69–78.

56.   Regarding the legend to the contrary surrounding Felton's Case (1628), see note 63 infra.

57.   Case 75, in April 1603, involving aspersions cast on the new King, and Case 76, Guy Fawkes.

58.   In Case 81 the warrant was issued by the monarch.

59.   See SPD 9:273; Spedding V:90–91; DNB 15:576.

60.   SPD 10:125.

61.   Spedding VII:77.

62.   SPD 10:336.

63.   This case gave rise to a legend that has been often repeated, even after Jardine set the record straight. The tale originated in Volume 1 of John Rushworth's *Historical Collections of Private Passages of State, Weighty Matters in Law, etc.* (1st ed., London, 1659). Rushworth's sources are unknown; he was a teenager in 1628 and could not have observed the events; see DNB 17:419. According to Rushworth

> *Felton* was called before the Council, where he confessed [his motives for] the Murder. The Council much pressed him to confess who set him on work to do such a bloody Act, and if the *Puritans* had no Hand therein; he denied that they had . . . . Dr. *Laud* Bishop of *London* [William Laud, afterwards Archbishop of Canterbury] being then at the Council-Table,

told him [that] if he would not confess, he must go to the Rack. *Felton* replied, if it must be so he could not tell whom he might nominate in the Extremity of Torture, and if what he should say then must go for Truth, he could not tell whether his Lordship (meaning the Bishop of *London*) or which of their Lordships he might name, for Torture might draw unexpected Things from him; after this he was asked no more Questions but sent back to Prison.

Rushworth, op. cit. (London, 1721 ed.) I:638 (italics original). It may well be that Felton's plucky response persuaded the Council that there were no conspirators to discover, or that examination under torture would in any event be futile. Rushworth's narrative continues, however:

The Council then fell into Debate, whether by the Law of the Land they could justify the putting him to the Rack. The King being at the Council said, before any such Thing be done, let the Advice of the Judges be had therein, whether it be Legal or no; and afterwards his Majesty the 13th of November [1628] propounded the Question to Sir *Thomas Richardson,* Lord Chief Justice of the Common-Pleas, to be propounded to all the Justices, viz.... Whether by the Law he might not be Racked, and whether there were any Law against it; for (said the King) if it might not be done by Law, he would not use his Prerogative in this Point....

First, the Justices of *Serjeants-Inn* in *Chauncery-Lane* did meet and agree, that the King may not in this Case put the Party to the Rack. And the Fourteenth of *November* all the Justices being assembled at Serjeants-Inn in *Fleetstreet,* agreed in one, that he ought not by the Law to be tortured by the Rack, for no such Punishment is known or allowed by our Law.

Id. at I:638–639 (italics original). Blackstone gave his imprimatur to this story, proud that the judges "declared unanimously, to their own honor and the honor of the English law, that no such proceeding was allowable by the Laws of England." Blackstone IV:321.

Jardine disentangled the story in a brilliant bit of analysis that deserves to be reproduced:

It is, however, probable that Rushworth, who was not a professed [*sic; professional?*] lawyer, and might therefore be technically inaccurate in his relation of a judicial proceeding, has mixed together two distinct occurrences in his account of this transaction. That Laud, or some of the Council, threatened Felton with the rack in the course of his examination, may readily be believed. But it is not credible that either Charles or his Council, who well knew the extent of the prerogative in this respect, and had actually exercised it in the case of Monke only two years before, should "fall into debate," as Rushworth represents them to have done, or consult the Judges respecting their power to administer the torture.... The course of the transaction ... was probably thus: Felton was threatened with the rack by the Council; but as he at once confessed his own offense, and there were no reasonable presumptions, or *indicia,* that he had any confederates, there was no ground for applying the torture to him in order to extract evidence. . . . After his examinations, and immediately before his trial, which did not take place for more than two months after his apprehension, Felton, though at first resolute in justifying his crime, is said by several historians to have expressed great remorse, and to have requested that his hand might be cut off before his execution as a part of his punishment, "which the King," says Whitelocke, "desired might be done; but the Judges said it could not be done by law, and he was hanged in chains." It can hardly be doubted that it was on this latter occasion that the Judges resolved that "no such punishment was known or allowed by our law;" and this would precisely correspond with the date of the resolution as given by Rushworth, namely, the 14th of November,—a few days only before Felton's execution.

Jardine 60–62 (italics original). Remarkably, Holdsworth carries forward the tale from Rushworth, remitting to a footnote the observation that Jardine "throws some discredit on Rushworth's narrative. . . ." Holdsworth V:186.

Whatever reservations the judges had about cutting off the hand of Felton did not restrain Chief Justice Richardson two and one half years later. "[A]t the assizes at Salisbury in the summer of 1631 [he] was assaulted by a prisoner condemned there for felony, who after his condemnation threw a brickbat at the said Judge, which narrowly missed; and for this an indictment was immediately drawn by Noy against the prisoner, and his right hand cut off and fixed to the gibbet, upon which he was himself immediately hanged in the presence of the Court." 2 Dyer 188b (Vaillant ed., 1794 ed.), 73 Eng. Rep. 416.

The John Felton in this case in 1628 is not to be confused with the suspect in our Case 27 (1570).

64.   Compare Coke's uneasy prescription argument, quoted supra text at note 2.

Index

Admiralty, High Court of, 131, 188 n. 5
Afflictive punishments, 27–28, 77, 213 n
Alfield, Thomas, 108, 124
Altham, ——, 119, 125
American Independence, War of, 43
Amsterdam workhouses, 34–38, 43
Andrews, Thomas, 80, 100, 124
Anger, Richard, Jr., 87, 118, 136
Antwerp, 34, 37
Apsley, Allen, 121, 123, 125, 130
Archer, John, 122, 124, 135
Asheton, Roger, 110, 124
Ashley, Anthony, 115, 125, 130
Ashley, Francis, 123, 125
Attorney General, 86, 92, 131
Austria: abolition of torture, 10, 63; galley
    sentence, 30–32; imprisonment, 39; cap-
    ital punishment, 39; torture in, 50; *poena
    extraordinaria*, 50. See also *Constitutio
    Criminalis Theresiana.*
Aysh, Henry, 114, 124

Bacon, Francis, 85, 117, 119, 121, 125,
    129, 139
Bagshaw, Edward, 114, 124
Bailly, Charles, 102, 124
Baker, John, 97, 125
Balfour, William, 123, 125
Bannister, Lawrence, 102, 124
Bamford, Paul, 32
Barberousse's case, 52, 173 n.43
Barker, William, 102, 124
Barkley, Richard, 85, 117, 125
Barton, ——, 96, 124
Bayles, Christopher, 112, 124
Bayles, John, 112, 124